Hangings and Lynchings
In Dallas County, Texas
1853 to 1920

Terry Baker

EAKIN PRESS Fort Worth, Texas
www.EakinPress.com

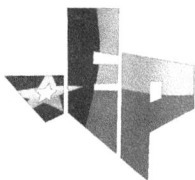

Cover Design by Flying Gorilla Studio
www.FlyingGorillaStudio.com

This book is dedicated to my father,
Henry "Hank" Baker
1907 - 1982

He grew up as a cowboy in North Dakota, and in 2013 he was inducted into the North Dakota Cowboy Hall of Fame in the Pre-1940 Rodeo category. He shared my passion for stories of the Old West in the 1800s, and the cowboy way of life. He sometimes said he was born fifty years too late, because he missed the great cattle drives of the 1870s from Texas to Kansas, North Dakota, and Montana.

Contents

Acknowledgements

The Texas and Dallas History Archives and the Genealogy Departments at the Dallas Central Library provided much of the research material for this book. I would like to thank all the staff at the library for the assistance they provided me over a period of seventeen years. They offered suggestions on how to locate the many hidden treasures in the library collections that were needed to complete the research. A special thank you to Carol Roark, Sharon Martin, Brian Collins, Bryan McKinney, Ed Boehringer, and many others at the Dallas library that made my job easier.

Gratitude is also extended to attorney-at-law Ron DeLord, the Combined Law Enforcement Officers Associations of Texas, and the Texas Peace Officers Memorial Foundation for their support over many years.

I would like to acknowledge the following for their suggestions and assistance: Robert W. "Bob" Stephens; Bob Alexander, former DEA agent; Donaly E. Brice, Reference Archivist at the Texas State Archives; and Rick Miller, former Dallas police officer, chief of police in Denton and Killeen, and former county attorney of Bell County, Texas. All are noted authors and historians of early Texas law enforcement.

Thanks to my daughter Cheryl, and son-in-law Denny Gorena, for their suggestions, and assistance with computer issues. Also thanks to longtime friends, Jim and Vicki Newman for their help with computer issues. Thank you to Leonard Knight, for his help searching old cemeteries for tombstones to photograph. And thank you to Harold Williams, caretaker, Oakland Cemetery, Dallas. Also thanks to Ed Clark, Dallas County Sheriff's Department.

I want to thank a longtime friend of over thirty years, retired Texas Chief of Police Phil Hambrick, who offered me encouragement to continue my research and document cases of Texas peace officers killed in the line of duty. Part of that research was used in the writing of this book.

And finally I would like to thank my wife Joyce Ann Greear Baker, for her patience and the time she spent with me in the upper floors of old courthouses going through dusty old criminal record books, and for the times we spent in old cemeteries searching for tombstones, and for offering suggestions and proof reading this book.

Methods of Execution

Lynching - aka: Judge Lynch and Lynch Law. Lynching is the illegal hanging of a person under the pretext as a service to justice, or revenge, without the due process of law. Usually the actions of a mob, or vigilantes.

Hanging - The legal execution of a person after a court trial, conviction and sentence to death. An execution could be ordered by a State recognized court of law. Legal hangings in Texas from 1836 to 1924 were conducted by the sheriff in the county where the trial was held, the accused was convicted, and sentenced to death.

Electrocution - In the early 1900s many states in the United States started requiring that executions be conducted by electrocution. During the summer of 1923, the Texas Legislature passed Senate Bill 160, which required that all future executions be held at the Texas State penitentiary in Huntsville. The bill also required that the executions be by electrocution. The first execution by electrocution at the Huntsville prison was on February 8, 1924, when five inmates were executed. The electric chair at Huntsville soon became known as "Old Sparky."

Lethal Injection - In 1964 the United States Supreme Court placed a moratorium, or temporary ban on executions. The ban was later lifted in 1976. New statutes were written in an attempt to comply with the Supreme Court ruling. In 1982, Texas resumed executions using the lethal injection method, which is currently in use today. Texas State ordered executions are still held at the State Penitentiary in Huntsville, Texas.

Hangings and Lynchings
in Dallas County, Texas
1853 to 1920

by Race and Sex

18 - Black males hanged, and or lynched.

1 - Black female hanged.

9 – White males hanged, and or lynched.

28 - Total.

12 – Black males hanged after trials.

1 – Black female hanged after a trial.

6 – Black males lynched by mobs.

3 – White males hanged after trials.

5 – White males lynched by mobs.

1 – White male robbed and then lynched [but he did not die].

28 - Total.

Introduction

Anglo Americans began arriving to settle in what was to become Dallas in the early 1840s. John Neely Bryan first visited in 1839 the place that would one day become Dallas. Bryan returned to Arkansas and settled his affairs, and returned in 1841 and built a small log cabin along the Trinity River. John Beeman arrived in April 1842 with his family, including daughter Margaret. Bryan married Margaret Beeman on February 26, 1843. As he was the first settler, John Neely Bryan became known to some as the "Father of Dallas."

Dallas County was created in 1846 from Nacogdoches and Robertson counties. Some believe Bryan named Dallas after his friend, Joseph Dallas, while others said he named the community after U.S. Vice President George Miffin Dallas. As other families came to the area a small community took shape along the banks east of the Trinity River.

At the time, Texas was a slave holder state with slaves legally bought and sold not only in Texas, but throughout the South. Some of the early settlers brought their slaves with them when they arrived in the area.

On March 30, 1846, after the annexation of Texas to the United States, the new Texas State Legislature passed an act creating the county of Dallas. On April 18, 1846, they named the city of Dallas the county seat.

The first Dallas County Courthouse was built in 1846. John Neely Bryan donated an entire block for a courthouse square. It was set in the center of the new town site. The courthouse was a ten foot by ten foot log building, with one door and two windows. It had benches made from logs and although crude, was good enough for a new frontier community. A building was later erected for the clerks of the county and district courts.

On September 28, 1846, the first marks and brands recorded in Dallas County were those of John Neely Bryan, John Beeman and John Young,

The Tonkawa Indians and the nomadic tribes were harassing the early settlers of Dallas County. After they were driven from the county they would often slip in among the settlers and steal their horses and destroy their property. If an opportunity presented itself they would murder the citizens.

When news of the Gold Rush in California arrived east in 1849, many men came through Dallas on their way to California. Several men from Dallas left to search for gold, including John Neely Bryan. He failed in his search and returned in 1850.

In the early settlement of the county, there were only a few people in Dallas. The 1850 Dallas County Census shows 435 families living in the county. Other than the Indian problem, crime was almost unknown among the early pioneers. But crime apparently had started to become somewhat of a problem because on December 9, 1850, the Dallas county commissioners court let a contract for the first jail. A full detailed description of the jail to be built was recorded in the minutes of the court. The jail was to be a sixteen foot by sixteen foot cedar log structure, with two floors, with nine feet between floors. The outside walls were to be eight inches thick, with one door, three and one half feet wide and five feet high. It had one window covered with slab iron bars that ran horizontally.

As Dallas grew crime became more of a problem and over the next few years the jail had to be expanded. The site of the first jail was built on land now occupied by the Union Train Station on Houston Street, at the west end of downtown Dallas.

The original hangings were conducted in an area below what is now known as the "triple underpass." It became known, according to some reports, as "Hangman's Hollow." Later the hangings were moved to the open courtyard next to the jail. The sheriff would have a scaffold built in the courtyard to carry out the order of the court. The sheriff, or one of his deputies, would conduct the hanging. The early hangings were open to the public and sometimes thousands of people would attend, including men, women and children. Still later, to provide some privacy and security, the hangings were moved to the stairwell inside the county jail.

On June 8, 1861, a state of war was declared between the North and the South with Dallas County voting 741 to 237 for secession. After the end of the Civil War, on June 19, 1865, Union General Gordon Granger arrived in Galveston and issued General Order Number 3, which declared "all slaves are free." The June 19th date became known as "Juneteenth," and is still celebrated in Texas.

Texas has a long tradition of capital punishment and in early Texas, hanging was the primary method of legal executions. In the early 1900s the frequency of local public hangings, as well as illegal lynchings, began to decline in the United States.

On June 4, 1923, the Texas State Legislature passed a statute which provided for the electrocution of convicts condemned to death. The condemned convicts would now be executed at the state prison, and not in the county where the prisoner was tried and convicted, as had been the past practice. By February 1924 the legal hangman's rope was replaced by the electric chair. Executions were moved from local communities to the state prison in Huntsville, Texas. The first two Dallas County prisoners sentenced to death, who were executed by electrocution in the state prison, were Blaine Dyer and Earnest Lawson. Both were charged with murder, and were electrocuted on March 28, 1924. The electric chair at Huntsville became known as "Old Sparky."

Not included in this book are suicides by hanging that may have occurred within Dallas County. This book is limited to hangings that occurred after a trial was conducted and a court ordered the sentence of death by hanging, and the execution actually took place in Dallas County. Also included are illegal lynchings that took place in Dallas County. The cases included in this book are from the years 1853 to 1920. At the end of the book are four chapters about four separate Dallas County sheriffs, assisted by sheriff deputies, other peace officers, and some civilians, who stood up to mobs and mob violence and prevented lynchings.

The jail currently known as the "Old Jail," at 505 Main Street in Dallas, opened in May 1915. From 1918 to 1920, five hangings took place in the Old Dallas County Jail. The gallows have long since been removed, but the three "death cells" are still there. They are on the 9th floor in the Old Jail. This is where the prisoners awaiting their sentences were held. In order to house more prisoners a jail annex was built next to the Old Jail and opened in August 1955.

The Old Dallas County Jail closed in 1967 when the new Government Center Jail at 600 Commerce Street opened. The Old Jail was reopened as needed for special events when large numbers of arrests [600-700] were made, such as Texas vs. Oklahoma football game celebrations, and protests at local colleges, etc. Later the Old Jail was opened or closed as needed, for housing inmates when the jail population grew or declined.

After twenty-six years of full time service the author retired from the Dallas County Sheriff's Department in 1994. He had served three years in the Dallas County Sheriff's Department Reserves prior to his twenty-six years full time service. Then he continued with the department for another ten years as a deputy sheriff in the sheriff's department mounted posse. After working for five Dallas County Sheriffs, Bill Decker, Clarence Jones, Carl Thomas, Don Byrd and Jim Bowles, he finished his service with a total of thirty- nine years as a sworn deputy sheriff in Dallas County.

In 1997, the author began researching cases of Texas peace officers killed in the line of duty. The officers' names were not on the newly formed memorial walls for peace officers killed in the line of duty. These memorials included the National Law Enforcement Officers Memorial, in Washington, D.C.; the Texas Peace Officers Memorial, on the Texas State Capitol grounds in Austin; and the Sheriff's Association of Texas Lost Lawman Memorial in Austin.

While conducting the research into officers killed in the line of duty, he began coming across information of hangings and lynchings that had occurred in Dallas County. He made files on each of these cases because the reason they were hanged or lynched may have been because they killed a peace officer. In fact two of the hanging cases he found were about men who had killed police officers in Dallas County.

After more than seventeen years of researching cases of peace officers killed in the line of duty, the author has submitted case files of 246 officers to the memorials in Washington, D. C. and Austin. Using information gathered over the seventeen years and conducting further research, he decided to write this book because the staff at the Dallas Public Library where the Dallas and Texas history is stored stated they had no file or book that told the story of all the hangings and lynchings in Dallas County. The information included in this book is a record of Dallas history the author felt should be documented and preserved for future generations.

The 1890 United States Federal Census was dated June 2, 1890. Most of that information was destroyed in a 1921 fire. With the loss of those records, valuable information is missing about some of the people included in this book.

Effective July 1, 1903, Texas State Senate Bill #168, required that births and deaths be reported and recorded in the county of the birth or death. Under the new law passed by the Texas Legislature, all physicians, surgeons, midwives, and coroners were required to make reports of all births or deaths under their personal observation, to the county clerk within ten days. Failure to make the report was a penalty of $5. Every county clerk in the state was to distribute report books of births and deaths to the doctors of their county. The county clerk was to report monthly to the newly created Texas Department of Public Health and Vital Statistics.

However, many of the newly required birth and death reports were not being made in the early years that this new law was in place. When death records were found, they were very useful in providing information for this book.

Some Texas cities and counties had started recording birth and death records as early as the 1870s. These records were made for their own information, and were kept within their own offices or departments and not submitted to the state. Some published a weekly or monthly notice of the births and deaths in the local newspapers, which has proved helpful to researchers.

The author believes that this book includes all the hangings and lynchings [not suicides] that occurred in Dallas County, Texas from 1853 to 1920. However, that doesn't mean that at some future date someone might not find and verify a case that has been missed.

The names of sexual assault victims have been used in this book only if they had been previously published in newspapers, court records, books or magazines.

In some of the cases, words, terms, quotations, descriptions, situations, sketches, and photographs have been used in this book that are not meant to offend anyone. They have been used solely in a historical context, and to provide an accurate record of this part of the history of Dallas County, Texas.

Terry Baker
Dallas, Texas

Chapter 1

Jane, a slave, aka: Jane Elkins

Black Female, age - about 53

Offense - Murder, occurred spring of 1853

Victim – Andrew C. Wisdom, white male, widower with 2 small children

Trial by jury

9th Judicial District Court, Judge John H. Reagan presided

Trial held in Dallas County, Texas

Indicted by Grand Jury May 10, 1853

Tried and convicted May 16, 1853

Sentenced May 17, 1853

Hanged on Friday, May 27, 1853, in Dallas County, Texas

Jane, a slave, *aka* Jane Elkins, was the first female to be legally hanged in the State of Texas. This is the story of Jane, the murder charge against her, and some of the people involved in her trial, and her execution.

The first bill of sale recorded in Dallas County was on August 9, 1846, [dated March 17, 1844] from Edward Welborn to John Young, and is as follows:

I have this day sold to John Young, a negro woman named Jane, and child about twenty years, which said negro I warrant to be sound both in body and mind, and a slave for life. The said John Young, in consideration of said property, has this day paid to me the sum of $400, I bind myself to warrant and defend the title of said negro unto said Young, his heirs and assigns forever. Given under my hand this 17th March, 1844.

Edward [his X mark] Welborn.

The 1850 U. S. Federal Census lists a Mr. John Young, age fifty, born about 1795, in Tennessee. John Young and his wife had four children living with them in Dallas. The 1850 U. S. Federal Slave Schedule has John Young listed as the owner of five slaves, a female age fifty, [this probably is the same negro woman named Jane, that John Young bought from Edward Welborn, and was recorded in the bill of sale dated, March 17, 1844], a male age twenty, a female age twelve, a female age eight, and a female age four. The names of the slaves are not recorded in the Slave Schedule.

Although the record has not been located that would show the date that John Young sold Jane, it seems evident that he did sell her to Smith Elkins. The Texas 1850 Census records show that Smith E. Elkins and his wife, America Elkins, were the only married couple with the last name Elkins living in Dallas County.

The 1850 U. S. Federal Census lists a Mr. Smith E. Elkins, age fity-seven, a lawyer, born about 1793, in New Hampshire, his wife America Elkins, age forty-eight, children Harrison Bowles, age ten, and Hannah Bowles, age seven, all living together in Dallas.

America Elkins was previously the widow of the Rev. William Bowles. The 1892 *Memorial and Biographical History of Dallas County* shows that Smith Elkins was elected chief justice in 1850, and quit the country under a domestic cloud. By 1853 America Elkins was a widow and died on March 3, 1856. Dallas County Probate Record Case #179, shows she left her remaining slaves and property to her children Harrison Bowles, Hannah Frances Bowles, and to the executor of her will J. M. Patterson.

In the spring of 1853, Andrew C. Wisdom, [the *Galveston Daily News*, August 28, 1880, reported his name as John Windom] a widower, was living north of downtown Dallas, somewhere in the area of Cedar Springs, between there and Farmers Branch on the W. C. Trimble property. The *Dallas Daily Times-Herald*, July 17, 1891, reported that the murder of Wisdom took place six miles north of Dallas on Buchanan Branch. Wisdom had hired Jane from the widow Elkins to help take care of his two small children, one who was an infant, and to keep house for him.

One night, Jane, for some reason, killed Wisdom while he was asleep by splitting his head open with an ax. It was first reported by Jane to the authorities that Wisdom had been killed by a prominent citizen of the county. The investigation quickly established that the guilty party was Jane.

Jane was arrested, jailed and tried for murder. It was reported that during her trial she slept the greater portion of the time, being perfectly indifferent to the proceedings. A witness stated that he saw Wisdom as he lay weltering in his blood and dying, and that Wisdom lived, but unconscious until about 8 a.m. the next day with a deep gash in his skull. The children were asleep as their father lay dying in an adjoining bed. The ax was found lying on the floor. One account had the reason that Jane killed Wisdom, was he had raped her.

The Dallas County Grand Jury on Tuesday, May 10, 1853, issued several indictments including the one against Jane charging her with murder. The case was assigned to Judge John H. Reagan, 9th District Court, and was heard in Dallas County.

District judges residing elsewhere and having large districts, presided successively in Dallas from the fall of 1846 to 1856. Judge Reagan also served as a judge in Dallas after he was elected district judge of the 9th district, at Palestine in 1852.

John H. Reagan was born October 8, 1818 in Gatlinburg, Tennessee. He came to Texas at age nineteen. He worked as a surveyor and then farmed for a time in Kaufman County. He studied law on his own and was licensed to practice in 1846. He was elected probate judge in Henderson County, and in 1847 went to the state legislature.

Reagan was elected a district judge in Palestine and he served from 1852 to 1857. Judge Reagan had a long career of public service serving as a United States congressman and then senator from the state of Texas. He resigned his senate seat to return to Texas and serve as chairman of the Texas Railroad Commission. He also served as Postmaster General under Confederate President Jefferson Davis. Reagan was imprisoned at Fort Warren, in Boston, Massachusetts, for his service to the South in the Civil War. He died in 1905 and is buried in East Hill Cemetery, near Palestine.

After Jane was indicted by the grand jury on May 10, 1853, Judge Reagan ordered that a special venire be issued for thirty-six jurors for the purpose of serving as jurors for the case, *State of Texas vs. Jane, a slave, Cause #188*. The case was set for trial on Monday, May 16, 1853 and the defendant being too poor to employ counsel, E. P. Nichols and B. W. Stone were appointed as counsel for the defendant. Dallas County District Attorney Nathaniel M. Burford, prosecuted the case against Jane.

Nathaniel M. Burford was born in Tennessee on June 24, 1824. He was raised in Tennessee and attended Irving College where he studied law and was admitted to the bar in 1845. Burford came to Texas in 1847. He settled first in Jefferson and later moved to Dallas in 1848. In 1850 Burford was elected district attorney for Dallas County. In 1856 he was elected judge of the Fourteenth Judicial District. In 1862 Judge Burford was made colonel in the Nineteenth Texas Cavalry in the Confederate army. In 1864 he left the army because of ill health. He resumed his legal practice and was elected a member of the Eleventh Assembly of Texas and was chosen speaker of the House. He was again elected district judge in 1876 and served in that position for two years. Nathaniel Burford married Mary Knight in 1854. She was a native of Tennessee and they had eight children.

On Monday, May 16, 1853, Judge John H. Reagan heard the murder case against Jane. The indictment was read to the defendant and Jane plead not guilty. After hearing the evidence presented by the district attorney and the rebuttal from the defending attorney, the jury retired to consider the evidence and returned to the court with the following verdict:

> *We the Jury find defendant guilty of murder in the 1st degree, we further find the defendant is a slave of the value of $700.00 and that the owner of defendant has done nothing to evade or defeat the execution of the law upon the said defendant.*
>
> D. R. Cameron, Foreman

On Tuesday, May 17, 1853, Judge Reagan issued the following order:

> *The State of Texas vs. Jane [a slave] charge murder.*
> *Pursuant to law, the prisoner Jane who has been found guilty of murder was brought into open court for the purpose of receiving the judgment thereof. She was asked if she had anything to say as to why the sentence of death should not be passed upon her and said nothing. Sheriff to keep her in close confinement in the common jail until Friday the 27th of the present month of May and that on said Friday Between the hours of 11 a.m. and 3 p.m. the sheriff shall take Jane from jail to a gallows erected for that purpose and he hang the said Jane by the neck until she is dead and that a certified copy of this judgment be delivered to the sheriff.*

Sheriff Trevevant C. Hawpe
Served 1950 - 1854
Courtesy of O'Byrne Cox, Jr.

Trezevant Calhoun Hawpe was the third elected sheriff, and fourth to serve as sheriff of Dallas County. He served as sheriff from August 15, 1850 to August 21, 1854. It became his responsibility to carry out the execution order of the court. He was born about 1820 in Franklin County, Georgia. The 1850 U. S. Census records show he was

Court Records of Trial, State of Texas vs. Jane (A Slave)
Charge - Murder • Date - May 16, 1853
Courtesy of the Dallas Public Library

living in Dallas with his wife, Electa Bethurum Hawpe, and son, John R. Hawpe. Also living with them were several children of hers from a previous marriage.

Sheriff Hawpe had a scaffold built in the yard next to the jail to carry out the execution order. On Friday, May 27, 1853, Hawpe read the death warrant to Jane, and then carried out the execution order. Jane aka: Jane Elkins, became the first female to be legally hanged in the State of Texas.

Magazine articles, news reports, stories in books and faded memories suggest that Jane was hanged in various years between 1851 and 1854, and one article even had her death as 1858. The correct date she was hanged in Dallas was on Friday, May 27, 1853. Microfilm court records of her murder case are on file on the 7th floor of the Dallas Public Library, 1515 Young Street, Dallas, Texas.

* * * * * * * * *

Josefa "Chipita" Rodriguez was for many years wrongly considered to be the first and only woman legally hanged in Texas. Chipita was accused of robbery and murdering a man named John Savage for the $600 in gold that he was carrying. Ironically, John Savage was also murdered with an ax. The murder took place along the Aransas River in San Patricio County, near the Texas Gulf Coast. District Court Judge Benjamin F. Neal heard the case. After Chipita pleaded not guilty, the jury recommended mercy, but Judge Neal ordered her executed on November 16, 1863. Her execution took place just over ten years after Jane Elkins was executed in Dallas County.

In 1985 Texas State Senator Carlos Truan of Corpus Christi asked the Texas Legislature to absolve Chipita Rodriguez of murder. The Sixty-ninth Legislature passed the resolution, and it was signed by Governor Mark White on June 13, 1985.

Chapter 2

"Uncle Cato" Miller, a slave
aka: "Old Cato," black male, age unknown

Patrick Jennings, a slave
aka: " Pat" Jennings, black male, age unknown

Samuel Smith, a slave
aka: "Sam" Smith, black male, age unknown

All three suspected of arson, and burning of downtown Dallas on July 8, 1860

*Committee of fifty-two citizens
selected to issue vigilante justice to slaves of the county*

All three lynched Tuesday, July 24, 1860, in Dallas County, Texas

On Sunday afternoon, July 8, 1860, the temperature was reported to have reached up to an unofficial 112 degrees in the small town of Dallas, population 678. Many of the residents were taking their afternoon nap, when the screams of "Fire . . . Fire" broke the early afternoon quiet. The fire originated between 1:30 and 2 p.m. in a pile of trash boxes in front of the new W. W. Peak & Brother Drug Store.

In just a few minutes the whole building was engulfed in flames and a strong southwest wind whipped the flames to other buildings. When the fire was finally over it had destroyed most of the downtown square. The courthouse which was made of brick was spared, along with a few other buildings. Thirty-two residences had also been consumed by the fire. No one lost their life as a result of the fire.

In a letter written the next day, on July 9, 1860, to Major John Marshall, editor of the *State Gazette* in Austin, Charles R. Pryor, editor of the *Dallas Herald*, wrote the following, and was published in the *State Gazette*:

State Gazette, Austin, Saturday, July 14, 1860, page 2

Dallas, July [misprinted as June in the Gazette] 9, 1860.

Major John Marshall—Dear Sir: A dreadful calamity has befallen us, our town is burned to ashes; every hotel, every business house, law office, phy-

sician's office, Herald office with all its material—everything gone… We have already ordered a new press and material, and in less than six weeks the Herald will be out again. The Court House is the only building left standing on the square, except on the south-east corner. The fire originated in Peak's new and elegant establishment, and spread with appaling [sic] rapidity. The fire originated only two doors above the Herald office. Hence we could save nothing but our books and subscription list. I have not even saved my clothing. I will write you more fully by next mail. It is not known whether it was the work of an incendiary or not.
Loss estimated at over $500,000.

Yours truly,   Chas. R. Pryor

Charles R. Pryor, age 28, was born in 1832 in Virginia. He was a physician and had received his medical degree from the University of Virginia. Pryor moved to Dallas in 1850. He followed his brother Dr. Samuel B. Pryor to Dallas. Samuel B. Pryor became the first mayor of Dallas in 1856.

In the 1850s Charles wrote articles for the *Dallas Herald* and when the paper's editor and publisher died, Pryor became the editor in 1859, and held the position until 1861.

With his newspaper office and four printing presses destroyed by the fire, Pryor turned to the *McKinney Messenger* for help. Using the *Messenger's* presses Pryor came out with a special edition titled *The Dallas Herald Extra*. In his *Extra*, Pryor detailed the destruction and damage to Dallas caused by the July 8th fire.

The only known copy of the *Extra* to exist was saved by a young girl in Lancaster. On December 14, 1890, on page 20, The *Dallas Morning News* re-printed, *The Dallas Herald Extra*, written by Pryor.

In July, August and September 1860, following the Dallas fire, Pryor wrote numerous letters that were published in the *Austin State Gazette*, *Houston Weekly Telegraph*, *Clarksville Standard* and the *Marshall Republican*.

Pryor's letters told of many prominent citizens that slaves had planned to assassinate when they tried to escape from their burning houses. Also firearms had been discovered in the possession of the slaves, and a plot was revealed for a general insurrection and civil war at the August election. Pryor's letters told of abolition preachers that were expected to arrive in Dallas at the head of a large force, and to warn the country of the dangers that threatened it.

Because of his letters being published and the unexplained fires, people across the state were on the lookout for abolitionists among them.

In 1860, and the months leading up to the Civil War, numerous fires were reported in north and central Texas. Unexplained fires occurred in Dallas, Denton, Milford, Pilot Point, Belknap, Gainesville, Black Jack Grove, and Waxahachie. There were also fires reported in Kaufman and Navarro counties.

Vigilance committees were formed to conduct investigations into the fires. The Denton and Dallas fires occurred on the same day at about the same time of day, which also led citizens to believe that they were not accidental. Some people thought that boxes of matches in the stores might have ignited due to the extreme heat. In Tyler a stranger was caught in the act of starting a fire. He was shot at but escaped.

Because of the hunt for African American suspects starting fires, terror was spread in the slave quarters, and northern ministers were implicated as the insurrection leaders.

In Dallas, a *Committee of 52* prominent citizens was selected to investigate the Dallas fires and issue punishment to those guilty. The fires were almost immediately laid to a slave plot. Two white abolitionist preachers, Solomon McKinney and William Blount, [or Blunt] from Iowa were arrested and held in jail. After being publicly whipped, they were told to leave the country.

On Monday morning after the Dallas fire, Judge Nathaniel M. Burford returned from holding court at Waxahachie to address the *Committee of 52*. For almost an hour, he counseled them on restraint and then departed.

The *Committee of 52*, had nearly 100 African Americans arrested and questioned. Several outhouses, granaries, oats and grain fields of Mr. Crill Miller, age thirty, were destroyed a few days after the Dallas fire. Several slaves belonging to Miller were questioned and a plot was discovered to destroy the land. The investigation revealed that after the July fires, the slaves were supposed to start a general revolt during the first week of August, on the day of the election for state officers. Many of the prominent citizens were marked for assassination. Poisoning was also a part of the plot. The old females were to be slaughtered along with the men. The young and handsome women were to be parceled out among the slaves.

Crill Miller's father, Wm. B. Miller, was shown to own thirteen slaves in the 1860 U. S. Federal Slave Schedule. Although not named in the Federal Slave Schedule, one of his slaves was "Uncle Cato."

A young slave boy was found who declared that Uncle Cato had told him there was going to be a fire downtown. Uncle Cato was a slave that was reported to have a bad reputation in the county. Uncle Cato was arrested and he implicated two other slaves, Pat Jennings and Sam Smith, a slave preacher.

After the *Committee of 52* decided to hang Uncle Cato, Pat Jennings and Sam Smith, there was much discussion on what to do with the remaining slaves in the county. It was finally decided that every slave in Dallas County was to be whipped for their part in the conspiracy. Another committee was appointed to whip the remaining slaves in the county.

Whether they were guilty or not, Uncle Cato, Pat Jennings and Sam Smith were taken to the bank of the Trinity River at the foot of Main Street, near the current location of the triple underpass and Dealey Plaza, and put to death on July 24, 1860, on newly constructed gallows.

When Texas Used the Whipping Post

"– TO·BE WELL LAID ON BY THE SHERIFF"

50 LASHES ON THE BARE BACK

Courtesy of the Dallas Morning News

On August 7, 1850, Wormley Carter was elected constable of Precinct 5 in Dallas County. In 1856 Carter was serving as a deputy sheriff under Sheriff Adam C. Haught, then on August 2, 1858, Carter was elected to a two-year term as sheriff of Dallas County. He served until the election on August 6, 1860. Carter was born on June 19, 1816, in Loudoun, Virginia. It is not recorded if Sheriff Carter had any part in the lynching of Uncle Cato, Pat Jennings and Sam Smith.

On October 31, 1860, Charles R. Pryor was back in the business of publishing a newspaper, when his *Dallas Weekly Herald* included an article about the lynching of Anthony Bewley in Fort Worth. Bewley was a Methodist preacher accused of participation in abolitionist riots and fires in Tarrant County.

In January 1861, South Carolina voted to secede from the United States of America. The secession of South Carolina was followed by the secession of six more states—Mississippi, Florida, Alabama, Georgia, Louisiana and Texas. Four more states followed including Virginia, Arkansas, Tennessee and North Carolina. These eleven states formed the Confederate States of America.

The Civil War began on April 12, 1861, when Confederate troops fired on Fort Sumter, South Carolina. After much suffering on both sides the Civil War ended four years later, with General Robert E. Lee's surrender at Appomattox, Virginia, on April 9, 1865.

It took more than two months, until June 19, 1865, for Union soldiers led by Major General Gordon Granger to arrive at Galveston with the news that the war was over and the slaves were now free.

June 19th became a celebration day for the freed slaves. It is still celebrated and is known as "Juneteenth." It is the oldest known celebration commemorating the ending of slavery in the United States.

* * * * *

Henry Miller was reported to be a descendant of Uncle Cato aka: "Old Cato" who was lynched on July 24, 1860. See Chapter 11 regarding Henry Miller who was convicted and hanged on July 28, 1893, for the May 24, 1892 murder of Dallas Police Officer C. O. Brewer. [See *Dallas Morning News*, July 10, 1892, page 12.]

Chapter 3

Josiah A. Record

White male, age 48, born July 12, 1813, in Ohio

Offense - Alleged to have made statements that the South did not have money or supplies to win the Civil War

Lynched by mob Tuesday, August 13, 1861, in Dallas County, Texas

By August of 1861, the South had been fighting the Civil War for four months. North Texas had some residents that supported the Union North, but most supported the Confederate South. If someone was suspected of supporting the North it could be fatal. This was reported to be the case with Josiah A. Record when he was alleged to have made statements that the South did not have the money or supplies to win the war.

Josiah A. Record was born, according to the Worcester Family Tree, on July 12, 1813, in Ohio. He married Lavinna Casey in 1834, in Ohio. In some of the records her first name is spelled as Levina and in other records Lavina.

In 1850 Josiah A. Record and his wife Lavinna Casey Record and their children were living in Gillam, Indiana.

The 1860 U. S. Census records show Josiah Record, age forty-seven, his wife Levina Record, age forty-one; children—Sylvester Record, age twenty-one; Frances [aka: Frank] M. Record, age nineteen; Jacob Record, age fifteen; Jno. Record, age thirteen; Hester A. Record, age eleven; Silas Record, age nine; and Otis Record, age three, were all living in Precinct 3, Dallas, Texas.

In August 1861, the Texas newspapers were filled with articles about the fighting in the Civil War. Articles titled such as: "The Victory in The West," "The Capture of Sherman's Battery" and the "Latest from Fort Smith" appeared in North Texas newspapers.

The *Dallas Herald*, August 14, 1861, published an article titled "Fight with Indians." A detachment of ten men escorting a wagon train from northwest of Camp Cooper to the Red River was attacked by an Indian raiding party of forty to sixty Indians. The fight lasted for six hours. Seven of the ten men were wounded. They lost four horses, and eight horses were killed.

The *Marshall Republican*, on August 17, 1861, published an article titled "Wholesale Hanging in Texas." Nine men were hanged at Gatesville in Coryell County. The nine men were hanged by the local citizens for attacking and killing one man and mutilating another man who had just moved into the county.

As seen in various newspaper articles published in the summer of 1861, Texans were in no mood to put up with those whom they deemed trouble makers, or with Indian raiding parties. When attacks were made on the citizens, the citizens often struck back using the bullet or rope to solve the problem.

A history was written about Josiah A. Record, and his wife, Lavinna Casey. The history was published in the book, *Proud Heritage II, Pioneer Families of Dallas County*, page 215, copyright 1993. The book was published by the Dallas County Pioneer Association. The article was submitted by Ima Faye Thomas Evans. The Dallas County Pioneer Association stated in their acknowledgments section, "No research has been made to verify facts. If any discrepancies have occurred, the name and address of the submitter is included at the end of each story."

Below is the article:

Josiah A. Record and wife, Lavinna Casey Record

Josiah Record was born in Ohio in 1813. He married Lavinna Casey in 1834 in Ohio. They moved with their children from Indiana to Dallas after 1856. He had a trading post near Farmers Branch.

In the troubled times of 1861, Josiah made a statement that the South didn't have the money or supplies to win the war. He was hanged near Keenan's Crossing and buried in Parrish Cemetery in what would become Coppell, Texas. In the Civil War, his son John served in Good's Confederate Regiment. Francis [Frank] served in Wells' Battalion of the Texas Cavalry. Sylvester served in Purcell's Company of the Ninth Regiment, and in Col. Sims' Regiment.

1n 1869, John and his younger brother, Silas, were found hanged at Hackberry Creek on Grapevine Prairie. Matt Russell, Benjamin Greer and an Akers or Baker were also found hanged, all reportedly by vigilantes looking for horse and cattle thieves. The Record brothers were buried at Parrish Cemetery in Coppell. Their mother, Lavinna, lived with her daughter, Eliza Jane, until 1910 when she was put in a poor farm at Hutchins. It was there she died. Relatives have been unable to find her grave or her death certificate.

Parrish Family Cemetery
Photo Taken by Author

Children of Josiah and Lavinna were:
- *Eliza Jane, born 1834 in Ohio, married: [1] James B. Parrish; [2] Henry S. Parrish; [3] John W. Askey, a Dallas County road builder; [4] Charles Carter [5] William Coffey.*
- *Sylvester, born, 1841, in Indiana, married Harriett.*
- *Jacob, born 1845, in Indiana.*
- *John, born 1847, in Indiana, died 1869, married Sarah S. Bullock.*
- *Hester Ann, born 1849 in Indiana, married Wright Tillery.*
- *Silas, born 1850, in Indiana, died 1869.*
- *Otis, born 1857 in Indiana, lived in Fort Worth in 1932.*

Submitted by: Ima Faye Thomas Evans
1001 Sherwood Dr.
Bedford, Tx 76022

* * * * *

Dallas County Sheriff Allen Beard was born in about 1820, in Tennessee. After spending several years in Missouri he came to Dallas with his family sometime prior to July 1848. Beard was elected justice of the peace, Precinct 1, in Dallas County in 1850 and served three terms in that office. He was elected sheriff of Dallas County on August 6, 1860,

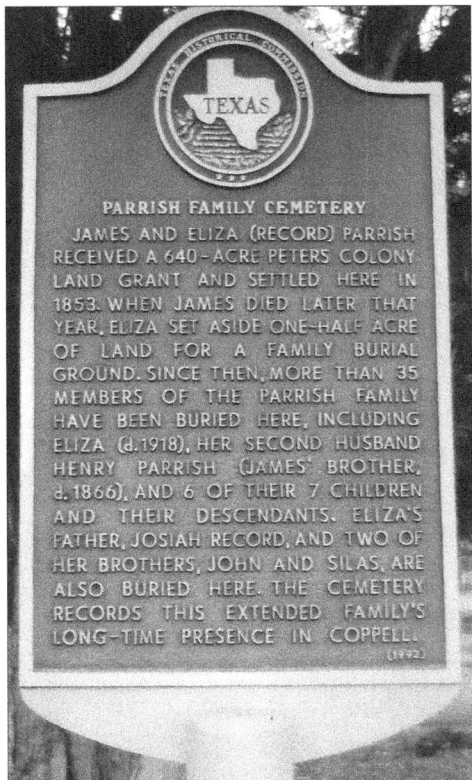

Parrish Family Cemetery in Coppell, Texas
Photo Taken by Author

and served as sheriff until August 4, 1862.

As sheriff of Dallas County when Josiah Record was lynched, it was Sheriff Beard's duty and responsibility to investigate the murder. No records have been found that anyone was ever arrested, charged, tried, or convicted, for the murder of Josiah Record.

The 1880 United States Federal Census records show that Lavina Record, age sixty-two, born about 1818 in Ohio, was a widow and head of her household, living in Precinct 8, in Dallas. Her son Otis Record, age twenty-three, was living with her.

Josiah Record is buried in the Parrish Cemetery, 746 Cardinal Lane, in Coppell, Texas. The dates on his tombstone are, 1819 – 1861.

* * * * *

Also buried in the Parrish Cemetery are two sons of Josiah and Lavinna Record, John Record and Silas Record. Both of these two sons were lynched on August 25, 1869. [See Chapter 4 for details].

Chapter 4

John Record
White male, age 23, born in Indiana

Silas Record
White male, age 16, born in Iowa

William James
White male, age 26, born in Indiana

Thomas Barkley
White male, age 20, born in Illinois

Offense - Suspected cattle and horse thieves

All four lynched Wednesday, August 25, 1869
in northwest Dallas County, Texas

On August 25, 1869, according to news reports and other accounts, John Record, age twenty-three; his younger brothers Silas Record, age sixteen; Otis Record, age twelve; William James, age twenty-six; and Thomas Barkley, age twenty; were working cattle on Hackberry Creek in far northwest Dallas County. By the end of the day, four of the five would be dead by the vigilante's rope.

Otis Record, the youngest of the group managed to escape the lynching party. But years later in 1882, Otis made the newspapers for shooting a man in Fort Worth.

Josiah A. Record, the father of the three Record boys was lynched on August 13, 1861, in Dallas County. *[See Chapter Three for the details of his death]*.

Here are some of the newspaper accounts of the lynchings that were published in September 1869. Also, there are accounts in books published by people who had memories of the lynchings.

The Dallas Weekly Herald

Saturday, September 4, 1869, reported in part:

Judge Norton informs us that four men named Baker, James, John Record and Silas Record were found hanging in the woods, on Hackberry Creek, 2 miles West of Keenan's Crossing on the Elm Fork of the Trinity River, They were hung by some unknown persons on Wednesday night and were not found until Saturday morning.

* * * * *

The *Galveston Daily News*, Friday, September 10, 1869, had this article under the title :

TEXAS NEWS.

The Dallas Herald, 4th inst., learns from Judge Norton, that four men, named Baker, James, John Record and Silas Record were found hanging in the woods, on Hackberry Creek, two miles West of Keenan's crossing on Elm Fork of the Trinity River, on Saturday week. They were hung by some unknown persons on Wednesday night and not found until Saturday morning, when they were cut down. The Herald learned no further particulars, as to who the parties were who hung them, or what they were hung for.

The *McKinney Messenger*, of the same date, has the same news and says "it is tolerably well authenticated." The *Messenger* says it is reported that the men hung were all horse-thieves.

* * * * *

The book, *History and Reminiscences of Denton County*, by Ed F. Bates, copyright 1918, and reprinted in 1976, gave the following account of the lynching:

Denton, Texas, September 18, 1869.

Ku Klux Klan or Vigilantes have been working down in Dallas County. If the reports that I hear are correct and I suppose they are. On the Third of this month five men and a boy were found hung on Hackberry Creek on Grapevine Prairie. Men named James, Akers, and Record, and his young brother, a boy about fifteen years old, were all found hanging on a pole stuck in the fork of a tree and then propped up with two forks like you were going to hang a hog. About three miles away a man named Russell and one named Greer were found hanging to a limb.

* * * * *

Anthony Bannon Norton was born in Mt. Vernon, Ohio, in about

1810. He was educated at Kenyon College, and admitted to the bar in 1840 in Ohio. He came to Texas in 1848. Judge Norton was elected to the Texas legislature from the Nineteenth District in 1857, and was re-elected in 1859. Judge Norton was considered a leading citizen in Texas and was appointed U. S. Marshal of the Northern District of Texas on April 2, 1879. How Judge Norton came to know about the lynchings of the Records and the other two has not been found. It was not recorded if he was the person that found the men who had been lynched, or if someone told him about the lynching. But, he was the person that informed the newspapers of the deaths of the four.

* * * * *

The *Dallas Weekly Herald* of Saturday, September 18, 1869, made this report:

> *The Denton Monitor gives the following version of the hanging which we mentioned week before last:*
>
> *Last Saturday morning, we are reliably informed, three men and a boy. . . John Record, his brother Silas Record, fifteen years of age, a Mr. Akers. . . were found on Hackberry Creek, Grape Vine Prairie, suspended by the neck from a pole, one end of which was adjusted on stakes and the other in the fork of a tree. Three miles from this point, near Keenan's Crossing, two others… Matt Russell and Benjamin Greer… were found dead, hanging to a limb. Greer, James and Akers were strangers, but Russell and the Records, we are told were raised in this section of Texas.*
>
> *From Appearance of their bodies it was supposed they were hung on the night of Wednesday, the 25th of August.*
>
> *We are told these men have been engaged in horse and cow stealing a long time, and though it seems almost impossible to bring a thief to justice; though it appears criminals invariably succeed in breaking jail before they can be tried, still we are opposed to mob law.*

* * * * *

The 1860 census records show that John Record and his younger brother, Silas Record were both born in Iowa. John born about 1847, and Silas born about 1851. However, The Mortality Schedule of 1870 which was made shortly after their deaths shows that John Record was born in Indiana, and Silas Record was born in Iowa.

* * * * *

The *Dallas Daily Times-Herald*, Saturday, July 4, 1891, published an article about the history of crime in Dallas County.

Here is part of that article titled:

MUST GO TO THE GALLOWS.

In 1866-67 there was a great deal of lawlessness in this portion of the state, and many outlaws rendezvoused in Dallas County. Cattle and horses were stolen and run off and the farmers suffered terribly at the hands of the marauders. One night a well-organized band of regulators swooped down upon Keenan's crossing, near Farmer's Branch, and captured John Record, his two younger brothers and two strangers who were herding 3,000 head of cattle which, it was claimed, they had stolen. The Records and their companions were all hanged on the same tree.

* * * * *

The *Dallas Daily Times-Herald*, Tuesday, July 7, 1891, printed corrections noted in part:

AN EARLY CHAPTER.

In Dallas History Repeated With Some Correction.

The "Recards," two of whom were hanged for stealing cattle, in the early history of Dallas County, were no relation to our Joe; in fact the names are spelled differently. Capt. Joe Record............

* * * * *

Actually the spelling of the last name of John and Silas was Record, not "Recard," as reported in the article of the *Dallas Times-Herald*, July 7, 1891. However there was no family connection to Captain Joseph W. Record.

Captain Joseph W. Record was a highly respected member of the community, and an outstanding leader in Dallas. He served in Company K, Nineteenth Texas Cavalry during the Civil War, and later was a Dallas County deputy sheriff under James E. Barkley. He also served four years as a Deputy United States Marshal under General W. L. Cabell.

* * * * *

John Record is shown to have enlisted in the Confederate Army in February 1861. He served in Captain Good's Texas Artillery, State Troops. Texas Light Artillery State Troops [Dallas Light Artillery.]

The U.S. Confederate Soldiers Complied Service Records 1861-1865, show John Record served in Captain Douglas' Co., Artillery and Capt. Greer's Rocket Battery.

The Texas Voter Registration Lists, 1867-1869, show that John Record, born in Indiana, was listed on the 1867 Dallas County Voter Registration List.

The Dallas County Marriage Records show that John Record married Sarah S. Bullock on January 1, 1868. J. M. Myers, M. G. performed the marriage.

* * * * *

The 1870 United States Mortality Schedule lists all deaths in each county, the cause of death and other information, for the one year period from June 1, 1869 to June 1, 1870.

Here is the information listed on the 1870 Mortality Schedule, in regard to the lynchings in Dallas County:

646 **Record, John** – *white, male, married, age 23, born Indiana,   death month August, hung by mob, homicide.*

646 **James, William** – *White, male, married, age 26, born Indiana, death month August, hung by mob, homicide.*

646 **Barkley, Thomas** – *white, male, age 20, born Illinois, death month August, hung by mob, homicide.*

646 **Record, Silas** – *white male, age 16, born Iowa, death month August, hung by mob, homicide.*

* * * * *

No record was found in the 1870 Mortality Schedule for a Matt Russell, Benjamin Greer or a Mr. Akers in the Dallas, Denton or Tarrant County Mortality Schedules. These three possible deaths have not been verified, and are not counted in this book as hangings or lynchings that occurred in Dallas County.

According to Dallas County Probate Records John Record signed and dated his Last Will and Testament on December 28, 1868. In his will John Record left everything in his estate to his wife, Sarah S. Record, and made her the executrix of his will. A copy of John Record's will is included in Probate Case file #555. The case was filed with S. S. Jones, clerk and County Judge A. Bledsoe, heard the case.

When he died on August 25, 1869, John and Sarah Record had been married just under one year and eight months.

* * * * *

Dallas County Probate Case #555
Application filed September 9, 1869
John Record, deceased, Aug. ___, 1869
Sarah S. Record, Executrix of the Will
Inventory of the Estate of John Record:

500 head of stock cattle worth $5.50 per head. $2750.00
8 head of horses worth $40.00 per head. 320.00
1 wagon and harness. 150.00
30 head of hogs worth $1.00 per head. 30.00
10 head of sheep worth $1.00 per head. 10.00
house hold and other sundries worth. 50.00

Total $3,310.00

Court filings were made in Dallas County Probate Case #555, John Record, deceased, on, September 9, October 19, and November 1, 1869.

* * * * *

In the book, *Historic Bethel Cemetery, Coppell, Texas, Dallas County*, there are handwritten pages that list the following:

Known dead buried in Bethel Cemetery, formerly Sands Cemetery, Coppell, Texas.
Akers. . . . . hanged by Vigilantes, 9/3/1869.
Barkley, Thomas. . . . . hanged by Vigilantes, 9/3/1869.
Greer. . . . . hanged by Vigilantes, 9/3/1869.
James, William. hanged by Vigilantes, 9/3/1869.
Record, John. . . . . born 1847 – Confederate Veter-
an-hanged – Marker in Parrish Cemetery, Coppell, 9/3/1869.
Record, Otis. escaped to Arkansas-Error in text-
died in Carrol City, Ark.
Record, Silas . . . . born 1851 – hanged, 9/3/1869.
Russell. . . . . hanged by Vigilantes, 9/3/1869.

* * * * *

According to the 1870 Mortality Schedules, John Record, Silas Record, William James and Thomas Barkley are the only ones verified as lynched/hanged. The hanging date of 9/3/1869 listed above is not correct. September 3, 1869, was the date the bodies were found and reported to the authorities and newspapers.

In 1869, the *Dallas Weekly Herald* was published once a week on Saturdays. The first article about the lynchings was published on Satur-

John Record's correct year of death was 1869 and not 1870 as noted on his grave marker, 1847 - 1869. Parrish Family Cemetery, Coppell, Texas. *Photo Taken by Author*

day, September 4, 1869. In the article it was stated that the bodies were found on Saturday morning last. [which was August 28th] They were hung by some unknown persons on Wednesday night [August 25th] and were not found until Saturday morning.

The correct date of the lynching of the four, John Record, Silas Record, William James and Thomas Barkley, was on, Wednesday, August 25, 1869.

* * * * *

The Parrish Cemetery on Cardinal Lane, Coppell, Texas, has tombstones for the following:

Silas Record . . . . 1853 – 1869
John S. Record . . . . 1847 – 1870
            [the correct year of his death was 1869]
Josiah Record . . . . 1819 – 1861
                [see chapter 3 for his story]
            [Josiah was the father of Silas and John Record]

John and Silas Record are buried in the Parrish Cemetery. Their sister Eliza Jane Record Parrish married James B. Parrish, thus they became related to the Parrish family by marriage.

Silas Record - 1853 - 1869 buried in the Parrish Family Cemetery, Coppell, Texas.
Photo Taken by Author

* * * * *

According to family history, Norval R. Winniford was born on December 25, 1823, in Casey County, Kentucky. He brought his family to Texas and settled in the southern section of Dallas County near Lancaster. Winniford was said to be a slave owner, but he refused to fight for the Confederacy. He hid out along Ten Mile and Bear creeks to avoid conscription. During the war he drove ox teams hauling timbers for the south to Mexico.

N. R. Winniford was appointed sheriff of Dallas County on November 13, 1867, by Major J. J. Reynolds, of the new Reconstruction government, and he served in that office until May 1870.

Because he was sheriff of Dallas County and the lynchings occurred in the rural section of the county, it was the duty and responsibility of Sheriff N. R. Winniford to investigate the murder cases. No records were found that anyone was ever arrested, charged, tried or convicted for the murders that occurred on August 25, 1869, of John Record, Silas Record, William James and Thomas Barkley.

* * * * *

The 1880 United States Federal Census records for Dallas County show that Lavina Record, white female, age sixty-two, [mother of John, Silas and Otis Record] was living in Precinct 8, in Dallas County. She was the head of the house hold and her son Otis Record, age twenty-three, was the only person living with her.

* * * * *

The *Fort Worth Democrat-Advance*, January 6, 1882 published an article in part, titled:

Dallas
Dastardly Shooting of a Prominent Citizen by A Drunken Rowdy
About one o'clock this morning, as Leopold Bohny, one of our most respectable citizens, was on his way home, he was run against by a drunken man from Grapevine, named Otis Record. Bohny remonstrated at the act when Record drew a pistol, fired and shot Bohny, the ball entering the left side, and was taken out of the right side. Record ran, but was captured by the police and jailed. Bohny is still alive, but his physicians make no predictions as to the final result of the wound. It is feared it is very dangerous.

* * * * *

Leopold F. Bohny, was born about 1843. He did not die from the January 1882 gunshot wound fired by Otis Record. Fifteen years later when he did die, Bohny was provided a headstone for deceased Union Civil War veterans. His date of death was recorded as January 15, 1897.

* * * * *

In 1989, Margaret Ann Thetford in her "Family Tree" column in the *Dallas Morning News* wrote two articles that mentioned the 1869 Dallas County lynchings. The articles she wrote were about burials in the Bethel Cemetery, and the ongoing work by the Historic Bethel Cemetery Association to identify the names and other information of persons buried in that cemetery. The articles by Thetford were published in the *Dallas Morning News* on June 29, 1989, and August 3, 1989.

The newspaper coverage of the deaths of four suspected cattle rustlers and horse thieves did not make much of a news story in the summer of 1869. No one was every arrested or charged with the murders.

Chapter 5

Reuben Johnson, aka: "Rube"

Black male, age 37, born about 1837, in Mississippi

Offense – None, he was a victim

Refused to commit perjury in a theft trial

Lynched Sunday, December 27, 1874, in Dallas County, Texas

Rube Johnson was a man of principal. He believed in standing up for what he believed was right, and in the end it led to his death. If only one man in this book can be called a hero, it should be Rube Johnson. This is the story of the circumstances surrounding his death, some of the people involved in the case, and how the criminal justice system, from his death in 1874 until the case was closed in 1881, failed him.

On Thursday, January 21, 1875, the body of Rube Johnson was found hanging from a tree in the Mountain Creek area of southwest Dallas County. His head and face were mutilated. He had been severely beaten with clubs, and his throat cut from ear to ear.

On Sunday night, December 27, 1874, Rube spent the night in Bill Reed's house on the property of a man named Marion Dill. Dill along with two other men came to Reed's house, called Johnson out and took him away. Rube Johnson was not seen again until his body was found on January 21, 1875.

James Edward Barkley was sheriff of Dallas County when Rube Johnson was killed. Barkley served as sheriff from December 2, 1873 to February 15, 1876. He was born in Scott County, Kentucky on December 19, 1824. He moved with his parents to Missouri, and in 1849 when he got "Gold Fever" he left for California. Barkley later returned to Missouri where he was a successful merchant.

He married Margaret I. Mobley. When the Civil War broke out Barkley served in the Confederate Army until the end of the war. Barkley lost his homestead, stock of goods and his slaves when the Union Army confiscated everything he owned. He then moved to Texas and settled

Sheriff James Edward Barkley
Served 1873 - 1876
Courtesy of O'Byrne Cox, Jr.

in Freestone County before moving to Dallas County in about 1867.

As the sheriff of Dallas County when Rube Johnson was found murdered, it was James Barkley's duty to investigate the case. Three men, Marion Dill, William Bell and Elijah T. Rice were quickly suspected of killing Johnson and were arrested. All three were charged with the murder of Johnson.

In 1874, William Dill, the brother of Marion Dill, was accused along with two other men named Shackelford and Longley, with the theft of wheat from a man named Harry Taylor. When the case was ready for trial, Rube Johnson was the only witness for the State.

On the night Johnson was murdered Marion Dill tried to get him to swear that on the night of the wheat theft William Dill was at his house, thereby providing an alibi for William Dill.

Rube Johnson refused to go along with the lie and in the end it cost him his life.

Ashley Pryor, bailiff for the Dallas County court, arrested Elijah T. Rice in the western part of Tarrant County and returned him to Dallas. Marion Dill, William Bell and Elijah T. Rice were all indicted by the grand jury for the murder of Rube Johnson.

Judge Silas Hare was assigned to hear the case against Dill, Bell and Rice. Judge Hare was born in 1827, in Ross County, Ohio. He moved to Indiana where he studied law and was admitted to the Indiana Bar Association in 1850. Hare served in the Mexican-American War. He also served in the Civil War as a captain and was promoted to major in 1863 and was stationed in Texas. Judge Hare also served as chief justice of New Mexico under the Confederate government. After the Civil War, Judge Hare settled in Sherman, Texas, and served as a district judge of the criminal court from 1873-1876.

The 1870 United States Census records provided the following information:

> *Reuben Johnson, mulatto male, age 37, born about 1837 in Mississippi, home Pct. # 2, Dallas, Texas. [victim of lynching on December 27, 1874].*

William B. Dill, white male, age 17, born about 1853 in Alabama, home Pct. # 3, Dallas, Texas. [brother of Marion Dill].

S. Hare, white male, age 42, born about 1828 in Ohio, home Sherman, Grayson, Texas.[Judge in murder trials of Marion Dill, William Bell and Elijah T. Rice].

Edward W. Hunt, white male, age 44, born about 1826 in Alabama, home Pct. # 1 Dallas, Texas. [defense attorney]

N. R. Winniford, white male, age 46, born about 1824 in Kentucky, home Pct. #2, Dallas, Texas. [A former sheriff of Dallas County from 1867-1870, he served on the jury during the trial held in 1878. See Dallas Daily Herald, February 24, 1878].

The 1880 United States Census Records show the following:

Marion Dill, white male, age 32, born about 1848 in Alabama, home Pct. #7, Dallas, Texas. He was the husband of Calarinda M. Dill. [Marion Dill was indicted and tried for the murder of Reuben Johnson].

Calarinda M. Dill, white female, age 48, born about 1832 in Tennessee, home Pct. # 7, Dallas, Texas. [wife of Marion Dill].

J. M. Thurmond, white male, age 41, born about 1839 in Tennessee, home Dallas, Dallas, Texas.

J. M. Thurmond served as lead defense attorney in the February 1878 trial of Dill, Bell and Rice. From April 1879 to September 1880 Thurmond served as mayor of Dallas and he was shot and killed on March 14, 1882 in a courtroom, by Robert E. Cowart, as the result of an argument between the two men stemming from the removal of Thurmond as mayor.

In September 1875, Dill, Bell and Rice were arraigned in District Court for the murder of Rube Johnson. The murder case against the three came before the court in December 1875 but was continued because of the absence of an important witness. Sheriff Barkley captured the witness, who was then placed under a $250 bond and ordered to appear in court on the 11th of January.

The State of Texas vs. Marion Dill, William Bell and Elijah Rice. Case #2734, Charge Murder, tried in Dallas County, Texas

The *Dallas Weekly Herald* of January 16, 1876 reported that testimony in the trial of Dill, Bell and Rice had been given by several witnesses. Headlines were:

The Dill, Bell and Rice Case
Bell turns State Evidence and Fastens the Horrible Crime on Dill

Reuben Johnson was on his way from Tarrant County to attend court in Dallas as a witness for the State in the case of William Dill, charged with the theft of wheat. Johnson stopped at the home of Bill Reed, but was taken from the house by Marion Dill and then horribly murdered.

William Bell testified that Dill and Rice came to his house and they wanted him to help them put Johnson out of the way. Bell further stated that he did go with Dill and Rice to Reed's house and they called Johnson out. Johnson went back in and put on his clothes and they told him he was under arrest and tied his hands.

"We hung him. Dill put the rope around his neck." Bell said. "Rice told him that he had told him when he was up in Tarrant County that if he came down here he'd be hung. Rice told him when he was let down that if he had anything to say, to say it. He replied that he had nothing to say. After we hung him, Rice cut his throat with my knife."

The trial began in mid-January 1876. The *Dallas Daily Herald* on January 21, 1876 reported that Marion Dill was sentenced to be hung for the murder of Rube Johnson. The 14th District Court minutes also show that Marion Dill was sentenced to hang for the murder of Reuben Johnson. For his part in the murder, Elijah T. Rice was sentenced to life in prison at hard labor in the State Prison at Huntsville. Judge Silas Hare overruled a motion by the defense for a new trial. The case was expected to be appealed.

In October 1876 the cases against Dill and Rice were reversed and remanded back to Dallas County for a new trial.

In the book, *Fugitives From Justice, The Notebook of Texas Ranger Sergeant James B. Gillett*, William Bell in February 1877 is listed as a murderer from Dallas County with a reward of $200 offered for his arrest. In the 1870s, Sgt. James Gillett carried in his saddlebags a handwritten notebook filled with the names of wanted persons, rewards offered, and sometimes a description of the wanted person.

In September 1877, Murder Case #2734, again came before the 14th District Court in Dallas. Attachments for the arrest of Marion Dill, William Bell and Elijah T. Rice were issued by the court. Bell could not be found and was believed to be hiding out in the Choctaw Nation or in Missouri. The case was again delayed.

In February 1878, the murder case against Dill, Bell and Rice again came up for trial in District Court in Dallas. After several days of testimony the courtroom was crowded and ready to hear the closing arguments. J. M. Thurmond for the defense spoke for nearly three hours devoting a good portion of his speech to vilifying The *Herald's* reporter for biased articles of testimony that appeared in that paper. Thurmond was followed by Colonel Hurt who gave the speech for the prosecution. Aldridge was the county attorney.

After the charge from the judge, the case went to the jury. The jury voted eleven for conviction and one for acquittal. The lone person voting for acquittal was N. R. Winneford, the former sheriff of Dallas County. The court discharged the jury and sent Marion Dill back to jail.

The *Galveston Daily News* in their July 10, 1878 paper noted the following:

> *Clarender Dill, the wife of the notorious Marion Dill, charged with hanging the negro, Reuben Johnson, has been arrested for keeping a disreputable house at Mountain Creek.*

On August 28, 1878, *Case #2734, State of Texas vs. Marion Dill*, William Bell and Elijah T. Rice, once again came before the court. The court ordered that bail for Marion Dill, the defendant, be fixed at $1,000, and that this case be continued by the State.

On February 10, 1879, *Case #2734, State of Texas vs. Marion Dill*, et al, charge murder, a special judge ordered sixty jurors be summoned for trial on March 4, 1879.

On February 11, 1879, *Case #3902, State of Texas vs. Elijah T. Rice*, charge murder, [the case numbers having been separated.] Special Judge R. E. Burke, upon agreement of prosecution and defense, disqualified Geo. Aldridge, presiding judge, having previously served as counsel in this case.

On March 4, 1879, *Case, #2734, State of Texas vs. Marion Dill*, was again continued by the court.

On March 4, 1879, *Case #3902, State of Texas vs. Elijah T. Rice*, was continued by the court.

On January 12, 1881, *Case #2734, State of Texas vs. Marion Dill, William Bell and Elijah T. Rice*, charge murder, E. C. McClure, special judge in the 14th District Court, held a hearing in regard to this case. The following information is recorded in part from the 1879 -1881 Minutes Book, Vol. M., page 621:

> *As such Special Judge, thence upon came the County Attorney for the State and by leave of the Court says he will no further prosecute herein. It is therefore ordered and adjudged and decreed by the Court that the defendant Marion Dill go hence without delay and of this cause stand fully acquitted. E. C. McClure, Special Judge.*

From the pages of the *Dallas Weekly Herald* dated January 20, 1881

DILL, BELL and RICE

One by one the roses fall, this perhaps the most important murder trial, and certainly one which created more intense than any other in the county, is finally off the docket. The state entered a nolle pros. in Bell's case, to secure his evidence against the other two. Dill and Rice were both convicted of murder in the first degree. Bell fled the state. The appellate court reversed and remanded. The state then entered a nolle as to Rice to secure his evidence against Dill. In the trial of Dill the jury disagreed. The state was unable to go to trial without the evidence of Bell and his wife. The case hung fire for nearly five years, and on yesterday morning the case against Dill was dismissed. While public opinion has been strong against these defendants, especially Dill, yet according to forms of law they are free. Judge Thurmond, the leading counsel for Dill, has justly received very high compliments for his able and successful defense of this important case.

None but the most skillful advocate it seems to us, could have succeeded in this case. The prosecution has been able, determined and tenacious. Judges Hurt, Bower, Seay and others fought ably but the defense has been victorious.

* * * * *

Reuben "Rube" Johnson died for what he believed was the right thing to do. When he refused to change the testimony he was about to give in court, he was taken out beaten, cut and lynched. After five years of trials and delays the charges were dropped against the men who murdered him.

Reuben "Rube" Johnson died a hero.

Chapter 6

Wesley Jones

Black male, age 27 or 28

Offense – Rape of Mrs. Sarah Benson

Rape committed November 2, 1875

Arrested in Jefferson, Texas, in late December 1875

Trial held in Dallas County, Texas
Judge Silas Hare 14th District Court presided

Tried and convicted for the rape of a white woman

Guilty verdict by jury January 18, 1876

Hanged Friday, August 11, 1876, in Dallas County, Texas

Mrs. Sarah Benson was a young woman of German decent. She and her husband were in their first year of marriage and she was pregnant with her first child. They lived on a farm on Rowlett Creek, some fourteen miles east of Dallas, in the eastern portion of Dallas County. On November 2, 1875, her husband was away on business, and she was alone at the farm.

On that day in early November 1875, Wesley Jones came to the Benson home. When he found out that Mrs. Benson was home alone he brutally assaulted and raped her. As a result of the attack on her by Jones, Mrs. Benson's baby was born premature. Jones then fled the Benson farm and the state of Texas.

James E. Barkley was elected sheriff of Dallas County on December 2, 1873, and served as sheriff until February 15, 1876. Sheriff Barkley conducted the investigation into the rape of Mrs. Benson and the search for Wesley Jones.

According to the *Dallas Daily Herald* of December 29, 1875, Sheriff Barkley tracked Jones more than 2,000 miles. Twice he tracked him to the Indian Nation, but every time Jones managed to elude the officers. Sheriff Barkley notified the sheriff of Marion County, at Jefferson,

Texas, to be on the lookout for Jones. The sheriff at Jefferson arrested Jones just after Christmas 1875, and held him for Dallas County. Dallas County Deputy Sheriff Tom Scott went to Jefferson and returned Jones to Dallas for trial. Jones had been on the run for seven weeks before he was arrested.

To prevent a mob from taking Jones out and lynching him, Sheriff Barkley called out two military companies, the Lamar Rifles and Stonewall Greys, to help escort Jones to the home of Mrs. Benson for the purpose of having her identify Wesley Jones as her attacker. Mrs. Benson identified Jones as her assailant and there were no problems with mobs. Jones was returned safely to the Dallas County Jail.

The case of *Texas vs. Wesley Jones*, charge—rape, cause #3196, was assigned to Judge Silas Hare, Dallas County 14th District Court, and the trial started January 18, 1876. After hearing the testimony, and arguments of the attorneys Fearn and Kearby for the defense, and Judge Hurt, the prosecutor, Judge Hare gave his charge to the jury.

After receiving the charge from Judge Hare, the jury was absent for about ten minutes when they notified the court that they had agreed upon a verdict. The jury sentenced Wesley Jones to be hanged by the neck until he was dead.

On January 21, 1876, the attorneys for Wesley Jones filed a notice of appeal to the Supreme Court. About this same time Judge Silas Hare retired from the District Court.

Judge Nathaniel M. Burford would then take over the case of Wesley Jones. Judge Burford was born on June 24, 1824, in Tennessee. He moved to Jefferson, Texas, in 1847, and then to Dallas in 1848. He was elected district attorney and then judge of the 14th District Court.

The Supreme Court refused to overturn the conviction and death sentence of Wesley Jones. On July 10, 1876, Judge Burford sentenced Jones to be hung on Friday, August 11, 1876.

William Marion Moon had replaced Sheriff Barkley as the sheriff of Dallas County. It would now be his responsibility to carry out the execution order of the court. As the day for the execution neared, Sheriff Moon had a gallows built in the bottoms above the Texas and Pacific Railroad bridge.

The night before his execution, Wesley Jones was visited by his wife and child, who had come from Upshur County to see him. They were allowed to see him again the morning he was to be executed. They had been married four years, and his wife said he had always been good to her.

The Lamar Rifles and Stonewall Greys were again present in case problems developed. On the day of the hanging the streets in Dallas became crowded with men, women and children who came from miles around in buggies, wagons, horseback and afoot. They came to shop, visit, and view the hanging. The *Dallas Daily Herald* reported that "There must have been fully five thousand persons from outside the city."

It had been years since a legal hanging had taken place in Dallas. There had been a number of lynchings that took place as reported in Chapters 2-5, but the last legal hanging was Jane Elkins, on May 27, 1853.

The *Herald* reporters said they saw no rowdy conduct, noise or disorder. They saw no drunkenness or lawlessness. They commented on the number of horsemen about the city, and that the average Texan is not afoot, but is well mounted.

Between three and four o'clock in the afternoon Sheriff Moon, assisted by two deputies and Dallas City Marshal Morton, brought out the condemned man, Wesley Jones was described as a burly negro with a coarse, sensual, brutal face, dressed in black, and wearing a white straw hat.

Judge Nathaniel M. Burford's tombstone in Greenwood Cemetery, Dallas. Born June 24, 1824 and died May 10, 1898. *Photo Taken by Author.*

They loaded Jones into the back of a two horse wagon and seated him in a chair. Accompanying the group were two African American ministers of the gospel, Rev. George Allen, and Rev. Marshall of Waxahachie. The rope was also loaded into the wagon. The Lamar Rifles and Stonewall Greys accompanied the procession from the jail past the courthouse square to the gallows.

About 3,000 people followed the procession to the gallows, where people had already began to assemble. One news report said there must have been 6,000 to 8,000 people present.

The military was described as providing a valuable service in keeping back the crowd, for only a limited number could be accommodated within the circle that surrounded the stand. Sheriff Moon escorted the prisoner up the steps of the scaffold. Along with the sheriff were his two deputies, Marshal Morton, Rev. J. R. Allen and two African American ministers. The prisoner's wife and child came forward and mounted the stand to give their last farewell. They were together about five minutes. After leaving the stand they left the scene.

The prisoner was allowed to make a statement. The *Dallas Daily Herald*, August 12, 1876, reported Jones did say:

> *You have come to see me die, I like all of you, have to die. I thank God I am going home to rest. I hope to meet you all in heaven. I know I have done wrong, as you all have. God will forgive me for what I have done, quick as for what you all have done. I feel that Jesus is with me. I hope this will be a warning to you all. May God be with you all forever and forever. You can persecute the body, but not the soul. Do not scorn me because I have to be hung. I have said about all that I have to or can say. I want you all to pray for me.*

> *There was a shaking of hands and bidding the last good-by, when all left the stand but the officers, Sheriff Moon then read the death warrant, after which he unshackled the prisoner and tied his arms behind him. He then had the prisoner step on the trap door, tied his feet, placed the rope around his neck and the black cap over his head. The trap door was sprung open. Five minutes after the body dropped through the trap and hung by the neck not a kick was perceptible, only a slight shivering. At the expiration of fifteen minutes he was pronounced dead, dead. At this juncture a few shouts went up from among the crowd, which did not appear in accordance with the awful hour.*

The *Dallas Daily Herald* of August 12, 1876, concluded their article with this paragraph:

> *The Law Vindicated - In conclusion The Herald congratulates the people of Dallas county upon their law abiding conduct from first to last, relative to this outrageous criminal. The law has been carried out. Justice had been done. A jury composed of twelve good citizens tried the case, and convicted the man, who confessed the crime. The case was appealed, and the decision of the District court here confirmed and the prisoner sentenced and executed accordingly.*

As a result of the assault and rape on Mrs. Sarah Benson that occurred on November 2, 1875, she was reported to have suffered both physically and mentally. Her baby was born premature, and at the end of December 1875, she had not recovered, and her health was reported to be in a dangerous condition.

Chapter 7
Allen Wright

Black male, age 21

Born about 1859, in Mississippi

Offense – Murder of Jesse Wicks, black male

Crime committed February 7, 1880

Indicted for murder March 16, 1880

Trial held in Dallas County, Texas

Trial- June 28 & 29, 1880

Tried by all black jury

Hanged Friday, August 27, 1880, in Dallas County, Texas

Sheriff William Marion Moon and Deputy Sheriff Jones had taken a number of people to the asylum in Austin and were returning to Dallas by train. At the Hutchins stop, in southern Dallas County, Allen Wright was turned over to the officers by Ben Perry and Mose Bledsoe. Wright's hands were bound by ropes, and a rope around his neck. The sheriff and deputy were told "he should be brought to Dallas and put in jail, as he had killed another colored man in a dispute."

Allen Wright and Jesse Wicks were both working as wood cutters. Wright and Wicks were working cutting rails and wood in partnership with a Dr. Mitchner. Wright decided he wanted to work cleaning out a well and hired a man named Mose Perkins to work in his place cutting wood.

On payday when they were considering the partnership settlement, Wicks objected to allowing Wright any money for Perkins' work. Wicks also wanted more than half the money. A quarrel ensued in which Wright alleged that Wicks attempted to brain him with an ax, but was prevented by Perkins.

The three went to Hutchins where the dispute continued and Wicks said to Wright that he had a good mind to kill him; that they would have a settlement next week and have no more to do with one another.

Wright went to the house of Dr. Stone where he got a shotgun loaded with buckshot. He returned to the Texas Central Stockyards where he shot Wicks. Wicks died an hour later.

Wright was taken to the Dallas County Jail by Sheriff Moon and Deputy Sheriff Jones and was charged with the murder of Jesse Wicks.

Sheriff William Marion Moon was born on March 18, 1830, near Independence, Missouri. He served as a deputy sheriff and city marshal in Dallas. He served as the elected sheriff of Dallas from 1876 to 1880.

Sheriff William Marion Moon
Served 1876 - 1880
Photo Courtesy O'Byrne Cox, Jr.

On March 16, 1880, Allen Wright was indicted for murder in the first degree. Case #4236 was to be tried in the 14th District Court in Dallas.

On May 20, 1880 the trial was set for June 28th and in open court on May 22, 1880 Allen Wright attempted to plead guilty to manslaughter. The county attorney refused to accept the plea because he wanted to charge Wright with first degree murder, which was a hanging offense. The trial date was again confirmed to start on June 28th.

On June 28, 1880, Wright was tried in Dallas County. The trial lasted almost two days. Wright was represented by appointed attorneys J. B. Simpson and A. H. Field. County Attorney Seay and Assistant County Attorney Morrow prosecuted the case.

At the time of his trial Wright was very sick. He had to be carried to and from the jail to the courthouse. Wright charged later that Mose Perkins gave false testimony against him, and that while in jail he wrote a letter to Perkins but Perkins never answered the note, in person or otherwise.

According to an article in the *Dallas Morning News*, on July 28, 1893, titled "Hangings in Dallas County" it was written about Allen Wright's trial, "It may be stated incidentally that this was the only negro jury ever impaneled in the county."

The jury was out only about fifteen minutes before they came back with their verdict. Judge G. N. Aldridge then issued his order.

It is therefore considered by the court and so ordered and judged and decreed that the verdict of the jury herein all things approved and confirmed, that the defendant Allen Wright is adjudged to be guilty of murder in the first degree and that his punishment be fixed at death, that he be hanged by the neck until he is dead, and that the State of Texas do have recover of the defendant Allen Wright all costs in this behalf incurred and that he be remanded to the custody of the sheriff of Dallas County to await the further order of this court.

The *Dallas Daily Herald*, July 9, 1880, reported that Wright took the verdict very coolly and positively declined to appeal his case. Judge Aldridge told Wright that he had the privilege to take an appeal, but Wright declined. The court then again appointed Judge J. B. Simpson and Judge Field, as counsel to continue to defend him. After speaking again with his attorneys, Wright still refused to appeal his case and said he was ready to die.

On August 18, 1880, Wright was taken from the jail, and under the guard of Sheriff Moon and jailer Dean, was escorted to a barber shop at the corner of Main and Field Streets where he was shaved. After getting shaved the officers escorted Wright to Freeman's Art Gallery, where he had four pictures taken. He was then escorted back to his jail cell.

Polly Williams, a sister of Allen Wright, who lived at Mineola, Texas, came to Dallas to visit him in the Dallas County Jail. Allen wrote his sister a letter, which he allowed the *Herald* reporter to publish in the newspaper on August 19, 1880. In the letter he seemed to be very sincere about his faith. He also was complimentary in the letter of the officers, and how they had taken care of him since his confinement. He mailed one of the photos he had taken to his sister.

At his request, Allen Wright had met with several ministers and expressed a desire to Rev. M. F. Smith and Rev. Parks, of a local Baptist church, to be baptized. The officers attempted to keep it as quiet as possible, but the news spread and within a short time several hundred people, both white and black, had gathered along the river bank. The prisoner was escorted to the Trinity River bank where Sheriff Moon tied a rope around the waist of Wright to prevent him from committing suicide, or escaping.

The Rev. H. S. Howell, of the black Christian church conducted the baptism. The two walked out into the water, Sheriff Moon held onto the rope that was tied to Wright's waist. The baptism was completed and the prisoner returned to jail. Wright stated, after being baptized, that he felt much better, and had a greater confidence than ever in obtaining everlasting life.

Two petitions were circulated by those in favor of commutation of the sentence of Allen Wright from death, to life in the penitentiary. Together about a thousand names were collected on the petitions.

The governor did not commute the death sentence, but did delay the execution date by one week, to give Wright more time to prepare himself spiritually for the next world.

On Thursday night, the night before he was to be executed, Wright had given up all hope of executive clemency by the governor. He slept soundly and appeared resigned to his fate.

On Friday morning Sheriff Moon received a dispatch from the governor, dated, August 27, 1880:

> *To Sheriff Moon, Dallas: The petition for commutation of Allen Wright presents no new facts. He has had time enough. It is therefore refused.*
> *O. M. Roberts, Governor.*

On the morning of the scheduled execution Mose Perkins, the witness against Allen Wright, was in town. He came to the jail because Wright had expressed a desire to see him. Sheriff Moon accompanied Perkins to Wright's cell, along with a *Herald* reporter. Perkins and Wright shook hands and Wright told Perkins, "Mose I'm going to die today."

Mose replied "Well I hate it Allen."

The two continued talking about the circumstances around Wicks' death. The conservation became one of contradictions, so Sheriff Moon asked them to stop. The conservation was terminated and Mose Perkins left.

On Friday, August 27, 1880, the gallows in "Hangman's Hollow" just above the Texas & Pacific bridge in the Trinity River bottoms, was in place and ready for the execution of Allen Wright.

Just after 1 p.m., all preparations for the execution were complete and awaiting the final hour. The city police force under Captain Morton, the Queen City Guards under the command of Captain Felton, and the Lamar Rifles under the command of Captain Morton, were all in uniform and ready to perform any duty that might be assigned.

Sheriff Moon, Under Sheriff Jones, jailer Dean, and the remaining deputies brought Wright out of the jail and placed him in a lumber wagon, for the trip to the gallows. The police and deputies marched on either side of the wagon, while the Queen City Guards followed. The group marched north on Houston Street, and then west down the bluff to the river bank, to the area known as Hangman's Hollow.

The crowd of people estimated at 5,000, lined both sides of Houston Street, and had to be pushed back by the officers as they moved toward the gallows. Men, women and children, black and white, made up the crowd of sightseers.

At the gallows, Sheriff Moon, Allen Wright and Marshal Morton ascended the scaffold. They were followed by deputy sheriffs Jones, Smith and Dean. Also, three ministers then climbed up the scaffold. Sheriff Moon read the death warrant issued by the court. Allen Wright was allowed to speak to the crowd of people. At first he refused and then decided to talk about his faith. Rev. H. S. Howell read the 86th Psalm. The ministers then shook hands with the condemned man and left the scaffold.

Sheriff Moon tied the rope around the cross-beam of the gallows, and placed the rope around Wright's neck. The black cap was placed over his head and face. At 1:15 p. m., Sheriff Moon said, "Good-bye," and at the same time dropped the trap door. Allen Wright fell to his death.

Wright had sent a letter of confession to the editor of The *Dallas Daily Times Herald*. The letter was published the day after his execution on August 28, 1880.

Allen Wright was buried in Potters' Field, in Dallas County.

Chapter 8

Adam Thompson

Black male, age about 26

Born about 1854-56, in Tennessee

Offense- Robbery and murder committed July 1, 1876

Victim – Joseph Schumaker, white male, over 50 years-old

Tried by two Dallas County juries

First conviction reversed by the Texas Court of Appeals

Convicted October 1876, and again in April 1880

Hanged Friday, July 1, 1881, in Dallas County, Texas

Joseph Schumaker, sometimes spelled Shoemaker, described as an "old and decrepit" German storekeeper, over fifty years-old, was found robbed and murdered about six miles southwest of Dallas, on the Cleburne road. His body was found outside the door of his store which also served as his residence. A pair of pants was found near his bed with nothing in the pockets. Another pair of pants was found in a box in the back part of the house, which he had probably worn the day before. In the pockets was $100. There appeared to have been a struggle in the room, as the lamp and furniture were turned over.

The next day, on July 2, 1876, G. W. Neely, Dallas County Justice of the Peace, held an inquest into the death of J. Schumaker. Judge Neely held the inquest at Schumaker's grocery store. Robert C. Lynch testified that on the morning of July 2nd, he found the body about 9 o'clock. As he sat on his horse he observed the body was lying face down in the mud, about ten feet from the door. The body was covered with bedding. Lynch also testified that J. L. Fudge and K. B. Archey were with him.

The cash box from the store was found in a field nearby, and the tracks of two men were found at the scene.

After hearing testimony, Judge Neely ruled that J. Schumaker came to his death on the night of July 1, 1876, by three blows to the head with an ax or some heavy weapon.

William Marion Moon, was elected sheriff of Dallas County on February 15, 1876, and served as sheriff until November 2, 1880. The murder of Joseph Schumaker occurred in the unincorporated area of Dallas County. Therefore, the case came under the jurisdiction of Sheriff Moon, and it was his responsibility to investigate the murder.

Sheriff Moon and his deputies, along with city police officers, had all been on alert since the murder of Schumaker. They were working hard to hunt down the killers. Within two weeks the officers had two suspects, Adam Thompson and Wesley Pollard, aka: West Pollard, or Wes Pollard. First they arrested West Pollard, and later Adam Thompson. Sheriff deputies, along with city police officers, and a citizen, Billy Myers, were all given credit in newspaper articles for assisting in the arrests.

Pollard and Thompson were arrested, indicted, and placed in the county jail. The murder charges were filed in the 14th District Court of Dallas County. *Case #3380, State of Texas vs. West Pollard and Adam Thompson* was set for trial and Judge Aldridge prosecuted the case.

On October 19, 1876, Wesley Pollard requested that he be tried separately from the defendant Adam Thompson. The request was granted by the court.

The trial for Thompson then began immediately. News accounts reported that a counterfeit half-dollar which was recognized by several witnesses as having been in the possession of Schumaker the day before his death, was found in the possession of Thompson.

News accounts also reported that "Old Man Schumaker" kept a little store a few miles across the Trinity River. He was found dead one morning at his store. His head was crushed with an ax, which was found near him covered with blood and hair.

Witnesses were introduced by the State who stated that on the evening Schumaker was killed, Pollard and Thompson were seen leaving the city, and were traced to near Schumaker's store. Also, that Thompson was overheard by a black woman confessing that he and Pollard had committed the crime.

On October 21, 1876, the jury came back with the following verdict:

We the jury find the defendant guilty of murder in the first degree and assess the punishment at death.

F. M. Ervay, Foreman

The murder conviction of Adam Thompson was appealed and the

appellate court reversed the finding of the lower court on a technicality.

Almost four years had gone by since the murder of Joseph Schumaker and the cases against Pollard and Thompson had been continued while the two men remained in the Dallas County Jail. On April 28, 1880, the case against Thompson came up for trial the second time. Special Judge Sawnie Robertson was assigned to hear the case. H. D. Morrow spoke for the State, and C. F. Clint spoke for the defense. Attorney Robert B. Seay gave the closing argument for the defense.

After hearing the testimony regarding the murder of Joseph Schumaker, the jury came back in an hour and a half with the following verdict:

We the jury find the defendant guilty of murder in the first degree and assess the punishment at death.
C. S. Mitchell, Foreman

Thompson had now been tried and convicted twice for murder in the first degree. He had been sentenced to death both times.

The murder trial for Pollard was set for June 30, 1880. Pollard had testified in Adam Thompson's trials, and Pollard's case was postponed until after the completion of the second trial of Thompson.

However, Pollard never went to trial. He died on June 27, 1880, of consumption while being held as a prisoner in the Dallas County Jail. Pollard died three days before his case was set to go to trial.

On November 2, 1880, Benjamin F. Jones, Sr. was elected sheriff of Dallas County. It would now be his responsibility to oversee the county jail and care and custody of the prisoners. Also, Sheriff Jones would be responsible to carry out the orders of the court, and any execution orders issued by the court.

Benjamin F. Jones, Sr., was born in 1835, at St. Joseph, Missouri. He came to Texas and settled in Grayson County in 1853. He later came to Dallas County. He married Sallie A. Beeler on October 13, 1858. They had four children. He served in the Confederate Army during the Civil War, and was awarded many honors for his actions during the war. He was elected constable in 1864, in Dallas County. He was serving as deputy sheriff under William Marion Moon in 1880.

In December 1880, the appellate court affirmed the death penalty case of Thompson. In January 1881, Adam Thompson filed an appeal and motion for a rehearing. The Texas Court of Appeals refused to grant him a rehearing, and informed him that he must hang.

On April 4, 1881, Judge Sawnie Robertson issued the following order regarding the murder trial and conviction of Adam Thompson, "I

Sheriff Ben F. Jones, Sr.
Served 1880 - 1882
Photo Courtesy O'Byrne Cox, Jr.

sentence you to be hung on Friday, the first day of July 1881, between the hours of 11 o'clock a.m. that day and sun-down."

The court asked Sheriff Jones if the prisoner could be executed within the jail yard, and the sheriff said he could, and that it had been his desire that the execution be as private as possible. The court then ordered that the scaffold be erected in the jail yard.

In an April 9, 1881, news article, Adam Thompson, under sentence of death for the murder of Joseph Schumaker, made a confession of sorts, in which he said he was an accessory, but had no hand in the murder. Thompson said that West Pollard and Jerry Grant committed the murder. His story was not believed because of the evidence and testimony which convicted him. Jerry Grant was a friend and sometimes associated with Thompson and Pollard.

The scaffold was erected on the west side of the jail in the jail yard, and in the same area which Allen Wright was hanged in August of 1880 for the murder of Jesse Wicks. The scaffold had a trap door with a seven to eight feet drop. Adam Thompson could see the gallows from his jail cell window. He asked one of the guards to spring the trap to see how it worked. When the guard sprang the trap door Thompson fell back onto his bed.

On July 1, 1881, the date the court ordered the execution of Thompson, he was dressed in a black suit and wore white gloves. Just before he was taken from his cell he was visited by two black preachers and two black women. They sang and prayed for him.

Just before 2 p.m., Sheriff Jones told him his time was up. He was escorted by the sheriff and surrounded by deputies as they left the jail. Sheriff Jones read the death warrant to the prisoner. There was more singing and some wept for him. The noose was placed around the neck of Thompson and he shook hands with the officers and his religious attendants, bidding them good-by. His hands and feet were then secured. He stepped onto the trap door, the black cap drawn over his face. Sheriff Jones sprang the trap. Thompson fell through the door. Six minutes after the trap was sprung doctors Field and Moore examined the body and pronounced him dead.

Joseph Schumaker was murdered on July 1, 1876. Five years later to the day, Adam Thompson was hanged on July 1, 1881, in the Dallas County Jail yard.

Chapter 9

John D. Hodges

White male, age unknown

Offense – None, he was a victim

Employed by the Houston & Texas Central Railroad Company

Robbed and lynched Thursday, August 4, 1881, in Dallas County, Texas

Did not die from the lynching

Story of a man who refused to die

Thursday night, August 4, 1881, John D. Hodges, a resident of Hutchins in southern Dallas County, was returning home from Dallas. Hodges was employed by the Houston and Texas Central Railroad Company. He had gone to Dallas to pick up his payroll check and had cashed it. He had about thirty-five dollars in his pocket. Hodges was walking home along the railroad track, near Miller's Ferry. He was still about two miles from Hutchins when two black males approached him from the opposite direction.

Hodges was not aware of it at the time, but he would soon be in a fight and struggle for his very life. As the two men walked past him he recognized one of them as Frank Bell, the other man he did not know. Hodges had walked about 300 yards after passing the two men when all of a sudden one of the men slipped up behind him, grabbed him around the neck and began to choke him.

The other man then began beating him about the head and face and knocked him down. Before he could recover they were on top of him and robbed him of his money. They then told him to come with them into the brush. When he refused they dragged him through the brush to a tree. Hodges begged them to spare his life, telling them that he wouldn't tell anyone about what they had done. One of the men then made the statement, "Dead men tells no tales."

They then stripped him of all his clothing. They tore up his blue flannel shirt and made it into a rope. Then they tied his hands behind

Sheriff Ben F. Jones, Sr.
Served 1880 - 1882
Photo Courtesy of O'Byrne Cox, Jr.

him. They tied one end of the rope around his neck, and threw the other end over a branch and tied it to the tree, leaving him to die.

His feet were left dangling two feet off the ground. He was experiencing terrible pain but never lost consciousness. With a desperate effort he reached the trunk of the tree with his right foot, then with his left foot. Using the tree for support he managed to work his way up the tree and untie the knot in the rope with his teeth.

Hodges managed to free himself and escape certain death. He made his way to a nearby cabin where the occupants who were black, untied his hands and furnished him with some clothes and a horse. Hodges rode to Hutchins where he notified Deputy Sheriff Perry of the crimes committed against him.

His neck was badly injured where the rope made its imprint. His eyes were blood-shot and his face swollen from the beating and lynching.

Deputy Sheriff Perry immediately started out with a posse of citizens to search for the two men responsible for the robbery and lynching of John D. Hodges.

Sheriff Benjamin F. Jones was the sheriff of Dallas County. He was elected sheriff on November 2, 1880. He had just presided over the hanging of Adam Thompson on July 1, 1881. It was now his responsibility to investigate the robbery and lynching of Hodges, and arrest the two suspects.

Frank Bell was arrested and jailed. He was charged with robbery and assault to murder. The other man with Bell at the time of the crime was later identified as Richard Bowen.

On November 28, 1881, *Case #5186, State of Texas vs. Frank Bell*, charge – assault with intent to murder, and *Case #5189, State of Texas vs. Frank Bell*, charge – robbery, were set for trial in the 14th District Court in Dallas. The jury was selected and the case ready when Frank Bell decided to plead guilty to both charges against him.

Judge Aldridge had the jury set the punishment for the crime of assault with intent to murder, to which Bell had just plead guilty. The jury retired and came back to report the following verdict:

> *We the jury upon defendants plea of guilty assess his punishment at seven years confinement in the State penitentiary.*
>> *J. E. Gibson, Foreman*

Judge Aldridge also had the jury set the punishment for the crime of robbery, to which Bell had just plead guilty. The jury came back with a new foreman. The jury gave their decision as:

> *We the jury upon the defendants plea of guilty assess his punishment at seven years confinement in the State penitentiary.*
>> *F. Cullen, Foreman*

Judge Aldridge then gave his order that Frank Bell, upon the verdict of the jury, be confined in the Texas State penitentiary for a term of seven years for the crime of assault with intent to murder, and for an additional term of seven years for the crime of robbery.

The court also ordered that the State of Texas recover all costs that the defendant incurred, and that the defendant be remanded to the custody of the sheriff of Dallas County to await the further order of the court.

On December 8, 1881, the two criminal cases of assault with intent to commit murder and robbery, *State of Texas vs. Frank Bell*, were again heard by Judge Aldridge in the 14th District Court. Regarding the assault with intent to murder charge, Judge Aldridge noted that no motion for a new trial had been made in behalf of the defendant.

Judge Aldridge pronounced the formal sentence of the jury, stating, "It is therefore ordered and adjudged and decreed by the court that the defendant Frank Bell be remanded to the custody of the sheriff of Dallas County, Texas and by said sheriff deliver to the State contractors for conveying prisoners and by said contractors convey to Huntsville, Walker County, Texas, and deliver to the keeper of the State Penitentiary, and by him confined at hard labor for the term of seven years."

Regarding the robbery charge against Bell, Judge Aldridge made a statement of fact that no motion for a new trial had been made on behalf of the defendant. Therefore the judge sentenced Bell to an additional seven years in the State penitentiary at Huntsville.

Frank Bell was issued convict #9887, when he was received at Huntsville prison in December 1881. His information was recorded in the prison ledger book as: age 18, 5' 10" tall, 150 pounds, copper complexion, black eyes and black hair. His occupation was listed as farmer. The offenses against him were listed as assault to murder and robbery.

The terms of his imprisonment was set at seven years for each offense. The expiration of his sentence was recorded as December 8, 1895.

On January 1, 1883, Bell was transferred to the newly opened Rusk Penitentiary, near Rusk, in Cherokee County. This was the state's second enclosed prison. It opened January 1, 1883 and closed in 1917. It was established in order to relieve overcrowding in the Texas State Penitentiary at Huntsville.

After the Rusk Penitentiary closed in 1917, the Texas State Legislature approved use of the property as an asylum for insane people and was named the Rusk State Hospital.

Richard Bowen, the other man involved along with Frank Bell in the robbery and assault with intent to murder, made his escape from the country. No record was found that Bowen was ever arrested or tried for the crimes he committed on August 4, 1881, against John D. Hodges.

Chapter 10

William Allen Taylor

Black male, age about 25

Charge – Burglary and attempted criminal assault

Offense occurred June 24, 1884 in Dallas, Texas

Victim – Mrs. W. H. [Lizzie] Flippin, white female, age 34

Trial – None

Taylor lynched by mob Friday, September 12, 1884, in Dallas County, Texas

In June of 1884 there had been a series of unsolved burglaries and criminal assaults on white women in the city of Dallas. During the early morning hours on June 24, 1884, between 4 to 5 a. m., Mrs. William H. Flippin [Elizabeth, or Lizzie as she was known], would become the next victim. The event would so traumatize her that she went into convulsions and was left in a "precarious condition."

W. H. Flippin, at age thirty-one, and Lizzie J. Lucas, at age twenty-six, were married on May 19, 1875 in Brazos County, Texas. W. H. Flippin was born in Tennessee. Elizabeth was born in Maryland. By 1880, W. H. was a banker and had moved his family, which included his wife and three small children, to Dallas.

After moving to Dallas, W. H. Flippin became the Dallas City Treasurer, and a partner with the banking firm of Flippin, Adoue, & Lobit. The bank was located at 616 Elm Street in Dallas. In June of 1884, W. H. Flippin traveled to Europe on business. In late June, when the attack occurred on Mrs. Lizzie Flippin, W. H. was still in Europe. It was not until the middle of July that W. H. Flippin sailed from Liverpool for home.

On June 24, 1884, Lizzie Flippin was asleep in her residence at 281 Ross Avenue in Dallas. Also sleeping in the same room was a young servant girl. An unknown black male entered the second floor bedroom and locked the door behind him. Mrs. Flippin became aware of his presence, but was so frightened she could not scream, or cry out in alarm.

The young girl awoke and screamed, and ran to the door, which she found locked. The black male then choked Mrs. Flippin and bruised her. He failed in his attempt to sexually assault her. The intruder made his escape by sliding down a post on the outside porch.

Doctor J. L. Carter, who resided two doors east of the Flippin residence, reported that his house was burglarized the same night as the assault on Mrs. Flippin. The thief stole a gold watch and four dollars in cash. Mrs. Mack Duncan, who lived just east of Doctor Carter, also reported an attempted burglary that same night, but the burglar was scared off when they heard him attempt to raise a window.

The suspect in the Flippin attack was described to Dallas police as a "copper-colored negro, with hair cut short as though done by a barber's clipper."

Detectives Duncan and Frisby set out to locate the wanted man. The two officers located and arrested Henry Broswell, a black male, on suspicion of being the wanted person. Word of the arrest soon caused an "intense excitement" among the citizens, and talk of a lynching went through the crowd. The officers kept Broswell hidden from the excited crowd, as they themselves were not satisfied that they had the right person. The officers had Mrs. Flippin look at Broswell, and she said he was not the man that attacked her.

When it became known the next day that the wrong person had been arrested, the excitement died out. The citizens appeared to agree to let the officials conduct their investigation into the burglary and assault. A $500 reward was offered for the arrest of the right person. The reward would later grow to $1,000.

Mrs. Lizzie Flippin was so traumatized by the attack on her that she went to stay with her sister in Bryan, Texas. Lizzie returned home to Dallas on July 11th, after she was reported to be "much improved physically." She was accompanied by another sister, Mrs. Scott, of Brownwood, Texas.

Here is an example of the fear that was gripping the citizens of Dallas County. Several days after the attack on Mrs. Flippin, a report came in that a widow lady living eleven miles south of Dallas had been assaulted and that the man, Tom Mayre or Morris, had been lynched. Dallas County Sheriff William H. W. Smith and Deputy Sheriff Winston went to investigate and the story proved to be false.

Tom Mayre was a tenant of William Bullock. Bullock was the father of Mrs. Joe Sprowles, a widow lady. Mayre and his wife slept in the same room as Mrs. Sprowles. Mayre had gotten up and was dressing when Mrs. Sprowles suddenly awoke, and saw Mayre near her bed.

When she screamed, a brother-in-law rushed in and knocked Mayre down. Bullock, after investigating the affair, decided it was a mistake all around. But somehow the report came into Dallas as an assault and lynching.

On July 23, a Dallas newspaper had the following headlines: "Caught At Last," and "The Dallas Monster Taken." The reports were that two suspects, Dick Sheppard, a mulatto, alias "Rube," and Louis Stokes, a black man, were arrested in Fort Worth as the suspects in the attack on Mrs. Flippin. Sheppard was reported to be the person that attacked Mrs. Flippin, and the other women in Dallas. Stokes was reported to be his partner in the Dallas burglaries. Sheppard had been in Dallas two weeks earlier and had worked as a porter at a local business named Craddock's.

The Courtright Detective Agency put four men on the case. The detective agency hired a black detective described as a "black leg," to work undercover to identify the suspect that attacked Mrs. Flippin. The black detective was directed to Dick Sheppard, as Sheppard had left Dallas and was reported to be a stranger in Fort Worth and staying in a cabin.

Mr. Courtright and a Captain Price, took charge of the case and put surveillance on Sheppard. Sheppard also had a bullet wound in the right lower leg. After his arrest Sheppard told different stories as to how he received the gunshot wound. By July 24, the *Galveston Daily News* reported that the two negroes arrested in Fort Worth, Dick Sheppard and Louis Stokes, turned out to be innocent, and they were released.

On August 29, 1884, Dallas police officer John Spencer arrived in Dallas with a prisoner, Allen Taylor, who he arrested in Fort Worth. Taylor also went by the name of Bill Taylor. As it turned out his full name was William Allen Taylor. Taylor was seen earlier by Dallas officers as acting suspicious, and they had looked for him the day after the attack on Mrs. Flippin, but Taylor was nowhere to be found. The officers felt certain he had left Dallas.

On August 28th he was spotted in Fort Worth, where he was working for a George Holland. When brought back to Dallas he could not explain why he left town suddenly.

William Allen Taylor was born in Alabama and had come to Texas in 1869. He had lived in Dallas about two years He was described as about twenty-five years old, weighing about 150 pounds, five feet ten inches tall, copper-colored skin, his hair close clipped. His description fit the description of the suspect in the attack on Mrs. W. H. Flippin.

The investigation of Taylor revealed that he was seen running out of the Fourth Ward in Dallas the night a Mrs. Getsell was assaulted. Alexander Boyd, a black man, gave a statement to Justice Kendall that the day after the Getsell attack in Dallas, he met Taylor at a gambling house in Fort Worth. Boyd said Taylor declined to go with him to break into some houses, and that Taylor told him he "had quite enough of that sort of thing in Dallas, and had to leave there to escape the officers."

Boyd went on to say that he asked Taylor if he had been assaulting the white women over in Dallas. Boyd said Taylor told him no, that he entered Mrs. Flippin's room in search of valuables. When she awoke and began to scream, he choked her into silence. Taylor went on to say that he was after money.

A Dallas bartender named Levison, and a black man working for him, both identified a coat which the man who entered the home of a Mrs. Benedict was wearing. They both said the coat belonged to William Taylor.

A witness attachment was issued for a black man named Jackson, who was employed by a Mr. Robertson. Jackson, it was understood, would swear that Taylor was seen running from the Fourth Ward in Dallas the night that Mrs. Getsell was assaulted.

Taylor was taken before Justice Kendall where sworn testimony was given. Taylor was identified by Mrs. Flippin as the person that attacked her. At the completion of the investigation on September 4th, William Allen Taylor was committed to the Dallas County Jail in default of a $1,000 bond, for "assault to commit outrage," and a $500 bond for burglary.

Now that William Allen Taylor was in the custody of Dallas County Sheriff William H. W. Smith, it became his responsibility to insure the safety of Taylor, and prevent any mob action as had been threatened shortly after the attacks on Mrs. Flippin and the other women in Dallas..

William H. W. Smith was born in Alabama in 1855. His father was a native of South Carolina and was a lawyer. His mother was also from South Carolina. Smith was the fourth of ten children and came to Dallas in 1873. In 1876 Smith married Fannie P. Sharpe and they had two sons and one daughter. He worked in a hardware store until 1878, when he became a deputy sheriff under Sheriff Ben. F. Jones. On November 7, 1882, he was elected sheriff of Dallas County and served in that capacity until 1886.

Sheriff Smith, fearing that Taylor would be mobbed, quietly had him taken to the Ellis County Jail in Waxahachie. A crowd of citizens found out that Taylor had been taken to Waxahachie, and began threatening to go to Waxahachie and lynch him. Learning of the latest threats, Sheriff Smith decided to take Taylor to Waco and place him in the county jail there. Sheriff Smith took Deputy Sheriff George Miller along with him to Waxahachie to make the transfer of Taylor to Waco.

George H. Miller, was twenty-five years old. He was born in Georgia, and was single. Miller had been a Dallas County deputy sheriff for at least four years. He served under Sheriff Ben Jones at the same time that W. H. W. Smith was a deputy sheriff under Sheriff Jones. Miller was also the elected constable of Precinct #1 in Dallas, having been elected constable on November 11, 1882. At the time it was not uncommon for law enforcement officers to be commissioned peace officers by two different agencies.

Sheriff Smith and Deputy Sheriff Miller left Dallas shortly after midnight on September 12, 1884. They were on their way to Waxahachie to pick up Taylor and take him to the county jail in Waco. The officers were driving a two-seated horse buggy. The sheriff and deputy were followed by three groups of citizens. One group was sent to watch the Ennis road, another group the Midlothian road and the third the Cleburne road.

Just after daylight the Midlothian group left the road and hid in the brush where they remained until noon. Sheriff Smith and Deputy Miller had left Waxahachie about 10 a.m. and were on their way to Midlothian to catch the Santa Fe train to Waco. Sheriff Smith and Deputy Miller were both in the front seat of the buggy and Taylor was sitting between them. At about noon the officers approached the area where the group of men was hiding. Without warning, nine masked men rode up and covered them with pistols, and demanded that they turn Taylor over to them.

Sheriff Smith's pistols were in the bottom of the buggy at his feet, and before he could get his hands on them, Taylor was taken from him. Deputy Sheriff Miller was sick and was unable to offer any resistance. The masked men took Taylor, Sheriff Smith and Deputy Miller as their prisoners.

The masked men took the three prisoners back to Dallas County where they stopped in the road just west of the Trinity River. Here they were met by a large mob of masked men. Sheriff Smith, standing in the buggy, addressed the masked men saying he was a prisoner in the hands of a mob. He asked them to stop breaking the law within the shadow of the Dallas County Courthouse, by lynching Taylor.

The mob placed a rope around the neck of Taylor and told him that he was to be hanged, and asked him if he had anything to say. Taylor protested his innocence. His last words were: "Boss, you're hanging an innocent man. I don't know anything about it and won't tell a lie by saying I do."

One account stated that Taylor was hung from the bridge, another account reported that he was hung from a tree next to the bridge.

After Taylor was lynched, the masked men told Sheriff Smith and Deputy Sheriff Miller they were free to leave and to get out of there.

The conduct of Sheriff Smith was reported in the *Dallas Daily Times Herald* as "very creditable to him as he used every endeavor to protect his prisoner, and only surrendered him when overpowered."

There was no record or information found that anyone was ever arrested or prosecuted for the lynching and murder of William Allen Taylor on September 12, 1884.

* * * * *

This would have ended this chapter, except that nighttime burglars continued to break into residences in the Ross Avenue area of Dallas. On January 22, 1885, seven months after the burglary and attack on Mrs. W. H. [Lizzie] Flippin, another attempt was made to break into the Flippin residence. This time Mr. W.H. Flippin was at home and able to protect his family.

The *Galveston Daily News* of January 23, 1885 reported in part:

A burglar secured an entrance last night to Mr. Flippin's residence, on Ross Avenue, by boring through the window blinds. Mr. Flippin awoke in time to send two shots after the scoundrel, but did not succeed in getting him.

Another burglar was shot at four times by another resident of East Avenue, and it is believed from blood traces that he is wounded.

Chapter 11

Henry Miller

Black male, age 33

Offense – Murder of a police officer

Victim – Dallas Police Officer C. O. Brewer, white male, age 42

Offense occurred Tuesday, May 24, 1892

Trial held in Dallas County, Texas

14th District Court Judge Robert E. Burke, presided

Convicted July 4, 1892 and sentenced to hang

Court of Criminal Appeals of Texas – Affirmed the case March 25, 1893

Hanged Friday, July 28, 1893, in Dallas, Texas

Henry Miller, a porter in a saloon in Dallas, was accused of slandering a respectable white woman several weeks prior to Dallas police officer C. O. Brewer being killed. Miller had circulated a report that slandered the woman's good name. Miller was arrested at the time and taken before acting Dallas Chief of Police Cornwell and questioned. Miller admitted to Chief Cornwell that he had been guilty of making the scandalous remarks. Miller further stated that a white saloon keeper had induced him to make the allegations. Chief Cornwell gave Miller a stern reprimand and released him.

The *Dallas Daily Times-Herald* of May 25, 1892, reported in part:

Two weeks ago Henry Miller who is coal-black and brutish-looking negro, stated in the presence of several white men that he had been hired by a white man to visit his wife's room for the purpose of having criminal relations with her. He stated that the white man forced him into the room occupied by the woman and watched the actions of the couple through a window. Miller also stated that the white man paid him $2.

The rumors finally reached the husband of the woman who had been slandered, and inquiries were begun at once. Dallas County authorities were consulted and they were determined to get to the bottom of the matter.

An affidavit charging Henry Miller with slander, and a warrant for his arrest, was prepared on May 23, 1892. Dallas police officers Ben Brandenburg and C. O. Brewer were detailed on the evening of May 24th, by acting Police Chief Cornwall to arrest Miller. The officers located Miller near the Union Depot in front of Alderman Lacy's saloon. Miller was placed under arrest at that time.

Miller asked Officer Brandenburg if he could make bond and not be taken to the jail. Brandenburg told him, "No, this is a county court case and we cannot take bond."

Miller had been arrested in the past, and since that arrest was a minor city court case, he was allowed to make bond on the spot. Miller wanted to do the same thing this time.

When he was not allowed to make an immediate bond, Miller whipped out a large caliber pistol and said, "Damn you." He then added, "I'll make a bond with this then."

Miller started firing, one shot struck a horse, another shot grazed Officer Brandenburg's scalp, and the third shot struck Officer Brewer. Brewer, who had been in close pursuit of Miller, fell about seventy feet from where the shooting started.

Several citizens ran to the wounded officer and picked him up, and took him to Johnson's Drug Store, where he died an hour later. In his last hour Officer Brewer expressed concern for his wife and babies. His wife was contacted and brought to the drug store to be with her husband.

Officer Brandenburg, along with Officer Jim Beard, who had been working close by, gave chase while exchanging gunshots with Miller. Officer Beard used a fire department buggy which happened by, to catch up with Miller and arrest him. They placed Miller in a patrol wagon and rushed him to the central police station and Dallas City Jail. A crowd of nearly 1,000 whites, blacks, men, women and children all gave chase.

The crowd at the city jail was without a leader, but the discussions were about taking Miller from the jail and lynching him. Before any organized attack could be made, Sheriff William Henry Lewis, along with several deputies and policemen, took Miller out the back way and placed him in the patrol wagon. They raced the heavy horse drawn wagon at full gallop to the Dallas County Jail. Miller was placed safely

OFFICER BREWER.

**Dallas Police Officer
C. O. Brewer**
Sketch Dallas Daily Times Herald

in one of the strongest secured jails in the South.

The crowd now moved down to the courthouse square and to the county jail. A young man got up and made a loud speech about demanding that the sheriff turn over the prisoner, or they would storm the jail and take Miller by force.

After talking to Sheriff Lewis, prominent citizens Captain Joe Record, Captain George A. Knight, and ex-United States Marshal Ben Cabell, spoke to the crowd and told them that Sheriff Lewis was going to protect the prisoner at all costs. The men urged the crowd to disperse and allow the law to take its course.

The angry crowd soon became a mob. There were shouts to blow the doors to the jail with dynamite. Other things were also suggested to break down the heavy doors and several men brought up a heavy railroad rail to knock down the door.

Sheriff Lewis addressed the mob through an open window. He told them they were friends of his, but he would do his duty and might have to kill some of them if they continued trying to break down the jail door. The mob tried using a crow bar to pry open the door, and then tried ramming the door with the railroad rail.

A shot rang out, then more shots. The mob was shooting at the deputies in the jail. The deputies returned the gunfire from windows inside the upper floors of the jail. In all about thirty to forty shots were fired. Three men in the mob were hit by gunfire. None of the officers were hit, but several shots missed by only inches.

When the shooting started most of the mob scattered. A few of them stood and fired a few more shots. One of the men in the mob was shot in the leg. Another was hit three times by the gunfire. Still another was hit by pellets from a shotgun. Their wounds were not serious.

Again, Captain Joe Record, Ben Cabell and Judge Charles Fred Tucker came down and appealed to the mob to disperse. Some of the mob tried again to storm the jail door before finally giving up.

The next day, excitement was still strong in Dallas over the murder of Officer Brewer. Officials were still trying to determine the facts. The

Dallas Morning News reported on May 25, 1892, in part: "Officer Brewer was shot in the left side. The ball passed through and lodged in the right side."

However, Justice of the Peace S. N. Braswell, Pct. #1, Place #1, on May 25, 1892, held an inquest over the body of C. O. Brewer. After viewing the body and hearing testimony, he stated in part. . ." the deceased came to his death from a gunshot wound inflicted on the right side of his breast by Henry Miller."

After a change of venue was denied, the trial, *State of Texas vs. Henry Miller*, charge murder, case #17010, started on June 27, 1892, in 14th District Court, Dallas County, Judge Robert E. Burke, presiding. The jury was impaneled and ready to hear testimony.

Trial judge Robert Emmett Burke was born August 1, 1847, near Dadeville, Alabama. He served as a private in the Tenth Georgia Regiment, Company D of the Confederate States Army during the Civil War. After the war, he moved to Jefferson, Texas, in 1866, and attended schools there.

Burke was admitted to the bar in 1870, and began his practice in Dallas in 1871. He served as judge of Dallas County from 1878-1888. Burke then served as judge of the 14th District Court in Dallas from 1888-1896. He also served as a United States Congressman from 1897-1901. Judge Burke died in Dallas June 5, 1901. He is buried in Greenwood Cemetery, Dallas.

The case for the State was prosecuted by Col. D. A. Williams, Mr. Harry Obenchain, Mr. Mann Trice and Judge Kenneth Foree. The defense was represented by Col. S. H. Russell, of the law firm of Bassett, Seay & Muse. The law firm of Kearby and McCoy also assisted with the defense.

The indictment was read and the trial began. Witnesses were heard from, evidence produced, speeches by both the prosecution and defense attorneys were offered to the jury.

On July 4, 1892, the jury came back with their verdict:

Dallas, Texas, July 4, 1892. We the jury find the defendant, Henry Miller, guilty as charged in the indictment of murder in the first degree, and assess his punishment at death.

    C. J. Green, Foreman

A formal application for a new trial in Henry Miller's case was filed July 6, 1892.

On March 25, 1893, the Court of Criminal Appeals in Austin affirmed the death penalty case against Henry Miller. On June 14, 1893, the Court of Criminal Appeals overruled a motion for a rehearing of the case against Henry Miller.

Ben Cabell was elected sheriff of Dallas County on November 8, 1892. It would now be his duty to carry out the order of the court and conduct the hanging of Henry Miller.

Benjamin E. Cabell was born on November 18, 1858, at Fort Smith, Arkansas. He was the son of William L. Cabell, who served in the Confederate Army. William L Cabell was promoted to Brigadier General during the Civil War. In 1874, General Cabell was elected mayor of Dallas, and in 1885 was appointed United States Marshal for the Northern District of Texas. Ben would follow in his father's footsteps, serving as a deputy U.S. marshal under his father. In 1892 Ben was elected sheriff of Dallas County. In 1900 Ben Cabell was elected mayor of Dallas.

On July 28, 1893, Henry Miller ate his final breakfast at 7:30 a. m. He ate fried chicken, tenderloin steak, coffee and cake. He was then allowed to receive visitors in the jail. Several ministers visited him that morning and he talked with reporters. Miller ate a hearty lunch. By the hour the execution was scheduled, the jail yard and surrounding streets were full of people. They took positions around the jail, but could see nothing.

The gallows had been put in when the jail was built. It was located in the jail stairway to the north of the jail office. It had a wood platform

Courtesy of the Dallas Times Herald

three foot square, with iron rods holding it together. Upright iron shafts extended from the floor to the roof of the second story. The rope was attached to a wooden cross beam near the roof of the second story. When the trigger was sprung, the platform would fall.

At 1:45 p.m., on Friday, July 28, 1893, Miller stepped onto the platform in the county jail stairway. Sheriff Cabell read the death warrant ordered by the court. He placed the rope and hood around Miller's neck, and sprang the trigger to the platform, sending Henry Miller to his death.

Tombstone of Dallas police officer C. O. Brewer who was shot and killed May 24, 1892 by Henry Miller. He is buried in Greenwood Cemetery in Dallas. *Photo by Author*

The *Dallas Morning News*, July 10, 1892, reported in part that Henry Miller was a descendant of "Uncle Cato", aka: "Old Cato," one of three slaves lynched on July 24, 1860, for the July 8, 1860, burning of downtown Dallas.

The *Dallas Times Herald*, July 19, 1893, reported in part that Henry Miller was the cousin of a famous Texas desperado named Commodore Miller, who was killed by citizens at Bardwell, Kentucky.

The *Dallas Times Herald*, February 6, 1894, reported in part that Bud Bell, age seventeen, was shot and killed while caught in the act of burglary of Cash's grocery store on Bryan Street. Bud Bell was the nephew of Henry Miller, who was hanged for the murder of police officer C. O. Brewer. Bud Bell's father, a notorious criminal named Jim Bell was in the penitentiary.

Dallas police officer Cassee Odorous "C. O." Brewer, age forty-two, was born in 1850, in Marshall, Texas. He was of Irish decent, and he came to Dallas twelve years prior to his death. When an infant he moved with his family to Gilmer in Upshur County, where in 1878 he married Miss Mollie Simpson, daughter of Judge J. M. Simpson, a respected citizen of Upshur County. Years later Brewer moved to Johnson County, and then to Fort Worth, before settling in Dallas. Brewer was in the business of house-moving, before he got a position with the Dallas Police Department.

Brewer had a $2,000 life insurance policy and he was survived by his wife Mollie, and two daughters, Hazel and Cassee, ages six and eight. C. O. Brewer is buried in the Greenwood Cemetery in Dallas.

Chapter 12

Joseph Malone

aka: "Dobie Joe"

Black male, age 22, born Harrisonville, Missouri

Offense - Rape and attempted murder

Victim – Mrs. Frederick [Catherine] Stein, white female, age 64

Offense occurred Friday, July 15, 1898

Indicted July 18, 1898

Trial held in Dallas County, Texas

Criminal District Court Judge Charles F. Clint, presided

Malone plead guilty at his trial July 25, 1898

Hanged Friday, September 2, 1898, in Dallas County, Texas

About ten o'clock on the morning of Friday, July 15, 1898, Mrs. Frederick [Catherine] Stein, age sixty-four, was working in her garden gathering vegetables and was home alone at the time. Her husband, Frederick Stein, and the Brock family members, had left to attend to other business. The Steins lived with the Brocks about four miles south of Dallas on the Houston and Texas Central Railroad line, near an area known as "Miller's Switch."

Mrs. Stein was born in Germany and spoke no English. The family came from Oklahoma to Dallas about a year earlier. They were in the truck gardening business. Mrs. Stein had no reason to believe that within minutes she would be brutally attacked and fighting for her life.

About an hour after Mrs. Stein was attacked, she was found unconscious in the garden by a family member. She was covered with blood. She had been choked into a state of insensibility, and then raped. Mrs. Stein resisted as best she could, but her attacker knocked her down with his fists, breaking her right shoulder. He then took a heavy shoe from her foot and using the shoe, he struck her in the head, causing ugly gashes. After raping her, the attacker left her for dead.

On Friday, July 15, 1898, Dallas County Sheriff Ben Cabell had just returned to Dallas from Galveston, when he was notified at 11:30 a.m. of the attack on Mrs. Stein. A full description of the attacker was obtained and the sheriff and two deputies immediately started out on horseback for the scene of the crime. After arriving at Miller's Switch, Sheriff Cabell telephoned for more posse members and four additional deputies to assist in the search for the attacker.

Will Moore, a member of the posse from Hutchins, came across the trail of the wanted suspect, Joseph Malone, and finally "treed" him in the river bottoms. Deputy Sheriff Fon Simpson arrived and Malone refused to surrender. Two shots were fired to let Malone know they were serious and he surrendered. Sheriff Cabell along with additional deputies arrived and took Malone into custody and had Malone taken to another city and placed in jail to keep a mob from gathering, and lynching him.

Between 9:30 to 10 p.m. that evening, Sheriff Cabell and five of his deputies returned to Dallas completely worn out. The sheriff told a reporter, "We came in to take a rest and to get fresh horses."

The reporter told the sheriff that it is rumored on the streets that they had made an arrest in the case. The sheriff replied, "Well, he is not here. We've just got in after riding through the brush and scouring the country since morning."

Sheriff Cabell said that Mrs. Stein, the victim, was in a precarious condition, but the doctors believed she would recover.

The attacker was identified as Joseph "Dobie Joe" Malone, a black male, age about twenty-two.

Judge Charles F. Clint called the grand jury to meet on Monday July 18th and hear the evidence against Malone. After hearing four hours of testimony they indicted Malone for the criminal assault on Mrs. Fredrick Stein.

Judge Clint appointed defense attorneys J. M. Minyard, A. T. Watts and A. H. Fields to defend Malone in the upcoming trial. On Monday, July 25, 1898, the case of *State of Texas vs. Joseph Malone* was called in Judge Clint's court. A special venire of seventy-five men had been ordered to appear for possible jury duty. Twelve men were selected to serve on the jury.

At least twenty deputy sheriffs were on duty during the trial. They were on alert for any signs of trouble. They were guarding all the entrances and exits to the courtroom. One hundred witnesses were called. After they were sworn in and placed under the rule, they could not stay in the courtroom and hear the testimony of other witnesses.

The indictment was read to Joseph Malone by Chandler, and he asked Malone if he was guilty or not. Malone's prompt reply was, "I am guilty."

Assistant county attorney W. H. Chandler then read the indictment to the jury. Judge Clint questioned Malone, asking him if he understood that under his plea the jury could not give him less than five years, and the jury might assess his punishment at death. Malone replied that he knew all about it. Malone also said that no one had advised him to plead guilty, and that he entered that plea because he was guilty.

Joe Malone
Courtesy of the Dallas Morning News

Judge Clint ordered the lawyers to proceed with the questioning of the witnesses, in order that the jury might be able to determine the severity of the punishment.

Mrs. Stein was the first witness. She was carried into the courtroom on a stretcher and appeared very feeble. She identified Malone as the man who had assaulted her, and then attempted to murder her. Doctor Robertson, who was called in to examine her and attend to her needs, was the next witness. He testified about the extent of her injuries. Sheriff Cabell then told the story of the chase to arrest the suspect, and presented the evidence he had gathered.

Judge Charles F. Clint gave the charge to the jury which included the statement, "Upon the defendant's plea of guilty to the crime of rape, find him guilty of rape as charged and assess his punishment at either death or confinement in the penitentiary for life or for any term of years not less than five, as you may determine and state in your verdict."

It required only twelve minutes for the jury to return with their verdict. Two votes had been taken and on the first vote, eleven ballots were marked for the death penalty; one ballot was blank. On the second vote all twelve ballots were marked for the death penalty.

The jury reported back to the court the following verdict:

We the jury, find the defendant guilty of rape, as charged in the indictment, and assess his punishment at death.
      W. T. Bryant, Foreman

Malone showed no emotion or fear when the verdict was read. After the crowd applauded the verdict, Judge Clint had the sheriff and deputies clear the courtroom. Constable Bolick and his deputies, along with Chief of Police Ed Cornwell, and a number of Dallas police officers assisted with the security in the courthouse, and the walking of Malone two blocks down Houston Street to the county jail.

Between 2,000 and 3,000 people were crowding the street in the area of the courthouse and jail. A few started yelling, "Hang him, hang him," but the larger crowd did not respond. Malone was safely placed in the Dallas County Jail and the crowd then dispersed.

On July 28, 1898, Malone was taken to Judge Clint's court to have the judge pass sentence. More than 100 spectators were present when Sheriff Cabell and his deputies marched Malone into the courtroom. After reviewing the case file, the judge asked Malone if he had anything to say as to why sentence should not be passed on him. Malone replied, "No, your honor."

Judge Clint read the following order, which was entered on the docket:

> It is ordered, adjudged and decreed by the court that the defendant, Joe Malone, alias Dobie Joe, be remanded to the custody of the sheriff of Dallas County, Texas, and by him confined until September 2, 1898, and by said sheriff on Friday, September 2, 1898, between the hours of 11 o'clock a. m. and 4 o'clock p. m. hanged by the neck until he is dead. And that the clerk of this court enter death warrant in accordance with this sentence, and direct and deliver the same to the said sheriff of Dallas County, Texas who shall execute the same in accordance with the law in such cases made and provided. Mr. Sheriff, remove the prisoner.

Sheriff Cabell and his deputies escorted Malone back to the jail. He was placed in the cell for condemned prisoners and a death watch was placed over him. Deputy sheriffs A. L. Ledbetter and Charles James were assigned to guard Malone.

During his final stay in the county jail, Malone had several visitors. He told a reporter from the *Dallas Morning News* that he was twenty-two years-old, and was born in Harrisonville, Missouri. Also, that his mother and father and a brother still lived in Harrisonville, and that he had another brother living at Little Rock, and a sister at Aberdeen, Mississippi. He also told the reporter that he had not written to any of his family and told them where he was.

Malone told the reporter that his full name was Joseph William Ambers Bird Malone, alias Dobie Joe. He also said he got the name Dobie Joe when he was a small lad and it always stuck with him.

With over a month to go, Joe said he had several visits from black preachers while in jail. Revs. Z. T. Pardee and W. H. Estees called on him. "But I didn't get religion," he said. Malone said he had been arrested before, but that he had always beat every case, until this one landed him in jail.

With only ten days to go before his execution, "Doba Joe is Getting Religion," was the headline of a *Dallas Morning News* report. The article went on to say he was now getting daily visits from black preachers and black women who had gathered at the fence outside the jail singing hymns.

Now with only a week to go before the execution, Malone had two white visitors come to the jail to see him. County Attorney Robert B. Allen and assistant attorney W. H. Chandler spent an hour of friendly chatting with Joe.

The day before he was executed, Malone decided he wanted to be baptized. On Friday morning, September 2, 1898, Sheriff Cabell ordered a large bath tub placed in his cell. After a breakfast of fried chicken, hot rolls, coffee and preserves, the Revs. Pardee, Rainey and Brooks conducted the baptism. A large crowd assembled outside the jail, trying to see through the windows of the jail to catch a glimpse of Dobie Joe, or of the gallows.

After the baptismal ceremony in which Joe was immersed in the big bathtub, and at about 11:30 a.m., he began to dress for the gallows. He dressed with great care, putting on his tie and white gloves. A lunch was delivered by a downtown boarding house, but Malone refused the meal because he didn't want to get his white gloves dirty.

Benjamin E. Cabell was elected sheriff of Dallas County on November 8, 1892, and served four two-year terms as sheriff. He served as sheriff until 1900, when he was elected mayor of Dallas. Ben was the son of General William A. Cabell and his mother A. A. Cabell.

General William. A. Cabell, was a graduate of West Point, and a general in the Confederate Army. He was appointed United States marshal for the Northern District of Texas, and served as mayor of Dallas. Ben Cabell served as a deputy United States marshal under his father.

Earle Cabell, [October 27, 1906 to September 24, 1975] was the son of Ben Cabell. Earle Cabell served as mayor of Dallas from 1961 to 1964, when he resigned to run for United States Congress. He won the election and served until 1972. The Earle Cabell Federal Building in Dallas is named after him.

Three generations of Cabells served as mayor of Dallas. They also

A newspaper sketch of Joe Malone on the gallows inside the Dallas County Jail.
Courtesy of the Dallas Morning News

held other elected and appointed positions of authority in Dallas and Texas.

Ben Cabell was the sheriff of Dallas County and conducted the hanging of Henry Miller in 1893. Sheriff Cabell would again have the responsibility to conduct another hanging, this time Joe Malone. The same gallows that were used to hang Henry Miller in 1893, would hang Joe Malone in 1898, in the Dallas County Jail stairwell.

At 12:15 p.m. Sheriff Cabell, along with his deputies and other peace officers, escorted Joe Malone from his cell to the gallows. Joe's hands were cuffed in front; his elbows were bound to his sides with strong twine. The gallows were located in the stairwell of the jail.

Sheriff Cabell read the death warrant, and then allowed Malone to speak a few words. Sheriff Cabell placed the noose around Malone's neck, and the black cap was drawn down over his head. The trigger on the trap door was pulled at 12:18 p.m., three minutes after the group left Malone's cell. At 12:37 p.m., doctors pronounced Joe Malone dead. Sheriff Cabell cut the rope and deputies carried the body to the jail hospital ward, where the doctors again inspected it. The body was buried in potter's field by an undertaker named Dunn.

The victim in this case, Mrs. Frederick [Catherine] Stein, died September 1, 1926, at the age of ninety-two. Her Texas death certificate, #31281, [1926] shows she was born March 14, 1834, in Germany. At the time of her death she was a widow and was living on Driskill Drive, in Dallas. She is buried in an unmarked grave next to her husband in Oakland Cemetery in Dallas.

Chapter 13

Holly Vann

White male, age about 28

Offense – Robbery and murder

Victim – Solomon "Sol" Aronoff, white male, 35 years-old

Offense occurred November 29, 1904

Trial by jury in Dallas, Texas

Criminal District Court Judge E. B. Muse, presided

Indicted by Grand Jury December 2, 1904

Tried and convicted December 21, 1904

Hanged Friday, May 12, 1905, in Dallas, Texas

Solomon "Sol" Aronoff, a white male, age thirty-five, operated a small grocery store in the 200 block of South Houston Street in Dallas. He and his wife, Fannie, and their two young children, Nathan, age eleven, and Lillie, age eight, lived in the back of the store. Census records show that Sol and his wife were both born in Russia, and they had been married since 1890.

On Tuesday evening, November 29, 1904, Sol Aronoff started to lock the store at 9 o'clock when two men, one a white man, and the other a black man, came in and ordered a sack of tobacco. As soon as Sol gave the tobacco to the white man, the man drew two pistols and said, "Hold up."

Sol apparently not understanding hesitated and was slow to respond. Mrs. Aronoff was looking at the men through a screen door from her room in the back. She said both men had pistols. The black man grabbed her husband by the hand. One of them fired a shot, and another shot was fired at her. She then grabbed her pistol and fired at the black man who was the closest to her, but missed hitting him because she was so excited.

Mrs. Aronoff stated later that when she fired at the black man, the white man then shot her husband. When Sol was shot, the bullet hit him in the left breast. He fell backward into the bedroom and fell dead on his own bed.

The Dallas police were notified immediately and Chief of Police Knight and his officers responded to the scene of the murder. Chief Knight called for Doctor Tipton to examine the body. Mrs. Aronoff had a hard time accepting the fact that her husband was actually dead. But, she gave a very good description of the two men involved in the robbery and murder of her husband. Somewhere between nineteen and thirty dollars was taken in the robbery.

Chief Knight called for Dallas County Sheriff J. Roll Johnson's bloodhounds to assist in the search for the killers. The bloodhounds followed the scent, and witnesses stated they heard the shots and saw the men run into the brush in the direction taken by the dogs. The dogs eventually lost the trail of the two men.

The next day after the murder of her husband, Mrs. Aronoff was brought to Dallas City Hall where a number of men who had been rounded up were brought before her to see if she could identify any of them. She immediately identified Holly Vann as the person who shot her husband. On December 2nd, three men were indicted for the murder of Sol Aronoff. They were, Holly Vann, a white male, age twenty-eight; Burrell Oates, a black male, age thirty-one; and Frank McCue, a white male, age twenty-two.

On November 30, 1904, Dallas County Justice of the Peace W. Edwards, Pct. #1, Place 2, held an inquest over the body of Sol Aronoff. After hearing testimony of Mrs. Aronoff and Doctor Tipton, Judge Edwards made his ruling:

> *I find that Sol Aronoff came to his death on the night of November 29, 1904, from the effects of a gunshot wound to the left breast, the pistol fired being in the hands of one Holly Vann, and that one Burrell Oats [sic] was present and aiding and assisting the said Vann.*
>
> *[signed] W. Edwards*

Judge Edwards in his official inquest record book listed the names of the three murder suspects being confined to the Dallas County Jail as Holly Vann, Burrell Oates and Frank McCue.

The trial of Holly Vann was the first one to come to trial. The case was assigned to Judge E. B. Muse of the Criminal District Court, and was tried in Dallas. The trial started on December 19, 1904 and the indictment was read and the defendant pleaded not guilty.

The attorneys for the State in the Holly Vann case were County Attorney Hatton W. Summers, Assistant County Attorney W. W. Nelms, and Phil Barry Miller. Counsels for the defendant were A. E. Firmin and Hyde and Latham.

The first witness to testify was Mrs. Aronoff. She gave a detailed description of the events and suspects. Her testimony was reported in the local newspapers.

O. L. Chittwood, a witness for the State, testified that he was working about thirty yards south of Anonoff's store the night Anonoff was murdered. Between 9 and 10 o'clock, he heard shots and saw two men run from Aronoff's door and down across the street. He could not tell if they were

Sol Arnoff
*Courtesy Dallas Times **Herald***

white or black men. Chittwood also said he telephoned the police station from Aronoff's store.

Holly Vann testified that he, along with Burrell Oates and Frank McCue, had been riding in a buggy together that evening. Vann further stated that he and Oates stopped at Aronoff's store and went inside to get some tobacco, and that he did not intend to commit a robbery. Vann said he didn't have a pistol and he was not the one that shot Sol Aronoff. He stated that Oates shot Arnonff.

Frank McCue testified for the State. He said he was going to tell all he knew, and they would then turn him loose. McCue said he, along with Vann and Oates, were riding in a buggy that Vann said he won by "shaking dice." They picked up the buggy and horse at Everett Hill's Saloon, in an area known as "the reservation." They went to Oak Cliff and were returning when Vann said something about holding up old man Aronoff. McCue said he told them he would not go along with their plan.

McCue further testified that Vann and Oates got out of the buggy near Aronoff's Store and that Oates told Vann he had better take a pistol. McCue said Vann told him to drive the buggy back to Everett Hill's Saloon and put up the horse.

Arthur Vann, testified on behalf of his brother Holly Vann. Arthur testified that on the night Sol Aronoff was killed, Frank "Mud" McCue drove up in a buggy to Everett Hill's saloon at between 9:30 and 10 p.m., and spent the night with him.

On December 21, 1904, after all the witness testimony was heard, closing arguments by the defense and prosecution were made. Judge Muse sent the case to the jury which gave its verdict:

We the jury, find Holly Vann, the defendant, guilty of murder of the first degree, and assess his punishment at death.

K. J. Kivlen, Foreman

The next day, on December 22, 1904, the jury selection for the trial of Burrell Oates began. The jury was selected. The same witnesses, which included Mrs. Aronoff and Frank McCue, testified in the case.

On December 24, 1904, the jury in the Oates case reported their verdict:

We the jury, find Burrell Oates, the defendant, guilty of murder in the first degree, as charged in the indictment, and assess his punishment at death.

F. G. Sharp. Foreman

On December 29, 1904, motions for new trials on behalf of Vann and Oates were overruled by Judge E. R. Muse.

"Holly Vann Met His Death Today," those were the headlines in the *Dallas Times Herald*, May 12, 1905. Vann was hanged inside the Dallas County Jail at 1:22 p.m. Dallas County Sheriff Arthur Lee Ledbetter went to Vann's cell and read the lengthy death warrant to him and asked Vann if he had anything to say.

Vann responded, "I never killed Aronoff...I never even had a pistol. All my trouble was caused by drink and evil associates."

Vann was led to the scaffold, his arms strapped to his side and his legs tied. Father Hayes conducted the religious ceremony. Sheriff Ledbetter placed the black cap over Vann's head, the rope was placed around his neck, and a minute later the trap was sprung. Holly Vann fell to his death.

With his death, Vann became the first white man to be hanged in Dallas, Texas, after being convicted and sentenced to death by a jury. As described in earlier chapters of this book, five white men were lynched by mobs, and one white man was robbed and lynched, but he survived.

This is not the end of this strange story.

On January 13, 1906, Frank "Mud" McCue, the witness who turned State's evidence in the case of Holly Vann and Burrell Oates murder cases, was sentenced to three years imprisonment for theft. Judge E. B. Muse was the trial judge in this case. In August 1907, McCue was pardoned by Governor Thomas Mitchell Campbell on the theft charge.

Tombstone of Sol Aronoff, robbed and murdered November, 29, 1904. Buried in Sherith Israel Cemetery in Dallas. *Photo by Author*

From 1904 to 1912, Oates was tried a total of seven times for the murder of Sol Aronoff. Five times, from 1904 to 1910, Oates was tried in Dallas and four of the trials resulted in convictions and a death sentence. Each time the case was overturned by the Criminal Court of Appeals. The fifth time the case was tried in Dallas, it resulted in a hung jury. Eleven voted for conviction and death, and one held out for a term of life in prison.

Finally, in 1911, the Oates murder trial was transferred to Waxahachie in Ellis County. The first trial held in May in Ellis County resulted in a guilty verdict and punishment set at death. Failure of the jury to indicate first degree murder caused Judge Hawkins to order a new trial.

On November 4, 1911, the second trial held in Ellis County ended, and again resulted in a guilty verdict and sentence of death. In June of 1912, the case and death sentence of Oates was affirmed by the Court of Criminal Appeals in Austin.

Sol Aronoff was robbed and murdered on November 29, 1904. Eight years to the day after his murder, Burrell Oates was hanged in the Ellis County Jail in Waxahachie.

Because Oates was not actually hanged in Dallas, he is not counted in the total number of hangings listed in this book. While the murder trials of Oates had been working their way slowly through the courts, another person involved with the Aronoff case was also making news reports in Dallas.

* * * * *

On Sunday, September 22, 1907, the body of a young man was found on the west side of the Trinity River. He had been stabbed seventeen times, his skull crushed, and throat cut from ear to ear. W. O. Norris, who said he had been searching for a stray yearling, found the body in the bushes along the river. Norris reported the discovery to the sheriff's office.

Letters and papers with the name Earl Mabry on them were found with the body. Also found were two watches and a pair of glasses. No money was found on the body. Officers believed the man had been robbed and then murdered. Deputies and police officers working on the case, located witnesses who said the young man had just arrived in Dallas by train from Jacksonville, Texas. Earl Mabry was seventeen years-old and was from the Mineola and Hawkins area of East Texas. His mother was in very poor health and living in Stonewall County fifty miles from Abilene, Texas.

Mrs. D. Rodgers, a friend of Earl Mabry's mother, came to Dallas and made arrangements for the body to be removed to Mineola for burial. Miss Beatrice Mabry, a sister of the murdered man, arrived in Dallas and said he was seventeen years-old, and had left home last April. He wrote home regularly and was last heard from while in Lufkin.

Within five days of Mabry's murder, Deputy sheriffs W. H. Chick and Joe Gable, arrested Frank "Mud" McCue and placed him in the county jail. The deputies made an affidavit charging McCue with the murder of Mabry. Two days later McCue and John Carrillo were brought before a judge on a charge of murdering Mabry, but the charges against Carrillo were dropped.

On November 19, 1907, the Dallas County Grand Jury indicted McCue for the murder of Earl Mabry. McCue was still in jail when he was indicted by the grand jury.

By November 1909, the Mabry murder case against Frank McCue had been transferred to Fort Worth, and tried three times there. In March 1910, after a mistrial, Tarrant County dismissed the murder charge against McCue. Dallas deputies were waiting for him and arrested him as he got up to leave the courtroom. McCue was re-indicted and placed back into the Dallas County Jail.

In February 1911, the Mabry murder case against McCue was transferred to McKinney, in Collin County. In July 1911, final arguments were heard in the Mabry murder case against McCue and he was convicted and sentenced to life in prison. McCue was released on $10,000 bond pending an appeal.

Finally, in December 1913, the murder conviction of Frank "Mud" McCue, was affirmed by the Court of Criminal Appeals in Austin.

In October 1917, after serving a total of eight years in jails and prison for the 1907 murder of Earl Mabry, Frank McCue was granted a full pardon by Texas Governor William P. Hobby.

* * * * *

The last note here is about Sheriff Arthur Lee Ledbetter. He was a former deputy sheriff and then Dallas County sheriff. He conducted the hanging of Holly Vann, the subject of this chapter. Sheriff Ledbetter left office in November 1910. On April 3, 1916, Ledbetter, at age fifty-four, was watching a parade in downtown Dallas when the wall of the old Fulton Market Building at Main and Market streets, fell on him. He died that same day at the old St. Paul Sanitarium, in Dallas. He was survived by his wife and six children.

Chapter 14

Allen Brooks

Black male, age, about 59 years old

Offense – Criminal assault/rape February 23, 1910

Victim – Mary Ethel Buvens, white female, age two and a half years old

Indicted – February 24, 1910

Criminal District Court Judge Robert B. Seay, presided

Trial not completed

On Thursday, March 3, 1910, mob action, Allen Brooks taken by force, thrown out a window of the "Old Red" Courthouse and lynched on a pole next to the Elk's Arch at Main and Akard Streets in downtown Dallas

The Elks' Arch, which read, "Welcome Elkdom," was constructed across Main Street, at the corner of Main and Akard streets in downtown Dallas. The Arch was built to welcome the Elks for their July 1908 Dallas convention. After the convention was over in July the Arch was left in place, as many citizens favored keeping it as a permanent structure, and just changing the wording for different festive occasions. No one could anticipate that is less than two years the Arch would stand as a reminder of the lynching of Allen Brooks, and the shame that followed.

On Wednesday, February 23, 1910, Allen Brooks, a black male, age about fifty-nine, was working for Henry J. Buvens. Brooks' duties were to attend to the furnace and keep the fires going. About 3 p.m. that afternoon, Mary Ethel Buvens, a white female, the two and a half year old daughter of Henry Buvens, age thirty-eight, and his wife Marie, age thirty-two, was playing in the yard at the family residence. The Buvens residence was at the corner of Ross Avenue and Pearl Street in Dallas. About 3:30 p.m., Mrs. Buvens noticed her daughter was missing and started searching for her.

Flora Dangerfield, a young black female who worked for the Buvens family as a cook, assisted in the search for the missing child. Flora found the child and Allen Brooks leaving the loft of the barn at the rear of the Buvens home. Flora took the child and ran with her into the house.

An examination of little Mary Ethel Buvens revealed that her underclothing had been torn and was covered with blood. The police were then notified and the search for Brooks started. Doctor W. W. Brandau, the family physician, was called and examined the little girl. The doctor also found the underclothing was torn and covered with blood, along with other evidence.

Brooks had fled, but was found in the boiler room at a nearby residence, and arrested by Dallas police officers Harrison, Dennis and Elmecke. Brooks was taken to the city jail where Doctor Brandau examined him, and found blood on Brooks' clothing. An affidavit charging Brooks with rape was filed, and he was then transferred to the Dallas County Sheriff's Department, where he was placed in the county jail.

The next day, on Thursday, February 24, 1910, the Dallas County Grand Jury met and returned an indictment against Brooks, charging him with criminal assault upon the person of little Mary Ethel Buvens.

Henry Buvens, along with Flora Dangerfield and Doctor Brandau all testified before the grand jury. Captain Theodore Harrison of the Dallas Police Department testified of making the arrest of Brooks, and was the last one to testify before the grand jury.

The case, *State of Texas vs. Allen Brooks*, charged with rape, was set for trial on Thursday, March 3rd, by Criminal District Judge R. B. Seay. A special venire of 150 men was ordered to be available for possible jury duty. In 1897, the Texas legislature passed article 246-a, of the Code of Criminal Procedure, which provided "prosecutions for rape shall take precedence of all cases in all courts."

A petition, dated February 24, 1910, signed by a number of prominent black citizens, was sent to Sheriff Ledbetter which read in part:

> . . . *having been informed of the alleged rape of the little girl yesterday by Allen Brooks, do hereby demand this said villain and assure you we will deliver him his just dues.*

On Thursday evening, a crowd of more than 300 men had gathered at the county jail. Later that night the crowd swelled to almost 1,000. The purpose of the crowd was to take Brooks out of the jail and lynch him. Chief of Police Ryan, along with fifteen to twenty of his officers, and four or five deputy sheriffs, all heavily armed, were on the steps leading to the jail. Sheriff Arthur Lee Ledbetter and a large number of deputies were inside the jail, all prepared for any sign of trouble.

Sheriff Ledbetter, age forty-seven, was born on a farm in southwest Dallas County. He was elected sheriff of Dallas County in November 1904 and served until November 1910, a total of three, two-year terms of office. He was an experienced officer having served six years as a deputy sheriff under Dallas County Sheriff Ben Cabell. Ledbetter had once been shot in the shoulder by a man he was trying to arrest. As sheriff, he conducted the hanging of Holly Vann in 1905. Vann had robbed and murdered Sol Aronoff in 1904.

The crowd soon became a mob. They obtained an iron rail about fourteen feet long and tried to break down the outer door to the county jail. Dallas Police Officer Caldwell was the

Sheriff Arthur Ledbetter
Served 1904-1910
Courtesy of the Dallas Morning News

only officer injured in the fighting with the mob when his hands were slightly cut and bruised.

Sheriff Ledbetter then called for Henry Buvens, father of the little girl, to be brought to the jail. The sheriff offered to let Buvens search the jail to satisfy the mob that Brooks was not in the jail. Buvens conducted the search and informed the mob that Brooks was not in the jail. When the mob was not satisfied, the sheriff allowed a committee of six mob leaders to conduct their own search of the jail. They also reported that Brooks was not in the jail. By early Friday morning the mob decided Brooks was nowhere in the building, and they left the area.

What the mob did not know was that at 10:30 p.m., Wednesday night, Sheriff Ledbetter had instructed Deputy Sheriff Bennett to take Brooks to Fort Worth and place him in the Tarrant County Jail, to prevent any miscarriage of justice. Brooks had been in the Tarrant County Jail for almost twenty-four hours, when the mob was making their demands at the Dallas County Jail.

Judge Seay appointed Dallas attorneys J. E. Thomas and William T. Pace to represent Brooks. Both of the attorneys were later excused by Judge Seay when Pace, "declared that he would not serve and said he had arranged to spend three days in jail if necessary."

Thomas said he would not refuse to obey the mandate of the court, but on account of a previous engagement in Hutchinson County it would be impossible to do so.

Judge Seay then appointed attorneys F. D. Cosby, R. H. Capers, and T. F. Lewis to represent Brooks. Clark would represent the State to prosecute Brooks. Judge J. C. Muse, a member of the law firm of Crawford, Muse and Allen offered the services of the law firm to assist as special prosecutors. The day before the trial, Cosby called Judge Seay and said he was ill and did not know whether he would be able to take part in the trial. Judge Seay then replaced Cosby with George Clifton Edwards to assist the defense team.

The day before the trial was to start, Judge Seay issued an order to Sheriff Ledbetter, which read:

In view of the fact that there will probably be a large number of people who desire to be present in the courtroom on Thursday morning, as there have been on other similar occasions, I desire that the Sheriff have enough deputies in the court room to preserve perfect order. No one should be permitted to block the aisles after the seats are filled, and order in the court room will be strictly enforced.

On Thursday, March 3, 1910, the trial, *State of Texas vs. Allen Brooks*, was scheduled to start in the district courtroom of what is now known as the "Old Red" Courthouse, at the intersections of Main, Houston, and Commerce streets, near historic Dealey Plaza, in downtown Dallas. This courthouse with its beautiful red sandstone construction and clock tower, opened in 1892. It is still standing, but not used as a courthouse. It is now open, and serves as the Old Red Museum of Dallas County History and Culture.

At 9 a.m., on March 3rd, a reporter for the *Times Herald* noted that the corridors, stairways and entrances to the courthouse building were crowded with men believed to be police officers and deputies that were mixed in with the crowd of people. Chief Ryan, with the police department, was present with his officers. Sheriff Ledbetter and his entire force of deputies was in charge of the situation.

Brooks was now being held in the jail at Sherman, in Grayson County. Early on the morning the trial was to start, Sheriff Ledbetter had his deputies bring Brooks to Dallas by the Interurban train. Brooks was placed in the jury room of the district court in the "Old Red" Courthouse.

As the trial was ready to start, the glass doors to the courtroom were covered with paper. Only the special venire of 150 men for possible jury duty, the officers of the court, attorneys for the prosecution and defense, and news reporters were allowed into the courtroom.

Judge Seay gave the defense attorneys time to confer with their client in the jury room, but denied their request for more time. The mob outside the courthouse continued to grow. Mob members rushed into the stairway and up to the second floor courtroom. When Brooks was brought into the courtroom, several members of the mob spotted him. Mob members used chairs to break the glass in the courtroom doors, and rushed in.

For ten minutes the deputies fought the mob. The fighting was hand to hand combat. The mob consisted of from 100 to 200 men and they overpowered the officers. The officers suffered bloody noses, cut faces, black eyes and bruises in the fighting.

Mob members found

An X marks the second floor window Allen Brooks was dragged through on the southwest corner of the "Old Red" Courthouse. *Photo courtesy of Dallas Times Herald*

Brooks in the jury room almost dead from fright. Three deputies made a stand to protect Brooks, but it was to no avail. Brooks was hiding under a table when mob members grabbed him. One mob member stuck Brooks' head out a window and a rope was thrown up from below and placed around his neck. He was then pushed and dragged out the second story window of the jury room, which was located in the southwest corner of the "Old Red" Courthouse.

Later reports stated that Brooks may have died when he hit the ground head first, or at least he was probably unconscious from that point on. The mob shouted to take him to the Elk's Arch. With the rope around his neck, he was dragged down Main Street to Akard Street. Someone climbed up and threw the rope around a spike in a telephone pole, that was next to the Elk's Arch. He was pulled up and left hanging with his feet about four feet from the ground.

Crowd scene of Allen Brooks lynching in downtown Dallas on May 3, 1910, with Brooks hanging in the background. *Photo courtesy of Lt. Bill Wiseman, Dallas County Sheriff's Office.*

Members of the mob began tearing off pieces of Brooks' clothing to keep as souvenirs. A photo of the lynching scene titled, "Lynching Scene, Dallas, March 3, 1910," shows the streets completely full of people standing around the body of Allen Brooks hanging from the telephone pole.

The mob was still not satisfied. Now they decided to return to the county jail and lynch Burrell Oates [see Chapter 13], "Bubber" Robertson [see Chapter 15], both of whom were charged with murder and were still being held in the Dallas County Jail. The *Times Herald* estimated the mob had grown to 5,000. At the county jail they wanted to break down the doors and seize Oates and Robertson.

After Brooks was seized by the mob, Sheriff Ledbetter had his deputies remove Oates and Robertson from the county jail and transport them by taxicab, followed by three other automobiles with men who were heavily armed, to the jail in Fort Worth. When the mob returned to the county jail, Oates and Robertson were long gone.

Sheriff Ledbetter allowed the mob to have a committee of twenty men look inside the jail, and satisfy themselves that Oates and Robertson were there. The search by the committee proved the wanted men were not in the jail.

In the meantime, the body of Brooks was being removed from the telephone pole, and was taken to the hospital. Chief Ryan of the police department ordered Fire Chief Magee to bring up the hose wagon, if needed to disperse the mob. Seeing what was happening, the mob scattered.

At about the same time, the mayor, Judge Seay and commissioners all met and agreed that all saloons should be closed. Chief Ryan was ordered to notify every saloon in town to close immediately. Later it was reported that the saloon operators were thanked for their immediate response.

In a statement to a news reporter, Sheriff Ledbetter said that in addition to his deputies and the police officers, he had at least fifty of the best citizens of Dallas to assist in the protection of Brooks. The Sheriff, who injured his wrist during the fight in the courtroom, said it was impossible to protect Brooks from the organized mob. The Sheriff also said he believed the mob was organized long before it reached the courthouse.

Dallas County Justice of the Peace, Q. D. Corley, Precinct 1, Place 1, who himself was a witness to the murder of Brooks, conducted the inquest into the death of Brooks. Here is his report in Inquest Minute Book 1909-1912, Vol. 1.page 26:

Allen Brooks, negro male, married, age about 59 years, residence County Jail.

Date of Death – 3-3-1910, 11:25 [A.M.] Location – Courthouse. Date of Inquest – 3-3-1910, 1:15 [P.M.]

Where inquest was held – Peoples Undertaking Co. Nature of information and by whom given,

Saw killing myself.

The inquest report of Justice of the Peace Corley continued as follows:

The State of Texas County of Dallas, In an inquest held by me, Q. D. Corley, Justice of the Peace and acting coroner in and for Precinct No. 1, Dallas County, Texas, over the remains of Allen Brooks, by viewing the remains and investigating the killing, I find that the deceased came to his death as the result of being thrown out of or pulled out of the second story window of the jury room of the Criminal District Court of the County Courthouse of Dallas County, Texas, by a mob, the names of the parties composing same being to me unknown. Said death occurring on March 3, 1910, at about 11:25 A.M.

Given under my hand this March 3, 1910, Q. D. Corley, Justice of the Peace and Acting Coroner, Precinct No. One, Dallas County, Texas.

The "Calm After The Storm," was the headline in one local paper the day after the lynching of Brooks. Militiamen had been called out to guard the jail that night. However, there was no need for them as the night passed without incident.

The body of Brooks was reported to be buried in the "Colored Cemetery," in Dallas.

On Saturday, March 5th, Criminal District Judge R. B. Seay, confirmed a report that he would order the Dallas County Grand Jury to investigate the mob actions of March 3rd. If indictments were returned by the grand jury, and convictions obtained, those responsible could be sentenced to prison, or in certain cases given the death penalty.

On Monday, March 7th, Judge Seay made it official and charged the grand jury with investigating three crimes related to the death of Allen Brooks, including riot, burglary and murder. On Thursday, the grand jury began its probe of the mob case. A long list of witnesses was provided to testify in the case. Every juror, judge, officer and newspaper man at the courthouse on March 3rd would be scheduled to appear in the case.

In the Sunday, March 13, 1910, issue of the *Dallas Daily Times Herald*, there was an open letter by James T. Stacey, foreman of the grand jury investigating the mob violence. Two of the headlines of the article were "James T. Stacey On Mob Law" and "Both Races to Blame for the Occurrence of Thursday, March 3."

The term of a grand jury was for three months. The grand jury charged with the investigation of the March 3rd violence, started their term of office on January 1st, and their term would end on March 31st.

On April 1, 1910, the Dallas County Grand Jury issued their report to Judge R. B. Seay, before being dismissed. The report talked about the number of cases reviewed, how many indictments, the condition of the county, the duties of the auditor, care for veterans and the courthouse needing to be cleaned. No mention was made of the mob violence and lynching of Allen Brooks on March 3, 1910.

The next Dallas County Grand Jury took office on April 1, 1910, and ended their term of office on June 30, 1910. In their report published July 3rd, they did not address the mob violence of March 3rd.

No one was ever arrested or held responsible for the mob violence, or the murder and lynching of Allen Brooks on March 3, 1910.

Chapter 15

Julius B. Robertson, aka: "Bubber"

Black male, age 28

Offense –Attempted robbery and murder

*Partners in crime: Walter "Shine" West, black male age 20,
and Eugene "Genie" Jones, black male*

Victim – Franklin F. "Frank" Wolford, white male, age 39, farmer

Wolford shot about 10:30 p.m. November 11, 1908

Wolford died 2 a.m. November 12, 1908

"Bubber" Robertson indicted –January 2, 1909

Trial by jury in Dallas County, Texas

Criminal District Court Judge Robert B. Seay, presided

Tried and convicted June 25, 1909, Dallas County, Texas

Hanged Friday, May 13, 1910, Dallas County, Texas

On Wednesday afternoon, November 11, 1908, Frank Wolford, a farmer who lived near the Rose Hill community in far eastern Dallas County, came to Dallas with his fifteen-year-old step-son, Epps Golson and a nephew named Wesley Anderson. Wolford had brought a wagon load of onions, which he planned to sell on Thursday. He often brought his produce to Dallas to sell.

Wolford had put up his team of horses and wagon at the Rupard Wagon Yard, near the Texas State Fair grounds. That evening Wolford, his step-son and Anderson, walked to downtown Dallas. At about 10:30 p.m., they were headed back to the wagon yard. They were walking at the east end of Main Street near Bopp Street, when they were confronted by three black males. One of the men pulled a pistol on Wolford.

While one of the robbers held the pistol on Wolford, and told him to throw up his hands, the other two went through his pockets. Wolford refused the command and happened to have a pocketknife in his hand. He thrust out with the knife and thought he had cut one of the robbers on the neck or face. The robber holding the pistol then shot Wolford. The bullet struck Wolford in the groin area. At the sound of the shot the three robbers fled.

Epps Golson ran to a nearby house to get assistance for his step-father. When he returned, Wolford told him to get a doctor, and gave him fifty dollars which he had in his pocket. Several men came to the scene and observed blood gushing from the wound. The bullet had struck an artery and was bleeding heavily.

Mounted Dallas police officers rushed to the scene, but the robbers were long gone. Because Wolford still had the fifty dollars in his pocket when attacked, it led officers to believe that the robbers did not take anything.

Wolford was transported by automobile to the City Hospital where Doctor Fisher, the city physician, cared for him. He remained conscious during the ordeal and gave officers a full account of the attempted robbery and shooting. Wolford told the officers he believed he had cut one of the robbers on the neck or face.

Frank Wolford died at 2 a.m. the next morning, on Thursday, November 12, 1908. He was survived by his wife and three sons. He was buried in the Lyons Cemetery, on Barnes Bridge Road in Sunnyvale, located in Dallas County.

Wolford was the son of Willis and Purdy Wolford. Willis Wolford was born in 1827 in Kentucky. In 1862, Willis joined the Confederate Army. He served in the Nineteenth Cavalry, Buford's Regiment. He died on August 7, 1869. His cause of death was reported as diarrhea. Frank Wolford was born on April 15, 1869, in Dallas County, and was only four months old when his father died. Willis Wolford is also buried in the Lyons Cemetery, Sunnyvale, Texas.

Dallas Chief of Police Ben Brandenburg, along with his officers, and Sheriff A. L. Ledbetter and his deputies, were all working on the case and a general roundup of suspects was made. Five or six black males were held in jail and questioned. One of the men was believed to know something about the case. One or two of the men being held were released on Thursday. A search was being made to find the robber with a cut or stab wound on his neck.

Golson came back to Dallas two days later to talk to the officers. He told the officers what happened when his step-father was shot, and that he believed he could identify the three men. The men being held in jail were shown to young Golson, but he failed to identify any of them as being involved in the attempted robbery and murder of his step-father. Young Anderson was also shown the men being held, but he could not identify any of them. All of the men except one, who was being held on other charges, were released.

Sheriff Ledbetter offered a $300 reward and the city of Dallas also offered a $300 reward. Governor Thomas Mitchell Campbell offered a $200 reward and others offered an additional $100. By November 20th, the reward had risen to $900. This amounted to $300 each for the arrest and conviction of the three persons responsible for the murder of Wolford.

Eugene Jones, aka "Genie," a black male, was being held in jail when he made an offer to the officers. Jones offered to give up the names of the other two persons involved in the murder of Wolford. Jones wanted a signed immunity agreement, and said he was willing to testify against the other two involved in the murder of Wolford.

Jones stated that Walter West was the person who Wolford had cut on the neck. West, aka "Shine," a black male, was also being held in jail on other charges. An examination of West's neck showed a healing scar.

Julius B. Robertson, aka "Bubber," a black male, was identified by Jones as the third person involved in the shooting. Jones said that Robertson was the one who shot Wolford.

Affidavits were filed with Justice of the Peace Q. D. Corley, charging Jones and West with the murder of Wolford. An examining trial was held before Judge Corley on November 28th and ordered the men to be held in jail.

Robertson, West and Jones were all indicted for the murder of Wolford. West and Jones were already being held in jail, and Robertson was still on the run.

In early December 1908, a person who fit the description and was suspected to be "Bubber" Robertson was arrested by Oklahoma authorities. Sheriff Ledbetter went to Oklahoma, but the person held was not Robertson and he was released.

Almost four months had passed since Wolford was murdered, and there was no sign of Robertson. Finally, in late March 1909, Robertson was arrested in Washington, D. C., by detectives Bauer and Cromwell of the Washington, D.C. police force. They learned that a black man answering Robertson's description was working on a farm in Maryland, just outside the district line. When Robertson came into Washington he was arrested by the detectives.

Robertson admitted his identity and to being present when Wolford was shot, but said he was not the shooter. He said that after the shooting all three ran and met up an hour later at a railroad crossing.

Dallas Chief of Police Ben F. Brandenburg was notified of the arrest of Robertson by telegram from Washington, D. C., and the *Dallas Morning News* reported the message was as follows:

> *Washington, D. C. March 28 – Ben F. Brandenburg, Chief of Police, Dallas, Tex., Julius Robertson, who is charged with the murder of Frank Wolford, November 11 [12th] 1908, in custody. Admits identify. Also send officer with requisition papers drawn on the chief Justice of the Supreme Court of the District of Columbia. Wire time of departure and arrival here. Answer. SYLVESTER, Superintendent of Police.*

Chief Brandenburg and another officer left for Washington, D. C., that night. The chief asked that the required paperwork from the governor be sent directly to Washington, D. C.

It was found out later that Chief Brandenburg had learned that Robertson was in the Washington, D.C. area, and had given that information to detectives there. Robertson was brought back to Dallas and placed in the Dallas County Jail. Chief Brandenburg had met several Washington, D. C., detectives at the July 1908 Elks Convention in Dallas, and contacted them with the information.

Walter "Shine" West was the first of the three to go on trial. Many of Wolford's friends and relatives were in the crowded courtroom the day of the trial. In the June 1909 trial, witnesses that testified for the State were Mrs. Addie Wolford, Dr. T. B. Fisher, Eugene Jones, Epps Gholson, Chief of Police Cornwell, now ex-Chief of Police Brandenburg and several others. West who testified on his own behalf, was the only witness for the defense.

In the West trial the jury came back with the following verdict:

> *We the jury, find the defendant guilty of murder in the first degree and assess his punishment at death.*
> J. M. Gamble, Foreman

As soon as the trial of West was completed, jury selection was started for the trial of Julius B. Robertson. District Judge Robert B. Seay presided at both the trials of West and Robertson. Jones turned State's evidence and testified for the State in both trials. For Jones' testimony, the charges of robbery and murder in the Wolford case were dropped against him.

On June 23, 1909, the trial began, and on June 25th the jury came back with their verdict which was reported in the *Dallas Morning News*: "State vs. "Bubber" Robertson brought in a verdict of guilty of murder in the first degree and assessed the penalty at death."

On October 8, 1909, West beat the hangman's rope. He died in the

Julius B. "Bubber" Robertson inside his jail cell. *Courtesy Dallas Daily Times Herald*

Dallas County Jail while waiting for the results of his appeal, and for his death sentence to be carried out.

Justice of the Peace Q. D. Corley, Pct. 1, Place 1, conducted the inquest into the death of West. The inquest was held on October 8, 1909, in the Dallas County Jail. Judge Corley ruled that West died of pulmonary tuberculosis and the body was turned over to Donovan Undertaking Company for burial.

In March of 1910, a motion for a rehearing filed by Robertson was overruled by the Texas Court of Criminal Appeals. A mandate was then issued by the District Court to bring Robertson before the court, and to set a date for his death sentence to be carried out. The clerk of the District Court was then instructed to draw up the "Death Warrant" for Robertson.

On April 4, 1910, Julius B. "Bubber" Robertson was brought before Judge Seay and told by the judge that he was tried by a jury, convicted of murder in the first degree, and his punishment set at death. Judge Seay asked Robertson if he had anything to say, which he did not.

On April 28, 1910, Jones was sentenced to fifteen years in the state penitentiary for his part in the November 8, 1908, robbery of H. M. Ramsey. Jones was also being held in the Dallas County Jail on a murder charge. He was charged with the murder of Holly Ewing, a black male, age nineteen, and was waiting to be tried on that case. Ewing was shot twice, at the corner of Elm and Walton streets, on the evening of October 20, 1908.

Judge Seay then set the date of Friday, May 13, 1910, for the date that Robertson was to be hanged by the neck until he was dead. The judge ordered Sheriff Ledbetter to take custody of the prisoner.

On the morning of Friday, May 13, 1910, Robertson ate his breakfast at 8 a.m. He was then allowed to put on a new suit of clothes which included a soft silk shirt, a tie and new shoes purchased by Sheriff Ledbetter. A number of people were allowed into the corridor of the jail to observe the hanging including Mrs. Frank Wolford, her daughter, several brothers of Wolford, Epps Golson, deputies, newspaper men and a few others.

A large crowd consisting of men, women and children had gathered outside the jail. All were trying to get some view of Robertson and the hanging.

The scaffold was set in the stairwell of the jail, only twenty feet from the cell where the prisoner was held. At 11:30 a.m. Sheriff Ledbetter read the death warrant to the prisoner. As soon as that was completed, Robertson was taken from his jail cell and walked to the gallows.

Elder S. G. George conducted the religious ceremony. He had baptized Robertson several weeks earlier. He was assisted by Mandy Ingraham and Ethel Jackson, two black women.

At the gallows there was a prayer, and the noose was placed around the neck of Robertson by Sheriff Ledbetter. The sheriff then placed a black cap over the head of Robertson. Robertson was heard to be praying when Sheriff Ledbetter threw the lever. The platform gave way and Robertson fell to his death.

State health officer, Doctor W. M. Brumby, city health officer, Doctor T. B. Fisher, and county health officer, Doctor K. W. Field were all present at the execution and pronounced Robertson dead.

Robertson's body was turned over to Peoples Undertaking Company, where it was prepared for burial. His body was sent to Paris, Texas, where he was born, for burial.

Chapter 16

John Roberson, aka: John Robinson

Black male, age 32

Offense – Assault, robbery and murder on May 4, 1911

Partner in crime - Will Flowers, black male,
sentenced to thirty years in prison

Victim – Otto Kalkhoff, white male, age 60, died May 7, 1911

Indictments returned by the grand jury June 1911

Trial by jury Dallas County, Texas

Criminal District Court Judge Robert B. Seay presided

Tried and convicted December 13, 1911

Death sentence affirmed by the Court of Criminal Appeals November 1912

Hanged Friday, January 10, 1913, Dallas County, Texas

Otto Kalkhoff, age sixty, and his wife Emily, decided to go to a "show" in downtown Dallas on Thursday evening, May 4, 1911. Little did they know what waited for them, and would happen as they walked back to their house at 1722 Chestnut Street. Two men had been watching the Kalkhoffs, and were waiting for them that night.

According to the Kalkhoff family tree, Otto's full name was, Christoph Friedrich Eduard [Otto] Kalkhoff. He was born in Germany in 1851 and arrived by ship in New York City on January 15, 1870. He married Emily Walke on January 22, 1879, in Illinois. By 1900, Otto was working as a machinist for the Bachman Foundry in Austin, Texas. In 1910 and 1911, he and his wife were living in Dallas, and he was working at the Murray Gin Company.

After leaving the "show," as the Kalkhoffs reached the intersection of Dawson and Chestnut streets, two men approached them from the front. Just as the men passed them, one of the men struck Mrs. Kalkhoff in the head with a heavy metal object. Then the other man began beating Otto about the head and face with a heavy metal object. The assailants took $2.40 and a plug of tobacco from Otto's pocket.

Because of the sounds made by Mrs. Kalkhoff, people came out of their houses and a crowd was at the scene within minutes. The Kalkhoffs were then assisted to their house. Otto didn't lose consciousness until he had unlocked the door to his house, walked inside, and fell across a bed. Otto was unconscious when he and his wife were rushed to the St. Paul Sanitarium on Bryan Street in Dallas.

Dallas police were called, and motorcycle officer Harr responded to investigate the assault. Two bloody, heavy metal coupling pins, about two feet long, were later found near the scene and taken by police as evidence.

Mrs. Kalkhoff had a deep scalp wound above the left eye. Otto had been struck four times over the head and his skull was fractured in one place. A piece of his skull the size of a half dollar was removed, and he had a wound around his eye. After being examined by the doctors, they did not expect him to live through the night.

Mrs. Kalkhoff was not injured as bad as her husband, and was able to give a description of the two attackers. She described them both as white, one "rather fleshy," and the other as "spare build." She said they were "smooth shaved." She also described their clothing and said they were well dressed.

Otto lay unconscious for several days until he died at 10 a.m., on Sunday morning, May 7, 1911. He had never regained consciousness after falling on his bed in his house after the attack. Two sons, one from Austin, and one from Oklahoma, came to Dallas when notified of their father's condition. On his death certificate the cause of death was recorded as, "Fracture of skull and injury to brain."

On June 2nd Dallas police detectives Scott Hall and Fred Lenzen arrested two black men, John Roberson and Will Flowers, and charged them with the murder of Otto Kalkhoff. They also charged the two with the April 23, 1911 robbery of Mr. and Mrs. I. Freedman, when they were robbed of $80, near the corner of Harwood and Eakins streets.

Although Mrs. Kalkhoff described the two assailants as being "white" males, witnesses were found that observed the attack on the Kalkhoffs. The witnesses knew the attackers to be Roberson and Flowers, both black males, who had put white shoe polish on their faces to make them appear to be white.

Roberson and Flowers were indicted in the June term of the grand jury for robbery, assault to murder and the murder of Otto Kalkhoff.

The trials for Flowers and Roberson were set to begin on Monday, December 4, 1911. Flowers' trial started first, and as soon as it was com-

NEGRO HANGED FOR MURDER IN DALLAS

John Roberson photo and headline from Dallas Daily Times Herald.

pleted, the trial for Roberson would commence. Special veni-res had been ordered to stand-by for possible jury duty.

The first witness to testify was Mrs. Kalkhoff. In her tes-timony she said the two men seemed to have "a sort of chalky white color."

Will Wright, a black man, testified that he knew Flow-ers and Roberson. Wright said that on the afternoon of May 4, 1911, they came to where he lived and asked him for a "skel-eton key" [a universal key that opened the locks to doors in many of the old houses]. They told him they found a house with two old people and no children, but they needed a key to get in. Wright said he did not give them the key they request-ed.

Wright also testified that Flowers and Roberson came back later and each had a coupling pin. They also had a box of white shoe polish. Wright said the coupling pins were made of steel and would weigh about ten or twelve pounds, and were about two feet long. He also said that Flowers and Roberson wanted him to go with them, but he refused.

Wright said he saw the two that night near the Wolf Saloon. They were coming down Chestnut Street, and they told him they were wait-ing for the old couple to come along. They wanted him to whistle if he saw the couple coming, which he said he refused to do.

Wright said when the couple came along he saw Flowers hit Mrs. Kalkhoff and knock her down. He said Roberson hit Mr. Kalkhoff and knocked him down. Roberson hit the man again after he was down. Roberson turned Mr. Kalkhoff over and ran his hands through his pockets. By then people started coming out of the house nearby. Rob-erson then hollered to Flowers to come on, and they ran off.

Wright also said that when he saw the two men just before the assault, they had white shoe polish all over their faces. When they came to his house later that night, the polish was just around the shirt collar and other places where they had failed to get it off. Flowers had cut out the front of his shoes where he had white shoe polish on them and could not get it off.

The coupling pins were shown to Wright by the police. He said they looked like the ones he saw in the possession of Flowers and Roberson. Dallas Police Officer F. A. Lenzen testified of arresting Roberson and Flowers on the charge of murder.

The cut-out shoes worn by Flowers were then introduced into evidence. Sheriff Ben. F. Brandenburg testified that the pair of shoes with the toes cut away were the same shoes he took off the feet of Flowers.

Edith Robertson, a black female, testified she was with Wright the afternoon and evening of May 4th. She testified to the same basic facts that Wright testified to.. She was also a witness to the actual attack on Mr. and Mrs. Kalkhoff. She said she heard Roberson say that he got $3.40 and a plug of Star Navy Tobacco, and if Flowers had hit the old lady hard enough to keep her from groaning, they would have gotten more.

Flowers had a number of his family and friends testify in his behalf, before the case went to the jury on Wednesday, December 6, 1911.

The jury was out a little more than an hour when they returned with their verdict. They found Flowers guilty and assessed his punishment at confinement for life in the Texas State Penitentiary.

The murder case, *State of Texas vs. John Roberson, Case #10990*, was next on the docket of Judge R. B. Seay, in Criminal District Court. By Friday, December 8, 1911, jurors had been selected. Dallas County Attorney Clark prosecuted the case. Roberson was represented by attorneys Wiley and Baskett.

The testimony in the trial of Roberson varied very little from the testimony in the Flowers trial. On Monday, December 11, 1911, the State rested its case. On Wednesday, December 13, 1911, the case went to the jury.

The jury was out a little less than an hour when it came back with its verdict:

> *We the jury, find the defendant guilty of murder in the first degree, as charged in the indictment, and assess his punishment at death.*
> *C. C. Wynn, Foreman*

On June 9, 1912, Will Flowers was transferred from the Dallas County Jail to the Texas State Penitentiary at Huntsville. He was issued

Sheriff Benjamin F. Brandenburg's tombstone at Wheatland Cemetery in Dallas. He served from 1910 to 1914. *Photo by author*

convict number 33384 and his age was listed as twenty-two. He was found guilty of murder in the first degree, and given a life sentence. The expiration of his sentence was shown as "Death." In the remarks column it was noted that he escaped on April 4, 1923. No record was found that he was ever re-captured.

In November 1912, the Texas Court of Criminal Appeals affirmed the death sentence for Roberson. Judge Robert B. Seay then set the date of the execution as Friday, January 10, 1913.

The early morning newspaper on the day of the execution, reported that all the arrangements had been made for the execution. The same rope that was used to hang Burrell Oates at Waxahachie on November 29, 1912, would be used to hang Roberson in the Dallas County Jail. A priest from the Catholic Church had spent time with Roberson the day before, and would again be with him at the execution. Sheriff Ben F. Brandenburg would act as the executioner for the first time in his term of office.

On the morning of the execution, Roberson struggled with the officers as they attempted to dress him for the hanging. After visiting with the Catholic priest he seemed to accept his fate and cooperated with the officers. Sheriff Brandenburg ordered a large steak, French fried potatoes and other side dishes, which Roberson quickly ate. He had not eaten his food since the previous day.

The execution was again held inside the Dallas County Jail. It was estimated that 250 people inside the jail saw the execution. In addition, a crowd of about 600 had gathered in the rain outside the jail, in an attempt to catch a glimpse of the hanging. Some people said it generally rained on "Hangman's Day."

Ed Roberson, a brother of the condemned man came to visit, but Roberson declined to see him. A black woman was inside the jail and stood near the scaffold. Officers at the execution said she was a sister of Roberson's.

Sheriff Brandenburg read the death warrant to Roberson, and Roberson asked permission to read the warrant himself. He only read a portion of the lengthy document before stopping. Roberson was led from his cell to the scaffold. He was placed on the trap door, with the rope around his neck and the black hood over his head.

At 12:51 p.m., on Friday, January 10, 1913, Sheriff Ben Brandenburg pulled the lever, and John Roberson fell to his death.

John Roberson's Texas Death Certificate 831 [1913], listed his personal information as male, negro, married, and his age as 22. The cause of death was recorded as, "Hanged by Sheriff."

Hundreds of people, both black and white, visited Peoples Undertaking parlor to view the body of Roberson. The body was sent to Hempstead, in Waller County, Texas, for burial.

Chapter 17

Floyd Stanton

Black male, death certificate shows his age as 38

Offense – Murder

*Victim – Naomi Stanton, black female, ex-wife,
death certificate has her age as 26*

Trial by jury in Dallas County

Criminal District Judge Barry Miller, presided

Murder occurred Tuesday, December 3, 1912

Indictment issued December 5, 1912

Tried and convicted December16 & 17, 1912

Case Affirmed by the Court of Criminal Appeals May 28, 1913

Hanged Friday, August 1, 1913, Dallas County, Texas

On Tuesday afternoon, December 3, 1912, at about 3:30 p.m., Naomi Stanton went to the Harry Harlan Commission House in the 2100 block of Main Street in Dallas. Her ex-husband Floyd Stanton, and his brother Sam Stanton, both worked at the Harry Harlan Company. Naomi and Floyd had been separated and divorced since April of 1912. Her side of the story and reason for going to Floyd's workplace is not known, as she didn't leave alive.

At the time Naomi arrived at the Harry Harlan Company, Floyd and Sam were trimming celery in the rear of the business. Several employees witnessed the conversation between Naomi and Floyd, and the shooting that followed. Sam Stanton said he paid no attention to the conversation, but when the shooting started he ran as fast as he could for a place of safety.

Dallas police responded to the call of a shooting and arrested Floyd Stanton within a few minutes. Officer W. W. Keatts went to the county attorney's office and swore out an affidavit charging Floyd Stanton with murder.

The *Dallas Morning News* reported a statement given to police by Stanton at the city jail.

I shot Naomi Stanton with a .32 caliber automatic. I do not know how many times I shot. She had come for more money. We were divorced, having been separated about last April, and she had kept on bleeding me for more money. I told her I could not give her any and she commenced to tell what she was going to make her man do to me. She said she had to have the money and she kept on talking that way and threatening. I drew the gun and shot her. I had not been carrying a gun regularly.. I do not know whether she had a knife or anything. I am 37 years old and she is 27 years old.

During the examination of the body of Naomi Stanton, nine steel nosed bullets were removed. The doctors reported that six or seven of the nine shots could have caused her death.

Naomi Stanton's Texas Death Certificate 27048 [1912], recorded the following information:

Deceased - negro female, married, age 26, born in Texas. Place of death – Dallas, Dallas County, Texas. Date of death – December 3, 1912. Cause of death – Gunshot. Place of burial - Terrell, Texas. Peoples Undertaking Company.

Two days after he was arrested, Floyd Stanton was indicted by the Dallas County Grand Jury for the murder of Naomi Stanton.

On Monday, December 16, 1912, the murder trial, *State of Texas vs. Floyd Stanton*, was ready for trial. Criminal District Court Judge Barry Miller would hear the case. County Attorney Currie McCutcheon, and Assistant County Attorney Noah Roark represented the State. Attorneys Thurmond Barrett and T. N. Simpson represented the defendant.

The attorneys for the defense attempted to enter a plea of not guilty on the grounds of insanity. This was rejected by the court. The jurors were selected and the trial began on the morning of December 16th.

The witnesses testified and evidence was presented. County Attorney McCutcheon closed for the State at 11:20 a.m., on Tuesday, December 17th. Judge Miller gave his charge to the jury.

The jury was out for only ten minutes when they came back with their verdict. It was reached on the first ballot. "We the jury find the defendant guilty of murder in the first degree and assess his punishment at death."

As reported in The *Dallas Morning News*, the murder trial of Floyd Stanton was one of the quickest on record in Dallas County, and shortest new case ever tried. He was tried and convicted in two weeks from

the date Naomi Stanton was murdered.

Stanton's case was appealed
to the Texas Court of Criminal
Appeals. Before the ruling came
down, Judge Miller retired and
on May 28, 1913, the Court of
Criminal Appeals affirmed the
death sentence of Floyd Stanton.

Judge Crawford, the new
judge, set the date for execution
of Floyd Stanton as August 1,
1913. The Board of Pardon Advisors agreed to make a favorable
recommendation on an application to commute the death penalty to life in prison. Several judges
and prominent citizens in Dallas
and elsewhere had endorsed the
application.

Floyd Stanton, Negro, Who Was
Hanged, and Spiritual Adviser

A photo and headline from the Dallas
Daily Times Herald of Floyd Stanton and
his spiritual advisor (standing).

However, on July 28, 1913, Governor Oscar Colquitt refused to
interfere with the death sentence and agreed to "let the law take its
course." The governor believed that Stanton had been properly represented in court, he had been given a speedy trial and the case was
affirmed by the appeals court.

On Thursday, the day before the scheduled hanging, Stanton met
with Catholic priest Father McSweeney, whom he thanked for his untiring work and the prayers in his behalf. Stanton said that he was ready
to die, he had no fear, and that God had saved his soul. Two days before
his execution Stanton made a written confession admitting his crime.

Stanton had been a model prisoner. He had been industrious
throughout his life and had not been in any serious trouble until the
murder of his ex-wife. He had three brothers and six sisters, most of
whom lived in Dallas.

Hundreds of people had asked Sheriff Ben F. Brandenburg for permission to witness the execution. The space in the jail stairway was
very small and only a few could be admitted to the jail.

Sheriff Brandenburg entered the cell where Stanton was being held
at 11:10 a.m. The sheriff provided Stanton with a new black suit of
clothes, shirt, collar and tie. At 11:30 a.m. he was taken from the cell and
allowed to kiss his relatives goodbye. Father McSweeney conducted a

farewell service.

Sheriff Brandenburg read the death warrant to Stanton. This was the second hanging that Sheriff Brandenburg would conduct. On January 10, 1913, he conducted the hanging of John Roberson.

The sheriff was assisted by his son, who was a deputy sheriff, and Deputy Sheriff John Chiesa. At the base of the gallows were deputies Preston, Roberts and Woolsey. Out of town sheriffs and their deputies from Grayson, Tarrant and Ellis counties were present, along with a deputy United States marshal. Also present were several Dallas County officials.

Sheriff Brandenburg allowed Stanton to speak through a window to the large crowd gathered outside the jail. Stanton admitted his guilt and said goodbye.

Stanton was taken to the gallows and stepped onto the trap door. Straps were placed around his arms and legs. Sheriff Brandenburg pulled the black cap over Stanton's face and placed the noose around his neck. The sheriff pulled the lever to the trap door at 12:02 p.m. Floyd Stanton fell to his death. Doctors Hale, Watson and Hendrix pronounced Stanton dead at 12:14 p.m. on Friday, August 1, 1913.

Stanton's Texas Death Certificate 17059 [1913] lists this information:

Male, colored, age 38. Place of death – Dallas, Dallas County Jail. Date of death – August 1, 1913, Cause of death – Hanged by the neck until dead. Place of burial – Woodland Cemetery, Dallas, Texas. Peoples Undertaking Company.

Chapter 18

Ed Long

Black male, age 34

Offense – Murder of a special officer

Partner in crime: Ed "Bright Eyes" Christian, black male, age 35

Victim – Special Officer Thomas Henry Bennett, white male, age 32

Officer Bennett was shot September 10, 1910, and died September 11, 1910

Indicted by the grand jury April 29, 1911

Trial by jury Dallas County, Texas

Criminal District Court Judge Robert B. Seay, presided

Tried and convicted February 7 & 8, 1913

Court of Criminal Appeals affirmed the case October 18, 1913

Hanged Friday, December 19, 1913 in Dallas County, Texas

Thomas Henry Bennett was born and raised in the Mesquite and Lawson areas of southeast Dallas County. Bennett worked for several years as a deputy sheriff in the Dallas County Sheriffs' Department. As a deputy sheriff he was the bailiff in the county court-at-law. It was while working at the courthouse that he met and made thousands of friends there. In July 1910, Bennett left the sheriff's department and went to work as a special officer for the Texas and Pacific Railroad Company.

His new duties at T & P Railroad Company included checking the railroad box cars that were parked in the railroad yards near the fairgrounds east of downtown Dallas. Box car burglars had been breaking into the cars and stealing the contents and Bennett was there to stop them. Those duties, in the early morning hours of September 10, 1910, would lead to his death.

Sometime after 2 a.m., and a short time before he was shot, Bennett was notified by a trainman that a boxcar had been broken into somewhere between Dallas and Mesquite. The train crew had just left the boxcar parked on a siding east of the fairgrounds, and several men seen in the vicinity were acting suspicious.

When Officer Bennett located the boxcar he saw what he thought were three men. Two were walking and one was driving a loaded express wagon pulled by a jennet [a female donkey], coming in his direction. Bennett knew they would be forced to pass through a nearby gate and he hid in the shadows behind a telephone pole. Bennett planned to wait until the men passed through the gate and then arrest them.

As the wagon was passing through the gate, one of the men saw Bennett, and without saying anything pulled a pistol and fired. The bullet struck Officer Bennett in the chest near

OFFICER SLAIN BY BOX-CAR BURGLARS

Special Officer Thomas Henry Bennett
Courtesy Dallas Daily Times Herald

the right nipple and proceeded downward. The bullet passed through his liver, and lodged near his spine.

The driver of the wagon whipped the jennet to a gallop as they fled. Bennett fired his revolver five times in the direction of the man who shot him as the man ran after the wagon. The shooting took place about 100 feet from the intersection of the Texas and Pacific Railroad and Dallas Avenue. Officer Bennett later described the man who shot him as a black man, short, and heavy set. He described the jennet as white or grey in color.

James Williamson, a dairyman, heard the shots and telephoned the police station. Night Captain Lynch answered the call and notified the officers in the city to be on the lookout for three black men and an express wagon pulled by a white jennet.

Citizens T. E Henry, James Williams and Luther Lagow, were the first three men to reach Bennett after he was shot. Henry was awakened by the first shot and before he was fully awake he heard five more shots. Henry said he was asleep about 150 yards from where the shooting of Officer Bennett took place.

Dallas Police motorcycle officers Phillips and Garrett, along with Doctor Reamer who lived nearby, located Bennett sitting up and in a "cheerful mood." The wound was bleeding heavily, and using a handkerchief, the doctor attempted to stop the bleeding. It was about a half hour before an ambulance arrived to take Bennett to the hospital.

The Dallas police officers observed hoof marks on the ground and measured the length of the stride and the shape and size of the small hoof prints to compare, if the jennet was located.

While at the hospital, Bennett expressed a determination to live. He told one of the doctors he was going to get well. He rallied for a while, and there was a belief he might live. Then at 7 a.m., on Sunday, September 11th, he began to sink rapidly and passed away.

Thomas Henry Bennett was born December 18, 1875. He was single and was survived by his parents Mr. and Mrs. John Bennett, of the Lawson community. He was also survived by four brothers and two sisters. He was a member of the Christian Church and the Lawson Camp of the Woodmen of the World.

The funeral for Bennett was held at the Christian Church in Mesquite. The Rev. C. G. Wright conducted the service and the funeral was under the direction of the Woodmen of the World. Burial was in the Mesquite City Cemetery.

A general roundup of suspects began almost immediately after Bennett was shot. Anyone that fit the description given by Officer Bennett was arrested, questioned and held in jail. When the arrested men provided alibis, and with no one admitting to the crime, they were released. Bud Tennison was arrested on September 26th, and charged with the murder of Officer Bennett. Those charges would also be dropped. The officers still believed that the white jennet would be the key to solving the case.

Months went by with no new developments in the case. Finally George Williams, a black man, was identified as the owner of the white jennet. When questioned he said he leased the jennet to Ed Long.

Ed Long, age thirty-four, was described as a black man with some Mexican or Indian blood. He was arrested and charged with the murder of Officer Bennett. Long admitted to being involved in the boxcar burglary and present when Bennett was shot, but said he was not the one who fired the shot that killed Bennett.

Long also gave up the names of the other two men involved in the burglary and shooting of Bennett. Ed Long, Ed Christian and George Williams, along with one unnamed man, were all indicted by the grand jury on April 29, 1911 for the murder of Bennett.

Ed "Bright Eyes" Christian, a black male, age thirty-five, was one of the two named by Long as being involved in the burglary of the boxcars and being present when Bennett was shot. But Christian could not be located. Sheriff Ben Brandenburg was given much credit for his untiring efforts to locate Christian. Almost a year and a half later, in September 1912, through Sheriff Brandenburg's efforts, Ed Christian was located and arrested in Limestone County, Texas.

In February 1913, the trial, *State of Texas vs. Ed Long*, began in Criminal District Court, Judge Robert B. Seay, presiding. The prosecution was conducted by attorney R. B. Allen as special prosecutor for the railroad company, and by County Attorney Currie McCutcheon and Assistant County Attorney Will Curtis. The defendant was represented by A. B. Baskett.

Long's trial started on Thursday, February 6, 1913, and was completed and submitted to the jury by 3 p.m. Friday afternoon. On Saturday morning at 9 a.m., the jury came back with their verdict of murder in the first degree and assessed the death penalty.

Ed Christian was the next to go on trial in Criminal District Court, with Judge Robert B. Seay also presiding in this case. After hearing the witnesses and evidence, the case was given to the jury. The jury returned their verdict after only forty-five minutes deliberation. They returned with a verdict of guilty and sentenced him to death.

In October 1913, the Court of Criminal Appeals of Texas affirmed the death sentence for Long. The date for the execution would be set as soon as a mandate from the higher court in Austin was received by Judge Seay. On October 22nd Judge Seay set the date of November 28, 1913, as the date Long was to be hanged. While Long was in court that day, he was found to have a sling-shot hidden in his clothing. It was suspected that he was planning to use it in an escape attempt, which failed.

On November 5th, 1913, the Court of Criminal Appeals of Texas affirmed the death sentence of Christian. Again Judge Seay would set the date for the execution for Christian as soon as the mandate was received from Austin. On November 9th the mandate for Christian was received in Dallas and Judge Seay set the date for Christian's execution as January 23, 1914.

Dallas County Sheriff Ben Brandenburg would again be called on to conduct a hanging in the Dallas County Jail. This time it would be Ed Long. This was the third execution conducted by Sheriff Brandenburg. The date was Friday, December 19, 1913.

On Friday, December 19, 1913, his last day, Long spent practically all morning singing, praying and talking. The Rev. J. T. Ramsey and a woman assistant were Long's spiritual advisors. The two spent most of the morning with him. Long took a bath and dressed for the final hour. He ate a healthy dinner thirty minutes before leaving his cell.

John Bennett, the father of Officer Thomas Henry Bennett, along with Officer Bennett's four brothers and several female relatives, were all present to observe the hanging.

Sheriff Brandenburg read the death warrant to Long before they left the jail cell. The scaffold was in place in the stairwell of the county jail. Ed Long said, "I cannot die with a lie on my lips, Ed Christian is not guilty. He was not even there."

Long walked through the crowd of people in the jail hallway on his way to the scaffold. When they arrived at the scaffold, Long stepped onto the trap door and began laughing and talking. Sheriff Brandenburg and his deputies strapped Long's arms and legs. The black cap was placed over his head and the rope was put around his neck. Sheriff Brandenburg pulled the lever to the trap door and Long fell to his death.

Doctor William Hale pronounced Long dead seven minutes after the trap door fell. The body was turned over to Peoples Undertaking Company. The county paid for the funeral expenses, as Long claimed he did not have a relative in the world that he knew of.

Ed Long's Texas Death Certificate 24953 [1913], listed the following information:

Male, negro, single, age 34, born in Texas, [no relatives are listed] Cause of death – Legally Executed.

On February 8, 1914, the death sentence of Ed Christian was commuted to life in the penitentiary by Governor Colquitt. On March 14, 1914, he was transferred to the State Prison at Huntsville. He was issued convict number 35808. Prison records show Christian died in prison on September 27, 1920.

The third party that Long named as an accomplice was never located or arrested for his part in the burglary of the boxcar and murder of Officer Bennett.

Benjamin F. Brandenburg served as sheriff of Dallas County from 1910 to 1914. During his term of office he served as the executioner for three Dallas county prisoners, who were sentenced to death by Dallas County juries. Ben Brandenburg died on September 7, 1951, in Dallas, at age eighty-nine. He is buried in the Wheatland Cemetery in Dallas.

Chapter 19
Walter Robert Stevenson

White male, age 34, born November 16, 1883, in Texas

Leonard A. Dodd

White male, age 30, born October 3, 1887, in Tennessee

Offense – Kidnapping and criminal assault, occurred June 25, 1917

Victim – Miss Florence Orcutt, white female, age about 18

Indicted by the grand jury June 28, 1917

Trial by jury in Dallas County, Texas

Criminal District Court No. 2 Judge Charles A. Pippin, presided

Walter R. Stevenson tried and convicted July 13, 1917

Leonard A. Dodd tried and convicted July 20, 1917

Both cases affirmed by the Texas Court of Criminal Appeals February 13, 1918

Stevenson and Dodd both hanged Friday, May 24, 1918, Dallas County, Texas

In June of 1917, Miss Florence Orcutt, who news reports described as a pretty eighteen-year-old stenographer, was living in Dallas. She had lived in Dallas for about three years. Both of her parents had died five years earlier and she came to Dallas to live with her sister. On the evening of June 25th she hired jitney driver E. J. Savage to drive her in his small bus to the home of Mr. Watkins who lived on the White Rock Road. Florence was familiar with Mr. Savage, as she had hired him several times previously. Before the night was over, E. J. Savage would be attacked with a hammer by two men posing as police officers, and Florence would be kidnapped, savagely beaten and criminally assaulted.

From her later court testimony Florence gave these accounts of the night she was kidnapped and attacked. She walked from her home on Cole Street to McKinney Avenue to hire Savage and his small bus. She got in and they first drove downtown, then out the Greenville Road.

After some time they saw another car and Savage seemed to be lost. He stopped and asked the other driver about the road. One of the men in the other car said something like, "It looks easy." Then Savage drove fast to get away from the two men.

The other car came after them and overtook the small jitney bus, and stopped them. The men in the car said they were officers and told Savage he was driving too fast. One of them showed a shield and Savage apologized and they began slapping him. Later one of the men said they were hold-up men and wanted $10. They had a hammer and began beating the car. They finally dragged Savage out of the jitney and Florence heard them strike him. It was dark, but she could hear him groaning.

The two men opened the doors and ordered her out of the vehicle. She got out and started to run, but a man she later identified as Stevenson, grabbed her and told her to get into their car or they would kill her. She got into the car and the men drove very fast toward town. She didn't know where they were, but thought about jumping out of the car and running. Finally one of them asked her if she had any money, and she told them no. Stevenson then gave her a dime and said they were going to let her out of the car.

Florence said she was scheming about how to get away. They turned down a dark street, stopped the car, opened the doors and told her to get out. She said Stevenson kicked her out of the car. She tried to run but the ground was too rough. They were screaming terrible language at her. They began holding her and one of them, she thought it was Dodd, hit her in the head with a hammer.

She said she fought and screamed until she was exhausted. She thought this lasted for about fifteen minutes. They beat her in the face. Her cheek was bleeding, and they pushed her face into the dirt. They held her down while attacking her.

Finally Dodd said, "Shall we fix her yet, or shall we kill her yet?"

Stevenson said "No."

She said she kept praying all the time for someone to help her. Finally a car drove up.

D. E. House, manager of the Kress Store, later gave his testimony at the trials. House said he and his wife were out driving that night. They turned off Haskell and onto Keating Avenue when they came upon the scene, and heard screams. House turned on his flashlight, and a man got up and ran away across the railroad tracks. In a moment he saw a girl get up and run to his car. The man who House later identified as Dodd, told him something to the effect that she was his girl and she wouldn't go with them.

Dodd then came to House's car, and between curse words told him to drive on, that this was none of his business. The girl began begging him to take her with him, and told him these men were trying to kill her. House took her into his automobile and drove her to the home of his sister, where she received medical attention.

E. J. Savage, the jitney driver, being half dazed from being hit in the head with the hammer, had already called the police station and reported that two men had stopped him and taken a girl away from his bus. Savage said it happened at Mockingbird Lane and the Greenville Road. Savage also said that one of the men had a police badge and a six shooter, and one of them struck him with a hammer when he tried to resist.

Chief of Detectives Charles Gunning of the Dallas Police Department immediately assigned detectives to work on the case. Savage's story was confirmed when police found that House had picked up a girl who was bleeding from a cut on her face, and had attracted his attention as he was driving by. House told the police that the two men appeared to be drunk.

Dallas police detectives Baird and Dillinger were assigned the case. The two officers searched the saloons in the city in an effort to find the two men who had purchased a case of beer that was in the vehicle described by Orcutt. Several brown beer bottles were found in the vicinity of the assault. Within twelve hours the saloon was found and the men identified.

Both men were arrested at their homes. Walter R. Stevenson was employed at the Dallas City Water Department and Leonard A. Dodd, was a painter. Both were charged with criminal assault, a capital offense. The charges were filed on June 28th in the Dallas County District Attorney's Office.

Stevenson and Dodd both gave written statements admitting their guilt, and stated they were drunk. They said they would not have committed the crimes if they had been sober. Stevenson and Dodd were identified by Orcutt the day after she was attacked. Police found that Stevenson had a criminal record, and that he had served two years in the penitentiary for burglary.

After the confessions were signed, Ludy Mayes, a black woman, came to the police department and asked to see the two men charged with the assault. She identified both Stevenson and Dodd as the two men who had dragged her from an automobile while driving on Lemmon Avenue two weeks earlier. Mayes said the two men beat and robbed her companion, Will Williams, and robbed her of $8 and assaulted her.

Stevenson and Dodd were both indicted by the Dallas County Grand Jury on Thursday, June 28th. They were both re-indicted on June 29th to correct the name of the victim on the indictments. They were indicted for criminal assault, a capital offense. The trials were to be held in Criminal District Court No. 2. Judge Charles A. Pippin would preside over the trials.

Dallas County Sheriff William Kary Reynolds had practically all his men on duty during the two trials. In addition, a large number of uniformed police officers were also on hand. Sheriff Reynolds had been first elected sheriff in 1914 and was re-elected in 1916. Before being elected sheriff he was a deputy constable, and prior to that he had been in the grocery business.

Stevenson would be the first of the two men to be tried. Judge Pippin ordered a special venire of 200 men to appear on Monday, July 9th for jury selection. District Attorney Mike T. Lively would prosecute the cases, with Assistant District Attorney A. H. Mount and W. L. Crawford, Jr. assisting. Attorneys Reid Williams and A. U. Puckett were appointed to represent Stevenson.

The first witness was Harry Knox, who had been out with Stevenson and Dodd the night of June 25th. Knox said they had been out driving around and Dodd and Stevenson were drinking, cursing and throwing bottles of beer at cars that passed by.

B. J. Savage testified about being hired by Florence Orcutt to drive her to the White Rock Road and him getting lost. Savage also testified about the attack by the two men, and them taking Orcutt with them.

Orcutt then took the stand and told the story of being attacked by the two men.. Much of what Stevenson and Dodd did to her was unprintable in the newspapers. The courtroom was filled with men spectators, all wanting to hear the details of the case. House testified as to his involvement in the case and what he observed that night.

The State called Detective Frank Smith; he identified the written confession of Stevenson. The defense objected to the confession, but Judge Pippin overruled the motion. District Attorney Lively read the confession to the jury.

A crowd of more than 1,500 people were gathered outside the courthouse, waiting for the outcome of the trial. The officers were on alert in case the crowd turned into a mob and tried to take the prisoner and lynch him.

Almost two days of the trial were used on hearing a change of venue motion. Wednesday was used for jury selection. The hearing of evidence began on Thursday morning and was completed by that afternoon. Arguments were completed shortly after noon on Friday.

The only plea offered by the defense was that of insanity caused by drink. A number of witnesses were called by the defense including Stevenson's family members.

Judge Pippin gave his charge to the jury, and the case *State of Texas v. Walter Robert Stevenson*, went to the jury the afternoon of Friday, July 13th. The jury took only one ballot before coming back with a verdict of guilty of criminal assault in the first degree, and assessed his punishment at death.

The trial of Leonard A. Dodd was set for Monday, July 16th, in Judge Pippin's court. A motion for a change of venue was denied by the court, and jury selection began and was completed by Wednesday afternoon. District Attorney Mike T. Lively prosecuted the case and Henry G. Willis represented the defendant.

Again, Sheriff Reynolds had many of his deputies on duty, and Dallas Chief of Police Ryan had a squad of police officers stationed inside the courtroom. Curious men from all walks of life packed and jammed the courtroom for the Thursday morning testimony. Scores of men were permitted to stand in the aisles and on both sides of the judge's stand.

The same principal witnesses who testified in the Stevenson trial again were called and repeated their testimony in the Dodd trial. Orcutt was again called upon to tell the story of her ordeal on the evening of June 25, 1917. She told her story in front of hundreds of men, who were listening as she told the details of the kidnapping, beating and criminal assault.

Doctor V. P. Armstrong was called by the State as an expert witness in insanity cases. District Attorney Lively asked a question to which the doctor answered, "These are the acts of a vicious criminal and not of an insane man."

Dodd's confession was read to the jury; after that the State rested its case.

Witnesses for defendant Dodd were his mother and father, and a woman who believed that he was of unsound mind. Several other witnesses were also called by the defense in an attempt to secure an insanity plea.

On Friday afternoon, Dodd was convicted and given the death penalty. The jury had been out only ten minutes when they reached their verdict. When Dodd heard the verdict he blinked and said nothing. The defense noted that a motion for a new trial would be filed on Saturday.

MEN WHO DIED ON DALLAS GALLOWS FOR BRUTAL ASSAULT ON YOUNG WOMAN

Headline and photos of Leonard Dodd (left) and Walter R. Stevenson from the Dallas Daily Times Herald.

In September 1917, motions for new trials in the cases of Stevenson and Dodd were denied by Judge Pippin. The cases were heard by the Court of Criminal Appeals in Austin, in January 1918. On February 13, 1918, the Court of Criminal Appeals affirmed both cases.

On April 1, 1918, Judge Pippin sentenced Stevenson and Dodd to be hanged on Friday, May 24, 1918. The Texas Parole Board had been reviewing the two cases, along with another Dallas County case. The day before the scheduled executions, Dallas City Attorney A. S. Hardwick went before the appeals board and assured them that Stevenson and Dodd had been given fair trials.

The morning of May 24, 1918, the gallows where Stevenson and Dodd would fall to their deaths were in place. The trap doors were examined and checked to see if they were working properly. The gallows had three trap doors. One of the trap doors was locked off as it would not be needed.

Early Friday morning the two men ate a hearty breakfast of steak, potatoes and some delicacies. They said they enjoyed their meal.

The last hours of Stevenson and Dodd were passed in religious services and talking to friends and family who were permitted to see them. Stevenson's aged father and mother came to see him but did not stay for the execution. Dodd's father came to see him and offered a prayer; his mother was too ill to visit him.

Sheriff Reynolds granted a re-

Tombstone of Walter Robert Stevenson, hanged May 24, 1918 and buried in Grove Hill Cemetery, Dallas, Texas. *Photo by Author*

quest that the two men and their families visit in the sixth floor reception room. The relatives did not want to visit the death cells on the 9th floor, or see the gallows.

Sheriff Reynolds came to the death cells and read the death warrants and pronounced the words, "You shall be hanged until you are dead."

They left the cells and it required only a few minutes to reach the scaffold. Dodd and Stevenson took their time walking. They stopped to shake hands with deputy sheriffs, assistant jailers and death guards, and others they knew personally.

The men walked up the scaffold to the trap doors where their arms and legs were strapped. The noose was placed over their heads; an audience gathered in front to observe the hangings, and stood in silence. Sheriff Reynolds pushed the lever up slightly and then pulled; the two trap doors opened and Walter Robert Stevenson and Leonard A. Dodd fell to their deaths.

There was no mention in news reports of Florence Orcutt being at the hangings, but someone remarked, "A telegram will inform her today that justice has been done in Dallas. Her wrongs avenged."

The bodies of Stevenson and Dodd were pronounced dead by Doctor William Hale. The body of Stevenson was taken by Brewer Undertaking Company. The body of Dodd was taken by Ed C. Smith & Brothers Undertaking Company.

Walter Robert Stevenson's Texas Death Certificate 20128 [1918] has the following information:

Male, white, single, born – November 16, 1883. Occupation – City Water Works, Date of Death May 24, 1918. Cause of Death "by Hanging [Legal]." Place of burial – Grove Hill Cemetery, Dallas, Texas.

Walter Robert Stevenson's tombstone at Grove Hill Cemetery is inscribed: W. R Stevenson 1883 – 1918.

Leonard A. Dodd's Texas Death Certificate 20127 [1918], has the following information:

Male, white, single. Born –October 3 1887. Occupation – Painter. Date of Death – May 24, 1918. Cause of Death – "Hanging by legal execution." Place of burial – Grove Hill Cemetery, Dallas, Texas.

Leonard A. Dodd is buried in an unmarked grave near the grave of Walter Robert Stevenson.

* * * * *

Convicted in a separate case, Emmett Vestal was scheduled to hang along with Walter Robert Stevenson and Leonard A. Dodd on May 24, 1918

In June 1917, Emmett Vestal, a white male, age about twenty-five, was hired by Roscoe Morrell to drive Morrell, a white male, age about twenty-six, from Weleetka, Oklahoma to south Texas. On the morning of June 13, 1917 the body of Morrell, was found on the Waco interurban rail tracks one half mile south of Lancaster, in Dallas County. Morrell, who was a resident of Weleetka, had been shot and robbed. The residents of Weleetka offered a $1,500 reward for the capture of Morrell's slayer.

Fifteen days after Roscoe Morrell was murdered, Dallas County Sheriff W. K. Reynolds, arrested Emmett Vestal at Victoria, Texas, and returned him to Dallas County. Vestal was also a navy deserter. Vestal was indicted for the murder of Roscoe Morrell. Prior to the murder trial, defense attorney J. T. Kelly announced that Vestal would claim insanity, and the issue of self-defense would enter into the case.

Judge Charles A. Pippin presided over the Vestal trial in Criminal District Court No. 2. Testimony showed that Morrell had left home with a considerable amount of money and a watch. When his body was found, all the money and the watch was missing.

Vestal took the witness stand at his trial and admitted fighting with Morrell and having the gun in his hand when Morrell was shot. Vestal also admitted picking up the watch at the scene of the shooting and said he thought it was his own. On August 23, 1917, Vestal was convicted of the murder of Roscoe Morrell and sentenced to death.

A motion for a new trial for Vestal was overruled in February 1918. The Criminal Court of Appeals in Austin affirmed the three death cases of Emmett Vestal, Walter Stevenson and Leonard Dodd.

Walter Robert Stevenson, Leonard A. Dodd and Emmett Vestal were all scheduled to hang together on May 24, 1918. Sheriff W. K. Reynolds had a scaffold built in the "Old Jail," which had opened in 1915. The jail was next to the Criminal Courts Building at the corner of Main and Houston streets. The new scaffold had three trap doors to accommodate the three men that were scheduled to be hung at the same time.

As the date for Vestal's execution approached, his mental condition continued to be investigated. As ordered by the courts Stevenson and Dodd were hung on May 24, 1918. Vestal was given a respite of twenty-one days by Governor Hobby to continue the inquiry of his sanity. In June 1918, Vestal was declared to be of unsound mind. In October 1919, Vestal was sent to the new Texas State Insane Asylum at Rusk, Texas.

In 1920, Emmett Vestal escaped from the State Insane Asylum at Rusk. In August 1926 Vestal was re-arrested in Queen City, Missouri, where he said he had been working as a railroad agent. He was given two more sanity hearings and then judged sane, but of "subnormal mentality."

In December 1926, Emmett Vestal was again given the death penalty by a jury in Judge Charles A. Pippin's District Court No. 2.

Since the summer of 1923 legal hangings were no longer held in the county where the trial was held. They were replaced by electrocution at the state penitentiary. The date for the electrocution of Vestal at the Huntsville prison was set for February 11, 1927. Dallas County District Attorney Shelby Cox; Judge Pippin; Doctor William Hale, the county health officer; and several other people signed a petition to Texas Governor Miriam A. "Ma" Ferguson. The petition requested that the death sentence for Vestal be commuted to life in prison. In less than a week Governor Ferguson commuted the death sentence for Emmett Vestal to life in prison.

Chapter 20

Will Jones, aka: Webb Nickerson

Black male, age 28

Offense – Rape and murder on July 16, 1918

Victim – Mrs. Anna Belle Sale Wolford, white female, age 21

Indicted by the grand jury July 17, 1918

Trial by jury in Dallas County, Texas

*Criminal District Court No. 2 Judge Charles A. Pippin, presided
Tried and convicted July 22, 1918*

Motion for a new trial overruled and execution date set by Judge Pippin

Hanged in the Dallas County Jail Friday, August 30, 1918, Dallas, Texas

Mrs. Anna Belle Wolford was at home the night of Tuesday, July 16, 1918, on the family farm two miles northeast of the community of Rose Hill, in far eastern Dallas County. At about 9:30 p.m. she was in bed with her two-year-old child. Her nephews, Dock Bryant, nine-years-old, and Volney Wolford, were asleep in another room in the house. Her husband, Eugene Wolford, was away working with a threshing crew harvesting grain in Collin County. Shortly, she would be attacked and fighting for her life. A fight she would not win.

Anna "Annie" Wolford was attacked while she was still in her bed. She was raped and stabbed in a number of places. Her throat was cut from ear to ear. She had a stab wound that extended from her right cheek downward across her breast. After the attack she was dragged through three rooms of the house and left on the front porch to die.

The nephews were awakened during the assault on Mrs. Wolford and were able to see her attacker and recognized him. The boys came to their aunt while she was lying on the porch. She pleaded with them not to leave her. It was about two hours before she became unconscious, and one of them finally left and went to a neighbor's house to get help.

The neighbor, Mr. Bryant, gave the alarm, and called Dr. J. H. Armstrong who then called for other physicians to assist. They were unable to stop the bleeding. She died at about 3 a.m. on Wednesday, July 17, 1918. He husband was called and told of the attack on his wife and she died a few minutes before he arrived home.

Before she died Mrs. Wolford made a statement to Doctor Armstrong. In her statement she went into the details of the assault, and it was put into writing. She told Doctor Armstrong that if she died before her husband came home, to tell him that "Will did it."

When the neighbors arrived at the Wolford home, Mrs. Wolford's two-year-old child was still asleep in the bed, which was saturated with blood.

Will Jones was arrested within six hours by Constable McCallum. Jones was in bed at the home of a black woman where he was living. She said he had been there for some time, but she did not know where he had been earlier. She said that when Jones came to the house he asked her for a clean undershirt and he went to the branch and washed out some of his clothing. He told her that he was going swimming and wanted the undershirt to wear when he got out of the water.

Eugene Wolford and his wife Annie lived on a farm owned by Claude Crabb, a former grand jury bailiff. Jones lived on another farm owned by Crabb, about two miles away. Jones had worked for the Wolford's off and on as a farm hand, so the Wolford's were well acquainted with him. When Eugene Wolford left to go to Collin County to work on the threshing crew, he hired Jones to feed and look after the livestock on the farm. The day of Mrs. Wolford's attack, she thought Jones had completed his work, and then left for the day.

Sheriff William Kary Reynolds was notified of the crime about 3 a.m. on Wednesday morning, when Jones was placed in the Dallas County Jail. Sheriff Reynolds immediately called for Deputy Sheriff Allen Seale, and they went to the Wolford home. Sheriff Reynolds was in charge of the investigation as it was committed in the unincorporated area of Dallas County.

They began their investigation and questioned all the witnesses, and summoned them to appear before the grand jury on Wednesday. Sheriff Reynolds and Deputy Seale also went to the home where Jones had been staying, and questioned the woman he was staying with. At the branch where Jones had washed out his clothing, they found a board with blood on it, where he had placed his bloody clothing. While in jail, Jones gave a written statement admitting he committed the crimes.

On Wednesday morning, Judge Charles A. Pippin instructed the grand jury to take up the rape and murder cases of Mrs. Wolford. In an attempt to stop any mob action, Judge Pippin, Judge Robert Seay and District Attorney Mike Lively met with a large number of farmers who lived in the Rose Hill community. The farmers assured the officials that they had no intention of taking the law into their own hands, and they intended to let the law take its course. J. A. Swawfar, owner of the general store at Rose Hill, said that he didn't think there would be any attempt to lynch Jones if he was given a speedy trial.

Jones was indicted for rape and murder on Wednesday. Judge Pippin set the trial for Monday, July 22nd. District Attorney Lively decided to try Jones only on the murder case. As the trial began, about 400 people were in the courtroom, and a large crowd gathered outside the courthouse. There was a heavy guard presence for the trial. A company of Texas Rangers, deputy sheriffs and police officers were all armed and in the courthouse to maintain order.

District Attorney Mike T. Lively would prosecute the case for the State. Attorneys J. W. Gormley, W. H. Graham and Alfred Crager were appointed to defend Jones. Criminal District Court No. 2 Judge Charles A. Pippin would preside over the trial. The jury selection was completed by noon on Monday.

Witness testimony and evidence were presented on Monday afternoon. Dock Bryant, the nine-year-old nephew of Mrs. Wolford, was called to the witness stand and pointed out Will Jones as the person that had murdered Annie Wolford. He stated that he saw Jones dragging Annie Wolford through the house and leaving her on the porch outside the house. Bryant also said he recognized Jones because he knew him, as Jones had worked for the Wolford family for about two years.

The written death statement made by Annie Wolford was read to the jury. The neighbor that sent out the alarm was called as a witness. Dr. V.P. Armstrong testified about the wounds and condition of Mrs. Wolford, and his knowledge of the case. Constable McCallum of Garland testified that he arrested Jones. Sheriff Reynolds testified as to his investigation into the murder of Mrs. Wolford. Sheriff Reynolds also testified regarding the written statement signed by Jones, admitting that he committed the crimes against Mrs. Wolford. The pocket knife used to murder Mrs. Wolford was never found.

The trial was concluded at 3:40 p.m. The jury returned their guilty verdict in eleven minutes. Jones was sentenced to death by hanging. No demonstration was made in the courtroom when the verdict was read.

After Jones was convicted of the murder of Annie Wolford and was

Tombstone of Mrs. Anna Bell (Sale) Wolford, Born Oct. 17, 1896 and died July 17, 1918. Burial was in the Wylie Cemetery, Wylie, Texas. *Photo taken by author*

sentenced to death, the defense attorneys filed a motion for a new trial. Two days later Judge Pippin denied the motion and the defense attorneys withdrew from the case. Judge Pippin read the death sentence to Jones and set the date for the hanging as Friday, August 30, 1918.

On the morning of Friday, August 30th, Jones' breakfast consisted of pork chops, eggs and French fried potatoes. He was also given a watermelon, which he had requested. Jones was allowed to have a minister he wanted brought to his cell.

Before going to the gallows, Jones wrote a note to Sheriff Reynolds. In the note he said his real name was not Will Jones. He said his real name was Webb Nickerson. Jones told of his relatives and asked a cousin to take his two small children, a boy of four-years and another of four-months, to his funeral. He also wanted the cousin to assist in raising his children.

Sheriff Reynolds then read the death warrant to Jones. It took about twelve minutes to read the warrant. Jones was asked if he had anything to say, and he said in part: "I realize I committed an awful crime, and one that calls for the extreme penalty."

Present in the jail to observe the hanging were several women who were relatives of Mrs. Wolford. Her husband Eugene Wolford, as well as her parents, Mr. and Mrs. Sam Sale, from Sachse, Texas, were present. A number of her other relatives and several people from the Rose Hill community were also there.

Jones stepped onto the trap door on the gallows at 10:58 a.m., Friday, August 30, 1918. At 11 a.m. the black cap was placed over his head and the noose around his neck. At 11:01 a.m. Sheriff Reynolds pulled the lever and the trap door opened and Jones fell to his death.

Doctors William K. Hale and J. H. Armstrong pronounced Jones, age twenty-eight, aka: Webb Nickerson, dead.

The funeral for Anna [Annie] Belle Sale Wolford was held on Wednesday, July 18, 1918, in the little Baptist church not far from the farm where she was murdered. The Rev. R. B. Keay, pastor of the church, conducted the service. She was buried in the Sale family plot in the Wylie City Cemetery, Wylie, Texas.

Death certificates for Annie Bell [Sale] Wolford and Will Jones, aka: Webb Nickerson were not found.

Her tombstone has the following inscription:

ANNIE BELL SALE WOLFORD. OCT. 17, 1896 – OCT. 17, 1918

The month of her death on her tombstone is incorrect. She died on July 17, 1918, not Oct. 17, 1918.

* * * * *

Sheriff William Kary Reynolds, who was in charge of investigating the Wolford rape and murder case, was born February 10, 1868 in Franklin County, Tennessee. He served as Dallas County sheriff from 1914 to 1918. On February 24, 1921, at age fifty-three, he was run over and instantly killed by a passenger train in the Texas and Pacific rail yards in Marshall, Texas. He is buried next to his wife, Sallie Copeland Reynolds, in Section 11, Oakland Cemetery, Dallas, Texas.

Tombstone of Sheriff William Kary Reynolds who served as sheriff of Dallas County from 1914 to 1918. Burial was in Oakland, Cemetery in Dallas. *Photo taken by author.*

Chapter 21

Green Hunter, aka: "James Brown"

Black male, age 26, born June 7, 1894, in Bryan, Brazos County, Texas

Offense – Criminal assault and robbery on May 28, 1920

Victim – Mrs. Hattie Carpenter, white female, widow, age 54

Indicted by the Dallas County Grand Jury May 29, 1920

Trial by jury in Dallas County, Texas

Criminal District Court No. 2, Judge Charles A. Pippin, presided

Tried and convicted June 4, 1920

Hanged Friday, July 9, 1920 in the Dallas County Jail, Dallas, Texas

At about noon on Friday, May 28, 1920, Mrs. Hattie A. Carpenter was at home alone. Her husband, John R. Carpenter, had died eighteen years earlier. She was living with her son William B. Carpenter. They lived five miles south west of Dallas on the Santa Fe Railway line, near Hale's Stop. In a few minutes she would be attacked and begging for her life.

The morning she was attacked, Mrs. Carpenter had been working outside in the garden at the rear of the house. At about 11:30 a.m. she went inside to fix dinner for her son. A tall black man came to the back gate and asked for a drink of water. She gave him a bucket, which he took to the well. When he came back to the kitchen door he hesitated and said he was looking for work. She told him he might find work at a neighbor that lived nearby.

Thinking that he had left, she went back into the kitchen. In a few minutes she went into the dining room. She saw the man standing there. He grabbed her arm and threatened to kill her with a large knife he had in his hand. She begged and pleaded for him not to kill her. The man dragged her into the next room and assaulted her twice. When he left the house he threatened to kill her if she cried out. As the man left he took a gold watch from a vest that was hanging on a chair.

Mrs. Carpenter then went over to a nearby neighbor's house and told the story of what had happened to her. The neighbor gave the alarm and soon a posse of enraged farmers and deputy sheriffs were hunting for the man. He was captured late Friday afternoon by two farmers on Beckley Road, near Five Mile Creek.

He was turned over to deputy sheriffs Allen Seale and Hal Hood. The two deputies took the man to the woman, who identified him as her assailant. When three vehicles full of armed men appeared and violence was threatened, the deputies hurried the man to the Dallas County Jail.

Dallas County Sheriff Dan Harston was in charge of the investigation of the case, because it occurred in the unincorporated area of Dallas County. The sheriff was also in charge of the county jail and it would be his responsibility to guard and protect the prisoner. The gold watch was later found under the back seat of the vehicle in which the prisoner was transferred to the county jail.

Statements were made by Mrs. Carpenter and the man, now identified as Green Hunter, aka: James Brown. Both statements were given before assistant district attorneys E. J. Gibson and Horace Williams.

In his statement, Green Hunter admitted he was guilty and said, "I don't know why I did such a thing, I hope I don't hang for it." Green Hunter signed his written statement by placing his mark above his name, which was written by Assistant District Attorney Gibson.

At the county jail on Saturday morning, Hunter, aka: Brown, said he was raised at College Station by a man named Dave Thomas. He said that he had worked on a farm in Rockwall County, and had lived in Dallas for about four years. He said he was living with a woman at 1010 South Akard Street, in Dallas. He again said, "I'm sorry I did what I did, I hope they won't hang me."

On Saturday morning, May 29th, Dallas County District Attorney J. Willis Pierson took charge and called the grand jury to hear the testimony in the case. After hearing the evidence, the grand jury returned a "true bill" and indictment for criminal assault. The case was assigned to Criminal District Court No. 2, Judge Charles A. Pippin's court. Judge Pippin set the date for the trial as June 4th.

On Friday, June 4th, a special venire of 150 men had been called to serve, if selected, as jurors in the case. District Attorney J. Willis Pierson and his assistants Arch. C. Allen and E. C. Gibson would prosecute the case for the State. Attorneys William McGraw and Thomas Kelley had been appointed by the court to defend Hunter.

Sheriff Dan Harston had sixteen deputies, in addition to a number of Dallas police officers, in the courtroom to maintain order and protect the prisoner. The jurors were selected in the morning. Seven jurors were dismissed because they were opposed to the death penalty. Two jurors were excused because they couldn't read or write. The courtroom was filled with spectators, which was described as "a solid mass of humanity." Judge Pippin instructed Captain Lane of the Dallas Police Department to stand by the prisoner and face the crowd.

The witnesses were sworn in, and the indictment was read by District Attorney Pierson. The defendant, Green Hunter, offered a plea of not guilty. Mrs. Carpenter was the first witness called to testify. She repeated the account of her attack as she had given in her written statement. Assistant District Attorney Gibson read the statement of confession that he had taken from Hunter.

NEGRO WHO DIED ON GALLOWS HERE FRIDAY AT NOON

Headline and photo of Green Hunter aka: Jim Brown from the *Dallas Times Herald*.

No other testimony was given. Short arguments were made by both sides and most of the day had been taken up by the selection of the jury. The case was given to the jury to decide their verdict at a little after 5:30 p.m. They returned with the verdict after only ten minutes of deliberation. The verdict was guilty and the entire trial lasted only one day.

On Saturday morning, the day after the trial, Hunter appeared with his attorneys before Judge Pippin and asked for a new trial. The request was denied. The judge then asked if he had anything to say before he passed sentence on him. Hunter faltered and finally said, "I acknowledge I am guilty; and I beg you to do the best you can for me."

Judge Pippin then said, "It is the order of this court and judgment of this court that you be taken in custody of Dan Harston, sheriff of Dallas County and by him safely kept in jail until Friday, the 9th day of July, between the hours of 10 a.m. and 4 p.m., at which time you will be taken by the sheriff to the place of execution erected in the Dallas County Jail, and there by him be hung by the neck until you are dead. May God have mercy upon your soul."

Friday was an unlucky day for Hunter. His comments on his bad luck day were, "Friday is my hoo-doo day. Friday was always a bad day for me. I was born on Friday and I will die on Friday. I committed my crime on Friday and I was found guilty by a jury on Friday. Now every day is Friday to me."

With only twenty-four hours to live, Hunter confessed to another crime. Hunter signed a full confession admitting that in 1912 he criminally assaulted an eleven-year-old white girl near Bryan, Texas. For that crime Ben Perry was tried, convicted, and had served the past eight years in the state penitentiary at Huntsville.

In his confession which was made public, Hunter stated: "I am guilty of the crime. It was I, and not Ben Perry who attacked the girl. I was eighteen-years-old at that time and the girl was about eleven or twelve years."

Hunter made this confession in the presence of Rev. J. D. Williams, a news reporter, Sheriff Dan Harston, Brazos County Attorney J. G. Minkert, Assistant District Attorney Grady Niblo, and J. M. Wilson, special assistant district attorney. Hunter asked the Rev. Williams to sign the confession. Hunter said he felt much better after making the confession, knowing that his confession would allow the freeing of an innocent man who had served eight years in prison.

Hunter slept soundly the night before his scheduled execution. He ate a hearty breakfast when he awoke Friday morning. Jailer Buck Parsons brought Hunter his "death suit," which consisted of a black suit, white shirt and white collar.

During the morning of his execution, Hunter was visited by newspaper men and several spectators. Black ministers J. D. Williams and A. F. Johnson visited him in his cell. Hunter was held on the 9th floor of the jail in an area of three cells known as the "death cells." They held services and sang with him until the hour of the execution.

An hour before he was to be executed, Hunter talked freely about his past life. He told a *Times Herald* reporter that he had committed several other crimes. These included the slaying of a Mexican near Robstown several years earlier. He said the Mexican attacked him with a knife, and he split the man's head open with an ax. He also told of an attack, about fifty miles from San Antonio, on another black man who he seriously wounded and possibly killed. Hunter said the man attacked him with a plow disk. Hunter said he had a cotton hook in his hand and ripped the man open.

As the time approached for Hunter's execution, Sheriff Harston read the death warrant. Hunter was led from his death cell to the scaffold and did not falter as he stepped onto the trap door. The jailers strapped his legs and arms to his body. Sheriff Harston gave him permission to make a last statement.

Hunter looked out over a crowd of over 200 who had gathered to observe the hanging. Six white women were among the crowd waiting to witness the execution.

Hunter admitted his guilt again, saying in part: "I'm a guilty man, I'm guilty of the worst crime there is—a crime against a white woman and a white girl. I'm also guilty of killing a man." Hunter went on to say that since he had been in this jail he had learned to repent and that they had been nice to him.

The death cap was placed over his head, and then the noose around his neck. Hunter's last words were, "If you're ready, I'm ready to meet my savior."

Sheriff Dan Harston pulled the lever, the trap door opened and Green Hunter, aka; James Brown fell to his death. Eight minutes later doctors Hale and Watson pronounced him dead. The body was placed in a casket and prepared for shipment to Bryan, Texas for burial.

Green Hunter's Texas Death Certificate #22000 [1920], has the following information:

> *Male, colored, single, born – 6-7-1894 at Bryan, Texas. Cause of death – "Legal execution by hanging." E. J. Crawford Undertaking Company handled the removal of the body. Place of burial, Bryan, Texas.*

* * * * *

In early August 1920, the Texas Board of Pardons completed its investigation of the application of the pardon of Ben Perry, who had received a life sentence from Brazos County in 1912, for the criminal assault upon a young white girl. According to the Texas State Penitentiary Convict Ledger, Ben Perry, convict number 33052, was pardoned on August 23, 1920.

In January 1921, the Texas House Committee on Appropriations killed a bill that would have appropriated $4,000 to Ben Perry, who served eight years in prison for a crime he did not commit. Judge Davis of Dallas introduced the bill. District Attorney Davis of Bryan appeared before the committee and presented the facts of the case, however the bill failed.

Chapter 22

Fred Douglas, aka: "Jobo"

Black male, age 22, born in Marlin, Texas

Offense – Robbery and murder July 5, 1920

Victim – Isaac T. Williams, white male, age 55, born in Tennessee

Indicted by the grand jury July 10, 1920

Trial held in Dallas County, Texas

Criminal District Court No. 2, Judge Charles A. Pippin, presided

Tried and convicted of murder July 15-16, 1920

Hanged in the Dallas County Jail Friday, August 27, 1920, Dallas, Texas

Isaac T. Williams was the station agent, or manager, of the Texaco filling station at the corner of Haskell and Ross avenues in Dallas. On the morning of Friday, July 5, 1920, Williams left his home at his regular time to open the filling station. At about 9 a.m., Williams was found dead in the back of the filling station.

H. D. Deacon, sales manager for Texaco, stated that he could not get an answer to his telephone calls to the station. Deacon called Williams' wife at home, and she said he had left home at 6 a.m. to open the station. Deacon then called J. D. Tripp, who managed the Magnolia station across the street from the Texaco station. Deacon asked Tripp to check on Williams. Tripp and A. W. Woodall went to the Texaco station to investigate the reason for the late opening. The window shades on the front windows were pulled down, and they were unable to open the front door. They went around back and looked through a window. There they saw the body of Williams lying in a pool of blood.

Dallas police were notified and they began their investigation. Williams was lying on the floor in the back room of the station. He had lost a lot of blood from a large gash on the back of his head. It appeared the weapon used to kill Williams was an ax, or some heavy iron tool used to change tires. No weapon was found at the scene.

Isaac T. Williams
Courtesy Dallas Daily Times Herald

The cash register and safe were both open. Bloody money and checks in the amount of $37.13, were scattered about the floor of the station. Bloody drag marks on the floor indicated that Williams had been standing at the cash register when he was hit from behind, and then dragged to the back room. His pockets had been turned inside out and it appeared to the officers Williams had been dead about an hour.

A check of the accounts showed that about $250 was missing. The sales leading up to the July 4th holiday had been heavy, which accounted for more money than usual being kept in the safe.

All chances to locate the murderer by fingerprints or bloody footprints were eliminated by the fact that hundreds of curious people had gathered around the doors and windows of the station. They had placed their hands on the window, by which the murderer was believed to have gained entry into the station.

After being told of the death of her husband, Mrs. Williams told her family and friends that she feared for his safety. She said, "I knew this was coming, my husband always carried so much money with him."

She told of the morning he was murdered. She said he got up at his regular time, ate his breakfast and started to the station. But, she did not know how much money he had with him that day.

The police got a break in the case when they located R. L. Selser. He told the police that he had passed the filling station early the morning that Williams was killed, and wanted to get air for his tires. The black porter was at work then, and told him they were out of air. Selser said he could see Williams in the front office counting the money. That was about 6:30 a.m. That corresponded with the time Williams should have arrived at work after leaving his home at 6 a.m..

Fred Douglas, the porter at the Texaco filling station, was nowhere around. The officers then went to the house of Douglas' sister, where he had been staying. As they were about to leave, the officers found two $5 bills under a match box and the bills had blood stains on the edges. The sister was not aware that the money had been left there.

Douglas' sister told the officers that her brother sees himself as a prize fighter, and that he was preparing to leave Dallas and go to Chicago to train under a white promoter. The detectives assumed that Douglas killed Williams for the money to make the trip.

The detectives found information that Douglas, after leaving the home of his sister, walked to Bryan Street, where he caught the interurban train to Denison, Texas. A nurse at St. Paul's Sanitarium saw Douglas walking on Bryan Street near the train stop, and gave his description to the officers. The conductor of the interurban train remembered selling him a ticket to Denison.

The detectives sent out a notice by telegraph to be on the lookout for Douglas, who was wanted for the murder of Isaac T. Williams. The Texaco Company that Williams worked for offered a $500 reward for Douglas' arrest, and Dallas County Sheriff Dan Harston added $100 to the reward.

A black man named Fred Douglas, was arrested in Fort Worth and placed in the city jail. He was arrested as a suspect in the Williams murder. However, he was in no way connected to the murder of Williams. This was not the same Fred Douglas; he did not even fit the physical description of the Fred Douglas that worked as the porter at the Texaco station. He was released on Tuesday night.

Fred Douglas had disappeared. The detectives again sent out telegrams to other cities and towns asking for assistance, and to be on the lookout for the wanted man. Reports came in on Wednesday afternoon of a man fitting the description of the wanted man, being sighted in the river bottoms near Miller's Switch. Officers and citizens conducted a thorough search of the brush and area before giving up when darkness fell.

Several other reports of the man in the river bottoms were given to Sheriff Harston and one of those reports came from a man living in the area, who said a black man fitting the description of Fred Douglas came to his place asking for water. Another report was from a young boy who was out looking for a lost horse, and saw a man jump up out of the brush and run when the boy spotted him. Another report came in from a person who believed they had spotted Douglas in the river bottoms near Metzger's Dairy. A search was made by Dallas police officers who found nothing. Other reports also produced the same results.

Dallas Detective Bert Dillinger located information that Douglas had purchased a ticket to Shreveport, Louisiana. Dillinger and S. H. Kirkman left by train for Shreveport. Kirkman was the cashier for the Texaco Company, and knew Douglas. He would be able to identify Douglas if they found him in Shreveport.

Detective Dillinger and Kirkman had searched every section of Shreveport where they thought Douglas might have gone. They gave up hope of finding their man, and returned to the train station to return to Dallas. They were standing on the platform waiting for the train when Douglas walked toward them. Kirkham pointed to Douglas and told Detective Dillinger, "There's Douglas now."

Before Douglas was aware of the officer's presence, the officer had his arms pinned to his side, and a pistol pointed at his back.

Douglas was taken to the parish jail in Shreveport, where he confessed to the murder of Isaac T. Williams. His confession was signed in the presence of Shreveport police officers. In his confession he stated that Tom Atkins, a black friend of his, was present during the murder, and that they had split the money and separated after killing Williams.

Detective Dillinger and Kirkman brought Douglas back to Dallas on the Texas and Pacific train. On the east side of Dallas, they left the train and completed the trip by automobile. This was an attempt to prevent any mob action against Douglas before they reached the Dallas County Jail.

Douglas gave a second written confession after arriving in Dallas. In the second confession he cleared Atkins of any involvement in the murder of Williams. Douglas now said that Atkins was not present and had no knowledge of the murder of Williams. Atkins, who had been arrested, was then released from jail.

The Dallas County Grand Jury was reconvened on Saturday, July 10th, to consider the case of Fred Douglas, charged with the murder of Isaac T. Williams. It took them only a few minutes to consider the case. The confession of Douglas was read and he was indicted for the July 5th murder of Isaac T. Williams.

The case was set in Criminal District Court No. 2. Judge Charles A. Pippin would preside over the trial. Judge Pippin set the trial for 9 a.m., Thursday, July 15th. A special venire of 250 men as prospective jurors was ordered to appear to be questioned for possible jury duty in the case *State of Texas vs. Fred Douglas*.

All the witnesses appeared to testify during the trial except Isabel Bennett, sister of Douglas, and her husband Jack Bennett. They were attending a religious convention in Waco. Sheriff Harston was making an effort to locate the two as the trial proceeded.

Dallas County District Attorney Pierson prosecuted the murder case against Douglas. Attorneys John A. Ballowe and W. E. Pinkston were appointed to defend Douglas.

During the trial District Attorney Pierson submitted an iron carpenter's level into evidence. The investigation had identified the level as the weapon that was used to kill Williams. J. W. Rule, a cement contractor, had been working on the driveway at the Texaco station. Rule had left his level in the back room of the station the day before the killing.

Douglas took the witness stand and admitted killing Williams, however, he claimed self-defense as his reason for the killing. The court was adjourned at 8:35 p.m. on Friday evening, until 9 a.m. on Saturday. The district attorney and defense attorneys gave their closing arguments which were completed by about 10:30 a.m. Judge Pippin gave his charge to the jury, and they retired to deliberate the case.

The jury deliberated for about an hour before returning their verdict of guilty, and the sentence as death. Judge Pippin set the date for the execution as Friday, August 27, 1920.

Sheriff Dan Harston and Deputy Allen Seale standing in front of the gallows in the Old Jail. Note Sheriff Harston holding the rope. *Photo Courtesy Dallas Public Library*

Douglas had a minister visit him in the days leading up to August 27th. Sheriff Harston reported that sheriffs from around the state had written him that they would attend the hanging. Harston said he expected to have about 200 people present to view the hanging.

On the morning of August 27th Douglas was very nervous, and he did not eat his breakfast. He dressed in a new suit, shoes and other clothing that had been provided by Sheriff Harston. Douglas spent much of the morning pacing his cell and smoking cigarettes. The Rev. J. C. Coleman of the Mt. Olivet Baptist Church and "Mother" Clark, a black prison worker from Corsicana, visited him in his cell and conducted a religious service. Other visitors were Douglas' mother and sister and a neighbor who spent a few minutes with him in his cell.

When the time came, Sheriff Harston read the court issued death warrant to Douglas. The corridors of the jail were crowded with those allowed to view the hanging. Douglas walked to the gallows and made a rambling short speech in which he said he was ready to die. He thanked the jail officers and deputies for their "kind treatment" while he was in jail.

Douglas stepped onto the trap door with his hands tied behind his back and his legs were strapped together. Deputy Sheriff Allen Seale placed the black cap over Douglas' head and placed the rope around his neck. At 11:25 a.m. on Friday, August 27, 1920, Sheriff Harston pulled the lever, the trap door opened and Fred Douglas, age twenty-two, fell to his death. Dr. William Hale and other physicians pronounced Douglas dead.

The $500 dollar reward for the arrest of Douglas was divided between Dallas Police Captain Gunning, Lieutenant Elmo Strait, Detective Bert Dillinger and Mr. S. H. Kirkman, the employee of the Texaco Company who identified Douglas in Shreveport.

Douglas' Texas Death Certificate 26075 [1920] has the following information:

Male, colored, single. Born on January 31, 1898, in Marlin, Texas. Date of Death – August 27, 1920. Occupation – laborer. Cause of death – "Legally Hanged." Burial - Mt. Auburn Cemetery, Dallas. Texas. Crawford Undertaking Company in charge of the arrangements.

Isaac T. Williams' Texas Death Certificate 22026 [1920] has the following information:

Male, white, married, born – March 9, 1864, in Tennessee. Date of death – July 5, 1920. Cause of death - "Skull split by sharp instrument – Homicide." Burial – Oakland Cemetery, Dallas, Texas. Ed C. Smith Brothers Undertaking Company in charge of the arrangements.

The exact burial location in Oakland Cemetery for Isaac T. Williams has not been found. The caretaker of Oakland Cemetery said some of the records had burned during a fire in the 1940s.

The hanging of Fred Douglas was the fifth held on the scaffold in what is now known as the "Old Jail" next to the Criminal Courts Building, at the corner of Main and Houston streets. This Dallas County Jail was built in 1913-1914 and opened in May of 1915. An annex to this jail was built in 1955.

* * * * *

Fred Douglas was the last person to be legally hanged in Dallas County, Texas.

In 1923, the Texas State Legislature passed an act requiring that all legal executions in Texas would be held at the Texas State Prison in Huntsville. The executions would now be by using the electric chair which later became known as "Old Sparky."

Lynchings Prevented By Dallas County Sheriffs

The following four chapters are the stories of Dallas County sheriffs who stood up to mobs and mob violence. They along with their deputies, and other peace officers and some citizens risked their lives to prevent lynchings.

Chapter 23
Sheriff William Marion Moon

White male, aka: Marion M. Moon

Born – March 18, 1830, near Independence, Missouri

Sheriff of Dallas County, Texas - April 18, 1876 to August 30, 1880

William Marion Moon, at age fifteen, along with his parents and siblings, moved from Missouri to Dallas County, Texas. The family moved to a farm located about six miles north of what is now downtown Dallas. In 1855, he began working as a clerk in the general store of Gold and Donaldson.

Later, Moon owned and operated a blacksmith shop which he ran until the start of the Civil War. In July 1861, he enlisted in the Confederate Army, and served in Company H., 3rd Texas Cavalry. He was involved in a number of battles and was wounded several times. He was captured just before the fall of Atlanta, and remained a prisoner until the close of the war. Moon entered the war as a private, but had been promoted to the position of lieutenant before being discharged when the war was over. He had never had a furlough or leave of absence during the war.

After returning home from the war he married Mrs. Nancy J. Knight, the widow of William A. Knight, who had died during the war. Moon farmed for a few years before working as a salesman in the hardware store of his brother-in-law, J. C. McConnell.

William Moon's career in Dallas County law enforcement was long and noteworthy:

- From 1856 – 1858 he served as a deputy sheriff under Sheriff Burnett M. Henderson.
- W. M. Moon was elected and served as sheriff of Dallas County

from 1876 – 1880.

- From 1882 – 1886 he served as a deputy sheriff under Sheriff William H. W. Smith.
- In 1886 he served as a deputy sheriff under Sheriff William Henry Lewis.
- In 1889 he was a Dallas police officer under Chief of Police J. C. Arnold.
- In 1892 he was a night watchman for the Texas and Pacific Railroad in Dallas.

In 1876 William Moon ran for, and was elected, sheriff of Dallas County. He served two, two-year terms as sheriff. It was for his actions as sheriff that he would be recognized after his death, in some news accounts, by the headline, "He Was A Famous Sheriff."

The Attempt to Lynch Jim Blake

On Saturday night, August 19, 1876, Dallas Police Officer John Carter, a worthy, respectable young officer, went to East Dallas to arrest a black man who was creating a disturbance at a black dance house near the old Central Depot. Officer Carter made the arrest and was transporting his prisoner to the jailhouse.

The *Galveston Daily News* reported that "several negroes – Jim Blake, Joshua Epps, Ed Harwood and another" waylaid and assaulted Officer Carter, "and received from one of them [Jim Blake] a terrible blow on the head with a large stick, which fractured his skull badly in several places. A piece of the skull was taken out, and it was found that the skull bone, where it was fractured, was pressing on the brain."

Officers arrested Blake and charged him with assault to kill and murder, for the attack on Officer Carter.

Doctors H. K. Leake and Graham did everything they could to save the life of Officer Carter. However, they felt the chances were against him for recovering from the injury. It was several days before Carter regained consciousness. A week later it was reported that Carter was still at "deaths door." His fate hung between life and death for several months.

On Sunday afternoon, the day after the attack on Officer Carter, small groups of men began gathering in different places in the business district of Dallas. They appeared to be organizing a lynching party and Sheriff Moon got wind that a lynching party was about to take place.

The sheriff set out to do everything possible to stop the mob action. He assembled all his deputies and organized a large number of special deputies. He placed his men in the corridors, and on the roof of the county jail. His deputies were all armed with double-barrel shotguns loaded with buckshot. The sheriff took up a position on the roof of the small jail office building, rather than the main jail building. A mob of 2,000 to 3,000 men, all wearing masks and carrying guns, marched up Lamar Street and then down Main Street, until they were within a block of the jail. There they were halted by Judge George A. Aldridge and other prominent citizens, who pleaded with them not to attempt to storm the jail. Captain Morton, the Dallas city marshal, told the crowd that Sheriff Moon would resist to the death any attempt to take his prisoner.

Some in the mob wanted the sheriff to come down to talk to them, which he refused to do. Their plan was to kidnap the sheriff so they could exchange him for the prisoner, Blake.

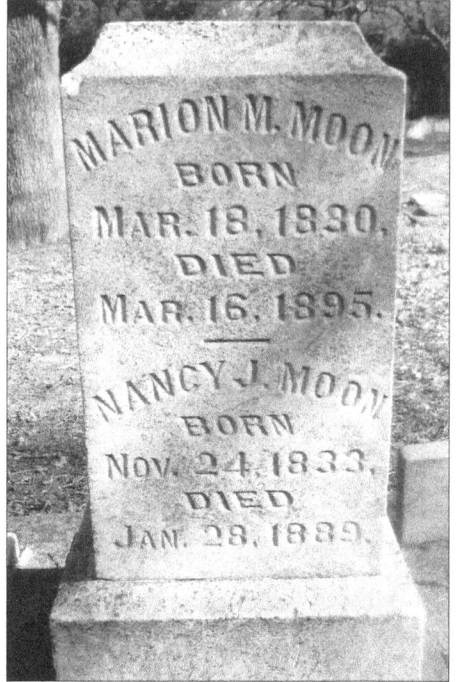

Tombstone of Sheriff William M. Moon who served as sheriff of Dallas, County from 1876 to 1880. Burial is in the Pioneer Cemetery, Dallas, Texas. *Photo taken by author.*

The mob began to show signs of weakening and Judge Aldridge again addressed the mob and told them if they persisted in their attempt to seize the prisoner, it would result in the death of a brave sheriff that they all loved.

Sheriff Moon was called for, and he gave a short statement. He said that he and his men "would hold the fort until death." The sheriff further went on to say he felt that he was personally acquainted with nearly every man in the mob, and that probably every one of them voted for him. The mob began to weaken.

A news account reported, "After a few speeches by some of the mob members, it was decided to let the law take its course."

The city was then quiet, and no more attempts were made to storm the county jail.

On Friday, August 25, 1876, seven days after the attack on Dallas Police Officer John Carter, the *Galveston Daily News* reported, "The negro dance house near the Old Central Depot, at which Policeman Carter was so nearly murdered last week, was burned this morning. No insurance."

On Friday, September 7, 1877, the case State of *Texas vs. Jim Blake, cause 3611,* was heard in the 14ᵗʰ District Court at Dallas. The court minutes recorded the following:

> *This day came the county attorney for the State and by leave of the court says he will no further prosecute herein. It is therefore ordered and adjudged and decreed by the court that the defendant Jim Blake go hence without delay and of this cause show fully acquitted.*

* * * * *

Policeman John Carter did not die from the wound suffered during the attack on August 19, 1876. The *Dallas Daily Times Herald* of March 18, 1895, reported that Carter was still alive in 1895.

William Marion Moon died on March 16, 1895, in Dallas. He is buried in Pioneer Cemetery, next to the Dallas Convention Center, in downtown Dallas. His tombstone has his name inscribed as, Marion M. Moon.

Chapter 24
Sheriff William Henry Lewis

White male, born March 11, 1851, in Franklin County, Georgia

First public office - Dallas County deputy tax assessor under R. D Rawlins

Dallas County deputy sheriff under Sheriff Benjamin F. Jones, Sr.

Continued as a Dallas County deputy sheriff under Sheriff H. W. Smith

In 1886 held the office of Dallas County constable, Precinct No. 1

Sheriff of Dallas County, Texas 1886 - 1892

William Henry Lewis, one of fourteen children, was born March 11, 1851, in Franklin County, Georgia. Lewis was raised on a farm in Anderson County, South Carolina, and completed high school in Anderson County. At age sixteen he decided he wanted to go to Texas. He spent his savings for a railroad ticket, and then split rails along the way to earn money. Lewis did some survey work for the Texas and Pacific Railroad Company, and worked on a farm to help make his living. He arrived in Dallas County in 1873.

Lewis was elected Dallas County Sheriff in November 1886. He served as sheriff for six years until leaving office in November 1892.

In his later years, Lewis was in the real estate business. He served on the City of Dallas Equalization Board, and was called on to assist the real estate condemnation and valuation committees.

The Attempt to Lynch Henry Miller

The story of Henry Miller murdering Dallas Police Officer C. O. Brewer was covered in Chapter 11 of this book. Also, the attempt to lynch Miller was covered in that same chapter. But, here again are the basic facts of those incidents to document that Sheriff William Henry Lewis, his deputies and police officers prevented the lynching of Henry Miller.

On Tuesday, May 24, 1892, Dallas police officers Ben Brandenburg and C. O. Brewer were assigned to arrest Miller for derogatory remarks he had admitted to making about a married woman.

The officers located Miller, and Brandenburg arrested him. When Miller was denied his request to make an immediate bond, he drew a pistol and fired, striking Officer Brewer. Brewer fell mortally wounded. After a brief chase, Miller was arrested and taken to the Dallas City Jail. A large crowd of men, women and children followed the officers and prisoner to the jail.

At the city jail the crowd was still unorganized and without leaders. Calls to break into the jail and "hang him," were starting to be heard. Sheriff Lewis, along with his deputies, and Dallas police officers brought Miller out the back door of the jail. They placed him in a heavy horse drawn wagon and raced with him through the streets to the county jail.

Sheriff William Henry Lewis served from 1886 to 1892. *Courtesy Dallas Daily Times-Herald*

Several attempts were made by the crowd, now turned mob, to storm the jail using a heavy railroad rail to break down the door. The attempts failed. Sheriff Lewis, along with respected citizens Joe W. Record, Ben Cabell and others, tried to reason with the mob and let them know that a trial would be held and justice would be done.

Some in the mob began firing shots at the officers inside the jail. The officers returned fire, and three of the mob members were wounded. However, none of the officers were hit by the gunfire.

After some time, the mob finally realized that Sheriff Lewis and the other officers would not give up the prisoner, and would defend him until the death. The mob members decided to leave and let the court system deal with Miller.

Miller was indicted for the murder of Dallas Police Officer C. O. Brewer. Judge Robert E. Burke presided over the trial. Miller was convicted on July 4, 1892. He then appealed the conviction. The conviction was affirmed on March 23, 1893, by the Texas Court of Criminal Appeals in Austin. A motion for a re-hearing was overruled on June 14, 1893.

Henry Miller was hanged in the Dallas County Jail on July 28, 1893, for the murder of Officer Brewer.

The Dallas Police Department recognizes C. O. Brewer, who was shot and killed on May 24, 1892, as the first Dallas police officer killed in the line of duty.

* * * * *

In the *1892 Memorial and Biographical History of Dallas County*, former Sheriff William Henry Lewis was described as being unmarried. Sometime after 1892, he married Julia Mister. She was born in 1871 and died in 1945.

Lewis was a member of the Presbyterian Church. He was one of the founders of Oakland Cemetery, and he assisted with the operation of the Texas State Fair.

William Henry Lewis died in Dallas on February 21, 1946, at age ninety-five. He and his wife are buried next to each other in Section 9, Oakland Cemetery in Dallas.

Tombstone of Sheriff William Henry Lewis and his wife at the Oakland Cemetery in Dallas, Texas. *Photo taken by author.*

Chapter 25

Sheriff Daniel S. "Dan" Harston

White male, born April 8, 1876 in Kentucky

Sheriff of Dallas County, Texas 1918 – 1924

Hanged two convicted felons on the gallows in the

Old Dallas County Jail at Main and Houston Streets, Dallas, Texas

Dan Harston, along with his family, came from Kentucky and settled in the Grand Prairie area of Dallas County. He received his high school education in Grand Prairie. In 1898 he married Mattie Curry of Grand Prairie. Harston worked on a farm before becoming a rural mail carrier, and later served as the assistant postmaster. Sometime later he moved to Dallas and went into the general merchandise and drug business.

Harston was elected sheriff of Dallas County in 1918. Harston and his deputies led raids on illegal whiskey stills, and arrested many bootleggers during the six years he served as sheriff.

While he was the sheriff, Harston pulled the lever on the trap door on the gallows for two prisoners in the "Old Jail" located at the corner of Main and Houston streets. These legal hangings led to the death of two convicted felons that had been sentenced to death by the courts in Dallas County.

Sheriff Harston and his deputies were able to save three prisoners from mobs and mob violence. The three separate cases are documented in this chapter where officers held off mobs and saved the lives of their prisoners.

The Attempt to Lynch Robert Grigsby on August 31, 1919

Robert Grigsby, a sixteen-year-old black male who lived at Wilmer in Dallas County, had a narrow escape with death on Sunday afternoon, August 31, 1919. A mob set out to punish him for attempting to criminally assault two young white girls.

Annie Dockery, age fifteen, and her sister, Mary Dockery, age thirteen, were walking alone along the Seagoville to Wilmer road that Sunday afternoon, when Robert Grigsby confronted the two girls. When Grigsby saw they were alone, he pulled a pistol from his shirt and told them to stop. The two girls screamed and ran. Grigsby again told them that if they didn't stop, he would shoot them.

The two girls saw their father coming and cried out, "Yonder comes papa now."

Grigsby then turned and ran. Mr. Dockery, who happened to be carrying his shotgun at the time, gave chase and overtook Grigsby and captured him. Mr. Dockery took Grigsby to Wilmer and turned him over to Constable Will Green.

Sheriff Dan Harston was immediately notified of the situation. Sheriff Harston hurriedly sent deputies Allen

Sheriff Dan S. Harston served from 1918 to 1925. *Courtesy Dallas Morning News*

Seale and Pat Richards to Wilmer. In a short time what had just happened became known, and angry men began to gather.

When deputy sheriffs Seale and Richards arrived at Wilmer, it looked as though violence could not be averted. However, the officers and a few citizens persuaded the men not to take the law into their own hands. Several times the officers attempted to take Grigsby to Dallas, but each time the group of angry men took Grigsby away from the officers.

Grigsby had a rope placed around his neck several times, and each time it was thrown over the crossbar of a telephone pole. The deputies were able to persuade the mob, now estimated between 300–500, to not lynch Grigsby. Finally, after an hour of pleading with the mob, Grigsby was turned over to the officers.

At one point, with Grigsby in hand, Constable Green and Officer J. C. Bramlett, started toward Dallas, but had a flat tire on their car. The officers crawled into a cotton field with hopes of hiding from the mob. They were soon discovered, and Grigsby was again taken from the officers. The officers were able to persuade the mob to release Grigsby back into their custody. Finally, the officers were able to transport Grigsby

Sheriff Dan S. Harston served as sheriff of Dallas County from 1918 to 1925 and is buried in Hillcrest Cemetery in Dallas, Texas. *Photo taken by author.*

safely to Dallas. The officers said later, that if it had not been for the assistance of some of the citizens, they would not have been successful in taking Grigsby to the county jail in Dallas.

District Attorney J. W. Pierson, after learning what had happened, praised all the officers for their work, and said, "This simply shows what a cool-headed officer can do."

A preliminary hearing was held inside the county jail on Thursday, September 4th. The two Dockery girls and their father were called as witnesses. The girls testified that they met Grigsby on the road and he pulled a pistol and told them to stop, but they started running and screaming. The younger girl testified that Grigsby said he would kill the older girl, if she didn't stop. The father testified that he saw the girls running and screaming. He said the black man was running away, and he chased and caught him.

In a statement following his arrest, Grigsby told District Attorney Pierson that it was his intention to assault both girls. At the preliminary hearing he changed his story, and said he did not intend to harm the girls. Grigsby's bond was set at $5,000.

On September 9th, Grigsby was indicted on two counts of attempted criminal assault, and on a charge of carrying a pistol.

When Grigsby appeared in court for the trial on September 16, 1919, the ring around his neck still showed where the noose of the rope had torn at the flesh when the mob tried to lynch him. The trial was held in Criminal District Court, with Judge Robert B. Seay presiding. District Attorney Pierson prosecuted the case.

The two Dockery girls and their father testified as to their previous testimony. Constable Green also testified as to his part in attempting to transport Grigsby to the county jail. The confession of Grigsby, that was taken a few hours after the crime, was read in court. Grigsby then pled guilty. He was not represented by counsel and he declined to make any further statement.

Grigsby, age sixteen, was sentenced to two ninety-nine-year sentences in the Texas State Penitentiary for attempted criminal assault. Grigsby died in prison on January 24, 1933, at the age of thirty.

The Texas Penitentiary Convict Ledger, 1849 – 1954, has the following information regarding Robert Grigsby:

> *Convict #44058, Robert Grigsby, black male, age 16, 5'6" 136#, Baptist. Charge: Assault with intent to rape, two counts. Sentence – 99 years and 99 years, total 198 years.*
> *County: Dallas, residence, Wilmer, Texas.*
> *Pled guilty: Sentence starts: October 5, 1919. Sentence ends: September 16, 2117.*
> *Comments: Died January 24, 1933. [in prison].*

The Attempt to Lynch David "Dave" Bunn on October 7, 1921

Late Wednesday, October 5, 1921, David Bunn, a twenty-one-year old black man, was arrested for robbing and terrorizing a house party at Lake Worth in Tarrant County. The robbery and attempted assault occurred on Tuesday night. Bunn not only robbed the men and women guests, who included members of prominent Fort Worth families, but he also dragged one of the young women from the house in an effort to assault her. He failed to accomplish the assault because of her screams and resistance.

Bunn made a confession to officers when he was arrested. He was immediately taken to the Dallas County Jail for fear of mob violence. On Thursday, Bunn was indicted by the Tarrant County Grand Jury, and a trial was set for the following week in Tarrant County District Court.

The day following his arrest, Bunn was connected with a number of other crimes that had recently occurred where white women were robbed and assaulted. One of these cases occurred at a home near the Fort Worth to Cleburne Interurban Railway. Another case occurred in a local park, where a black man waylaid a young couple and forced them at gunpoint into the woods, where he gagged and tied them. He then terrorized them for an hour before releasing them.

A mob of about 500 gathered at the Tarrant County Jail on Friday. They were seeking to take Bunn out of the jail, and issue a quick justice for his crimes. Tarrant County Sheriff Carl Smith finally allowed a committee of fifteen members of the mob to search the jail to prove that Bunn was not there.

After failing to find Bunn at the county jail, the crowd gathered at the Fort Worth City Jail, and made demands to search that jail for Bunn. Mob members were escorted through the city jail by Chief of Police Harry Williams, where they failed to find their wanted man. Next the mob gathered at the Fort Worth City Hall to discuss going to Dallas to look for Bunn.

At about 1:30 a.m. on Friday morning, Tarrant County Sheriff Smith called Dallas County Sheriff Dan Harston. He warned him that about twenty vehicles, loaded with men armed with rifles and shotguns, were on the way to Dallas.

By 2 a.m. the mob members began arriving in Dallas. Sheriff Harston was ready for them. He had deputies armed with rifles and shotguns at all the entrances to the Old Jail, at the corners of Main and Houston streets.

Two separate attempts were made by the mob that Friday morning to seize Bunn from Dallas County Sheriff Harston and his deputies. Both efforts failed. Sheriff Harston told the mob that it was no use to try to storm the jail again. He refused to allow anyone inside to search for Bunn. Harston told the mob members to go home, that Bunn would be tried in Tarrant County. The mob members began breaking up into smaller groups, which were then dispersed by Dallas police officers.

The Texas National Guard had stored a machine gun and two bandoliers of ammo in the sheriff's office the previous week. They had been displayed for recruiting purposes at the courthouse. The deputies brought out the machine gun and ammo belts and placed them where the mob could see them. . Many of the young men in the mob were believed to have served in World War I a few years earlier, and had a great respect for the firepower Sheriff Harston now held. It was believed the machine gun and ammo added much weight to quieting the mob.

Bunn was now charged with nine indictments issued by the Tarrant County Grand Jury. Bunn's trial was set for October 14th in Fort Worth.

On Tuesday, October 11th, Tarrant County Sheriff Carl Smith and Deputy Sheriff Tom Snow, went to Dallas to transfer Bunn back to Tarrant County for trial. The two officers left Dallas County with their prisoner, and crossed into Tarrant County at about 5:20 a.m.

In later news accounts, Sheriff Smith and Deputy Snow stated that the prisoner, upon seeing several oncoming cars, pointed ahead and said, "There's a mob." When the officers looked up, the prisoner jumped out of the car. According to the officers, David Bunn was shot and killed by them when he attempted to flee.

David "Dave" Bunn's Texas Death Certificate 29112 [1921] verified his place of death as Tarrant County. It listed his information as follows:

> *Full Name: Dave Bunn, male, negro, married, age 21, Occupation: laborer. Date of Death: October 11, 1921. Cause of Death: Affects of gunshot wound in hand of officers. Place of Burial: Trinity Cemetery, Ft. Worth, Texas. Peoples Undertaking Company.*

The Attempt to Lynch Frank Fennell on June 15, 1924

Jack Kendall, a white male, farmer, age thirty-two, lived about a mile south of Garland. He and a partner named Pace owned Pace and Kendall Company that bought and sold mules. Their ad in a Garland newspaper stated that their reputation of twenty-five years was behind every sale.

At about 9:30 p.m. on Saturday evening, June 14, 1924, Kendall went to a cafe in the black section of Garland to collect a debt. Eye witnesses said that Kendall went to the cafe to collect some money from a man who owed him for a stove. When leaving the cafe Kendall saw Frank Fennell, a forty-three year old black man, "standing on the porch drunk, and talking insolently." Kendall jokingly told Fennell that he was preaching too soon, that the next day was Sunday. Fennell then cursed Kendall, and Kendall struck at Fennell.

Fennell dodged, drew a revolver, and fired one time. The bullet struck Jack Kendall in the chest, mortally wounding him. Kendall ran through the cafe and out the back door, where he fell on the ground. Kendall never spoke after being shot, and died before the doctor arrived.

Mules!

We keep on hand at all times a large number of GOOD MULES, and can supply your needs for any kind of single animal or team you want. Our reputation of 25 years is behind every sale.

Heavy Hauling of All Kinds

PACE & KENDALL

Pace & Kendall ad from the Garland News.

Fennell ran away immediately after the shooting. A large crowd quickly gathered and searched for him, to no avail. The Dallas County Sheriff's office was notified of the shooting. Deputy sheriffs Hal Hood and Walter Taylor were sent from Dallas to the scene of the shooting and arrived about 11 p.m.

Several black men, including George Dudley, helped move

Kendall to Dyer's Drug Store, where Dr. Ogle pronounced him dead. The body was then removed by Williams Undertaking Company.

The Dallas deputies were assisted in the search for Fennell by Constable E. Harris and Deputy Brite, along with Garland posse men S. D. Smith, Jr. and Boone Cooper.

After searching all night, Fennell was arrested at 5 a.m. the next morning by deputies Hood and Taylor. When arrested, Fennell still had the .38 cal. revolver in his pocket that he had used to kill Kendall. The arrest was made on the Lum Weaver farm about one mile north of Garland.

News of the arrest preceded

Jack Kendall's tombstone is located in Garland Memorial Park Cemetery in Garland, Texas. *Photo taken by author.*

the arrival of the officers and their prisoner in Garland. By this time a crowd had gathered and turned into a mob and threats of lynching Fennell had been made. The officers were able to evade the leaders of the mob and outdistance them. A large number of automobiles chased the deputies' car in an effort to seize Fennell and carry out the threats to lynch him.

When Sheriff Hartson was notified of the arrest and threats of lynching, he ordered all deputies to the Criminal Courts Building and the Dallas County Jail. Many members of the mob which had formed at Garland, went to the sheriff's office and county jail in Dallas. The fact that Fennell was now in the Dallas County Jail and Sheriff Harston had the jail heavily guarded by armed deputies, seemed to quiet the mob's mood for violence.

The complaint charging Fennell with murder was filed in Justice of the Peace Court in Garland on Sunday, June 15th. Fennell was indicted for murder on June 17, 1924.

The trial charging Fennell with the murder of Jack Kendall was underway within two weeks. The trial was held in Judge Adams' court. The jury trial was completed and Fennell was sentenced to life in the Texas State Penitentiary. The attorneys for Fennell made a motion for a new trial, which was denied. A notice of appeal was then given.

On December 3, 1924, the Court of Criminal Appeals in Austin affirmed the life sentence for Fennell for the murder and on January 6, 1925, Fennell was transferred to the Texas State Penitentiary.

The Texas State Penitentiary Record Ledger book has the following information recorded:

Frank Fennell, Convict number 51986, age 43, black male, L. Bro. Gray hair, No Church. Born 1881. Occupation: farmer. Conviction: July 5, 1924, December 3, 1924 and December 20, 1924. Offense: Murder. Plead: Not guilty. Sentence: 5 to Life. County: Dallas. Residence: Garland. Received at Ramsey Unit: January 6, 1925. Expiration of Sentence: Death. Remarks: Cond. Pardon on April 13, 1939.

Frank Fennell was given a conditional pardon from the Texas State Penitentiary on April, 13, 1939.

* * * * *

Jack Kendall was survived by his wife and three-year-old child. He is buried in Garland Memorial Park Cemetery, Garland, Texas.

Chapter 26
Sheriff Schuyler B. Marshall, Jr.

White male, born March 3, 1895 in Dallas County, Texas

Died – April 9, 1982, in Dallas County, Texas, at age 87

Sheriff of Dallas County, Texas January 1, 1925 to December 31, 1926

Schuyler B. Marshall, Jr. only served one two-year term as sheriff and was only twenty-nine-years-old when he took over the office of Dallas County sheriff, on January 1, 1925. A newspaper reported that at his swearing in ceremony he wore khaki trousers, a badge pinned to his shirt, a belt and holsters with two six shooters. Some said he was too young to keep the peace in Dallas County. That was before he stood off a lynch mob estimated at 4,000 to 5,000, rounded up a gang of outlaws in a shoot-out in Denton while assisting the sheriff there, filled the county storerooms with stills, and jailed the bootleggers.

Marshall was born on his father's 3,000 acre ranch on Scyene Road, between Dallas and Mesquite, in Dallas County. He lived on the ranch with his parents and a brother and sister. He attended a boys' school in Dallas, and then attended Kansas State College at Manhattan, Kansas.

He was a member of the ROTC in college and in 1916 he was on the Mexican border with the Kansas National Guard. Marshall was commissioned a 2nd Lieutenant in the regular Army in 1917. He served with General John J. Pershing's expeditionary force chasing

Sheriff Schuyler B. Marshall, Jr. served Dallas County from 1925 to 1927. *Courtesy Dallas Morning News*

Pancho Villa, the Mexican bandit. Later he served in France and was a captain when discharged.

After World War I, he returned to Dallas County and began farming. He was elected sheriff in November 1924, and took office January 1, 1925. Four months after he took over as sheriff, he and his deputies would receive the test of a lifetime, a mob out to lynch their prisoners.

The Attempt to Lynch Brothers—Frank and Lorenzo Noel

On Sunday, April 12, 1925, at about 8:30 p.m., a young lawyer, H. Ryan Adkins, white male, age twenty-seven, and his female companion, Mrs. Mary Steer, a widow, white female, age thirty, were riding slowly on Airline Road north of Southern Methodist University. Two black men with pistols suddenly jumped onto the running board of the car, and forced Adkins to stop the vehicle.

Mrs. Steer later said that the two men beat Adkins to death with their pistols and some type of metal object. She heard them cursing because Adkins only had a few dollars in his pockets. Mrs. Steer was assaulted and beaten. She received a severe head wound along with cuts and bruises. The two men put her back into the car and drove it about a mile away, and over an embankment. She believed the two men thought she was dead.

A short time later, a Dallas man with his wife and daughter were driving along the road, when they saw the car in the ditch and a woman in the road. The Dallas man drove the body of Ryan Adkins to St. Paul Hospital on Bryan Street. Another man drove Mrs. Steer to her home. Police were notified of the attack on the couple and Mrs. Steer's doctor ordered her taken to Baylor Hospital, where she was admitted for treatment.

Sheriff Marshall, along with six of his deputies, four Dallas police detectives and Highland Park police officers, immediately began an investigation. They found the location of the attack on the couple. There they found evidence of a struggle, blood on the ground, a hammer and a piece of a metal spring. Police began rounding up the usual suspects and placing them in jail, in hopes that someone would know something and talk.

Two weeks after the murder of H. Ryan Adkins and the attack on Mrs. Mary Steer, another attack on a young couple in Dallas again put citizens in fear for their safety.

At about 8 p.m., on Saturday night, April 25, 1925, Walter L. "Larry" Milstead, a white male, age thirty, who was the district superintendent for the Corona Typewriter Company, had been to dinner in Dallas with his female companion, Mrs. Mable Berry, a twenty-eight-year-old white female.

Milstead and Berry were driving on Goodwin Avenue in Dallas near the home of Mrs. Berry's sister, when a black man leaped onto the running board of their car and pointed a pistol at Milstead and forced him to stop the car. The assailant made Milstead get out of the car and then shot him. Milstead was left lying on the sidewalk. The man got in the car, forcing Mrs. Berry to keep quiet by threatening her. He forced her to remain with him for over two hours, while beating and assaulting her. Mrs. Berry was finally abandoned and left for dead. She walked barefooted to a telephone and called the police department.

The officers interviewed Mrs. Berry and went to the location where Milstead had been shot. His body was found still lying at the location. The body had been undiscovered for three hours. Dallas police Captain Will R. Moffett found a .45 caliber automatic pistol casing at the scene where Milstead had been shot.

When Milstead's body was examined by doctors, they found that the bullet entered his body near the heart, passed through the body, and stopped in his back just under the skin. The lead bullet matched that of the shell casing found at the scene of the shooting.

Other recent reports of white couples being robbed and assaulted had been compared with the murders of Adkins and Milstead. On the Thursday night before Milstead was killed, C. K. Bullard, a local attorney, was robbed of a small amount of money. The black man who robbed him tried to force Bullard to drive him to Mockingbird Lane. Bullard said he swerved his car into the path of another car, and the man jumped from his car and fled.

In another case, Mrs. Oswin King foiled an attack while driving on Gaston near White Rock Lake. A black man attempted to jump onto the running board of her car. She swerved the car, and the man fell to the ground as she sped away.

Rewards were now being offered for the arrest and convictions of the parties responsible for the murders of H. Ryan Adkins and Walter "Larry" Milstead. Dallas Police Sergeant Will Henry put up $100 and Dan Harston, former sheriff of Dallas County, also put up a $100 reward. Texas Governor "Ma" Ferguson, at the request of Sheriff Schuyler Marshall, Jr., put up $250 for the capture of the killers of Ryan Adkins, and $250 for the capture of the killers of Larry Milstead. The bellboys of the Southland Hotel collected $50 for the reward and a group of leading Dallas black citizens put up another $100 for the capture of the criminals. The Scottish Rite Masons offered a reward of $1,000, while

W. H. Adkins and A. C. Adkins offered $1,000 for the capture of the killers of Ryan Adkins. The Corona Typewriter Company offered $500 for the capture of the killer of Larry Milstead. The combined rewards now totaled $3,350.

In the three days following the murder of Milstead, the roundup of suspects continued. Approximately one hundred black men were arrested and questioned by officers. The wanted killers still had not been identified and were at liberty.

By May 5, 1925, Mrs. Mary Steer and Mrs. Mable Berry were both still under care of their doctors for the injuries they received from the beatings at the hands of their captors. Several times, officers asked the women to view suspects in hopes that they could identify the killers.

Finally, on Friday, May 15th, Mrs. Mable Berry positively identified Frank Noel as the person who killed Larry Milstead and attacked her. Photographs were shown to Mrs. Berry and she quickly pointed out Noel as the wanted person. Noel was arrested on Friday and his brother Lorenzo Noel was arrested by detectives Leonard Pack and Walter Hanson on Saturday. Lorenzo attempted to disarm Detective Hanson, but was quickly subdued when Detective Pack rushed to assist his partner.

The officers now believed they had the two men responsible for the recent murders and attacks in Dallas. The two Noel brothers were also identified by several other victims who had been robbed and beaten. During a search of the Noel brothers' residence, and a former residence, officers found a .45 caliber automatic pistol and a shot-filled pouch used as a club. Also found were two skull caps and bloody underclothing. The evidence was found hidden under a stairway and in the ceiling. Officers also found a watch that had been taken from Vernon Wood in a robbery, when he and Miss Jewel Young were robbed near the Lakewood Country Club.

Officers found a small white gold wrist watch that had been taken from Mrs. Mary Steer the night Ryan Adkins was murdered and she was attacked and assaulted. The watch was found embedded in refuse in the sewer in the home of the parents and sister of the Noel brothers. Lorenzo Noel had given the watch to his sister, and she hid the watch in the sewer.

On Tuesday, May 19, 1925, Frank and Lorenzo Noel were transferred from the Dallas City Jail to the county jail. The transfer was made after the police department had received several anonymous calls that the Noel brothers were going to be taken from the city jail by a mob and lynched. The transfer to the county jail was made at 4 o'clock in the morning to avoid as many problems as possible. Sheriff Marshall had been notified and he was prepared to receive the prisoners.

Frank Noel gave a written statement to Dallas Police Detective Captain Will Moffett in the presence of District Attorney Shelby Cox, Sheriff Marshall and two police detectives. In his statement Frank Noel admitted killing Ryan Adkins and assaulting Mrs. Mary Steer. Lorenzo Noel gave a written statement in which he admitted his part in the murder of Ryan Adkins and the assault on Mrs. Mary Steer. Lorenzo, in his signed statement, stated that Frank Noel told him that he shot Mr. Milstead and committed the attack on Mrs. Mable Berry.

On May 20th, the Dallas County Grand Jury indicted Frank and Lorenzo Noel in six separate indictments. Frank Noel was charged with the murders of Ryan Adkins and W. L. Larry Milstead, and the assaults on the women in both cases. Lorenzo Noel was charged with the murder of Ryan Adkins and the assault on Mrs. Mary Steer.

On Wednesday evening, May 20th, a crowd estimated by the police department at 5,000, gathered at the county jail. By midnight the crowd was made up of predominately young people, including young women. Sheriff Marshall, assisted by the Dallas police and fire department, made every attempt to keep the crowd from approaching the jail. Heavily armed deputies and police officers were posted inside and outside the jail.

The fire department had their hose line laid out near the courthouse to be used to keep the crowd in check. Constable Buck Parsons headed a group of constables who came to the courthouse to assist the sheriff and his deputies.

Earlier in the evening, about fifty people in the crowd who were agitating, were arrested by police and placed in the city and county jails. More than twelve firearms were taken from the agitators when they were arrested. The officers on the street had been directing traffic and kept asking the crowd to stay back. It was apparent to the officers that many of the young people were there just to watch.

When the crowd refused to disperse, the fire hoses were brought out and turned on the crowd. Some in the crowd were cheering and laughing when the water was sprayed in their direction.

Shortly after 1 o'clock on Thursday morning, another group of approximately fifty men attacked the jail, hurling bricks, rocks and other objects. Before the night was over, officers fired about fifty shots from the jail entrance. The attackers withdrew toward the Trinity River. One of the wounded attackers was brought into the jail and treated for a gunshot to the arm. Two others were carried to the Emergency Hospital by ambulance. By daylight Thursday morning, the crowd had quietly dispersed.

Some estimates of the crowd size were now as high as 10,000. Additional help came to assist the Dallas officers when the Texas National Guard assigned forty men to assist in guarding the jail. Texas Ranger Captain Frank Hamer and Sergeant J. B. Wheatley were ordered to Dallas from Austin.

Thursday morning, Dallas Mayor Louis Blaylock issued a proclamation forbidding any assembly in or around the county jail or any place in the city for the purpose of inciting a riot, or aiding and abetting any person to commit mob violence.

Sam Gross, United States marshal for the Northern District of Texas, issued a statement on Thursday afternoon stating that the security of federal prisoners in the county jail must not be jeopardized by any attacks on the jail. Marshal Gross said that Federal Judge Atwell had made it very clear that if any violence was made against a Federal prisoner, that person committing the violence would be subject to investigation by the federal grand jury and federal statutes.

On Friday, May 22nd, the *Dallas Morning News* had an editorial titled "Dallas County Has A Sheriff." In the editorial, Sheriff Marshall, his deputies, Dallas police officers, Dallas firemen and all the other officers that assisted, were all given credit for stopping the mob attack on the county jail.

Dwight Moody Stewart, an eighteen-year-old white male, was shot shortly after 1 a.m. on Thursday morning by officers who were defending the Dallas County Jail during a mob attack. He died Friday evening at a local hospital. His death certificate number17263 [1925] has the following information:

> *Occupation: Drug Business, Date of Death: May 22, 1925 and Cause of Death: - Gunshot wound. Stewart was survived by his parents, a brother and a sister. He is buried in Grove Hill Cemetery, Dallas, Texas.*

The situation at the Dallas County Jail was now quiet. The mood in the city seemed to be to let the Noel brothers be tried in court. The National Guard troops that had been guarding the jail since Wednesday, were relieved on Saturday. Texas Rangers now took over the guard duty at the jail.

The Dallas County Grand Jury began an investigation into the shooting death of Stewart at the county jail on the morning of Thursday, May 21st. The sheriff, marshall, deputy sheriffs John Rowland and S. F. Pickens, United States Narcotic Agent H. S. Brown and M. T. Gon-

Dwight Stewart's tombstone who was shot and killed by officers while a mob was attempting to storm the Dallas County Jail. He is buried in the Grove Hill Cemetery in Dallas. *Photo taken by author.*

zaullas, a former prohibition agent, were among the officials who went before the grand jury.

On Wednesday, May 27th, five additional indictments were returned by the Dallas County Grand Jury. Frank and Lorenzo Noel were now charged with robbery with firearms.

City and county officials were now preparing for the trial of the Noel brothers. Judge Charles A. Pippin, Criminal District Court No. 2, would preside over the trials. A special venire of 300 men was summoned to appear on Thursday, May 28th, for possible jury duty.

District Attorney Shelby Cox would represent the State, and prosecute the cases. Attorney J. H. Beall was appointed by the court to represent Lorenzo Noel. Attorneys J. Hardy Neel and Henry Yeager were appointed by the court to represent Frank Noel. The defense attorneys agreed with the State to have both Noel brothers tried at the same time on the charge of criminal assault on Mrs. Mary Steer on the night of April 12, 1925, when Ryan Adkins was murdered.

Judge Pippin issued an order that only special venire men, regular officers, witnesses and newspaper reporters would be permitted inside the Criminal Courts Building on May 28th, during the trial of the Noel brothers.

On the morning of Friday, May 28, 1925, Judge Pippin took the unusual step of ordering that all venire men be searched for firearms as they entered the courthouse. The jury was quickly accepted by both the prosecution and defense. District Attorney Cox stated his case to the jury. Judge Pippin ordered Frank Noel to stand, and asked, "Are you guilty or not guilty of the charge you heard read to the jury?"

"I admit it," said Frank Noel.

Judge Pippin asked if he had been forced by cruel treatment or any other means to enter the plea.

Frank Noel said, "Of my own free will."

Mrs. Steer was the only witness called. She told her story of what happened the night of April 12th. She told of the two black men pulling Ryan Adkins out of the car, beating him, leaving him on the ground, and stealing her watch. She said the one named Frank told her he was going to kill her. Mrs. Steer said that she was only conscious part of the time, but that both of the men assaulted her. She went on to tell of the beating she suffered, and that she was struck in the head and face causing her eye to be partially paralyzed.

The defense announced that they would not cross-examine, and the witness was excused temporarily. Judge Pippin sent the case to the jury. The jury returned in two minutes with a verdict of guilty, and Frank Noel was given the death sentence.

Mrs. Steer waited in the witness room for half an hour before she was called back to repeat her story. A new jury was selected for the trial of Lorenzo Noel. The second trial was mostly a repeat of the first trial. The defense in the Lorenzo Noel trial also announced that they would not cross-examine the witness. The second jury was out thirteen minutes before they returned with their verdict of guilty, and punishment of death was also given to Lorenzo Noel.

Judge Pippin pronounced the sentences of the two men given by the juries:

> *You will be remanded to the custody of the sheriff until your commitment papers can be made out, and then, with these papers, you will be taken to the Texas Penitentiary at Huntsville, there to be confined in the death cell until June 28, when at some hour before sunrise you will be taken to the electric chair and currents of electricity will be sent through your body and continue until you are dead, dead, dead.*

Judge Pippin ordered the prisoners be taken from the courtroom and placed in the death cell of the county jail. At the conclusion of the trial, Judge Pippin made an address where he thanked the people of Dallas County. He also thanked Governor Miriam "Ma" Ferguson for sending the Texas Rangers to Dallas.

The Dallas County Grand Jury commended Dallas County officials for their vigilance in connection with the arrest and conviction of Frank and Lorenzo Noel.

When it was pointed out to Judge Pippin that he had sentenced the Noel brothers to be executed on June 28th, a Sunday, he said he overlooked that fact, but "if the officials at Huntsville don't want to execute them on Sunday I'll go down and do it myself."

On May 30, 1925, Frank and Lorenzo Noel were transferred to the Texas State Penitentiary at Huntsville. Governor Ferguson, who opposed executions on Sunday, granted a five-day respite for the Noel brothers. Judge Pippin had ordered the executions on June 28th and the new date for the execution was set as Friday, July 3, 1925.

Dallas County District Attorney Shelby Cox went to Huntsville to question the Noel brothers in hopes of gaining confessions in unsolved crimes. The brothers refused to admit that they were involved in any other crimes the offices believed them guilty of.

Letters were sent to Governor Ferguson asking her to commute to life imprisonment the death sentences for Frank and Lorenzo Noel, but the governor refused to interfere with the order of the court at Dallas.

John Tipps and Robert Perry, assistant district attorneys, and Dallas police detectives Leonard Pack and Walter Hanson were in Huntsville to witness the executions. Through information obtained from Frank and Lorenzo Noel just before they were executed, a valuable watch was later located that was taken in a robbery the previous March.

Shortly after midnight on Friday, July 3, 1925, Frank Noel was the first of the two brothers to die in the electric chair at the Huntsville State Penitentiary. He made a short statement admitting his guilt and made his peace with God before stepping into the chair. Within a few minutes his body was carried out.

Lorenzo was next; he also made a short talk declaring he made peace with God and was ready to die.

With their deaths on July 3, 1925, Frank and Lorenzo Noel became the third and fourth prisoners from Dallas County to die in the electric chair known as "Old Sparky," at the Huntsville State Penitentiary.

The first to die in the electric chair from Dallas County was Sidney Welk. He was convicted of murder in Dallas County and was executed on April 3, 1925. The second from Dallas County was Lavannie Twitty. He was convicted of murder and was executed on June 5, 1925. All previous court ordered death sentences in Dallas County were carried out by the sheriff, using the hangman's rope. The last court ordered person to die by the rope in Dallas County was Fred Douglas on August 27, 1920.

* * * * *

H. Ryan Adkins, who was killed by the Noel brothers, was born May 26, 1897. His occupation is listed as "lawyer" on his Texas death certificate number 13565, [1925]. The cause of death was listed as "fractured skull from blow of some blunt instrument, homicidal."

He was beaten to death on April 12, 1925, during a robbery and criminal assault on his female companion.

H. Ryan Adkins was survived by his mother, a brother and two sisters. Adkins is buried in the Brady Cemetery, formerly Live Oak Cemetery in Brady, Texas.

* * * * *

Walter L. Milstead, who was killed by Frank Noel, was born in March 1895. Texas death certificate number 13510, [1925] has his occupation listed as "salesman." He was shot and killed April 25, 1925, during a robbery and criminal assault on his female companion. The cause of death on his death certificate is listed as "Gun Shot Wounds, Murder."

Milstead's military Service record shows his rank and assignment as "PFC FLYING CADET AIR SERV D C DETCHMENT." Milstead is buried in Arlington National Cemetery, Arlington, Virginia.

* * * * *

In November 1926, at Houston, Texas, The Texas Commission on Interracial Relations voted to award Dallas County Sheriff Schuyler Marshall, Jr. a medal in appreciation of his efforts in repulsing a mob which stormed the Dallas County Jail on May 21, 1925. The mob attempted to lynch the Noel brothers, two black men being held on murder charges.

Schuyler B. Marshall, Jr. died on April 9, 1982, in his home at age eighty-seven. He is buried in the Calvary Hill Cemetery Mausoleum, Calvary Hill Cemetery, Dallas, Texas.

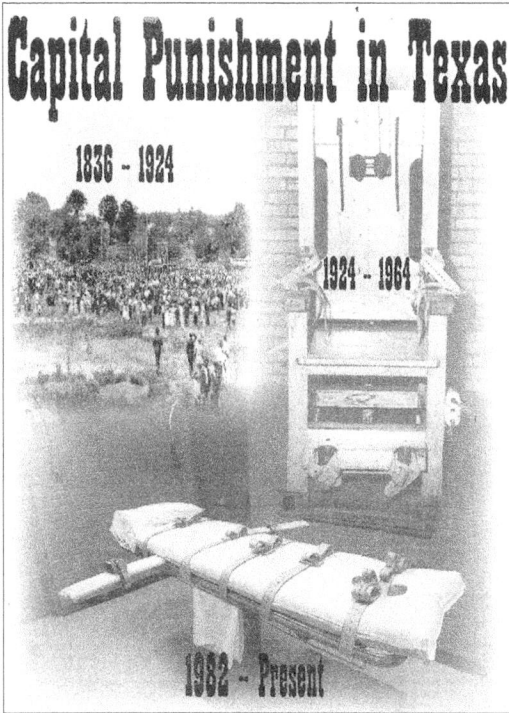

Capital Punishment in Texas
1836 - present
Legal Hangings - 1836-1924
Electric Chair - 1924-1964
Lethal Injection - 1982 present
Courtesy Texas Prison Museum

Texas Electric Chair
aka: "Old Sparky"
Used in Texas from 1924-1964
361 men died in the chair
Courtesy Texas Prison Museum

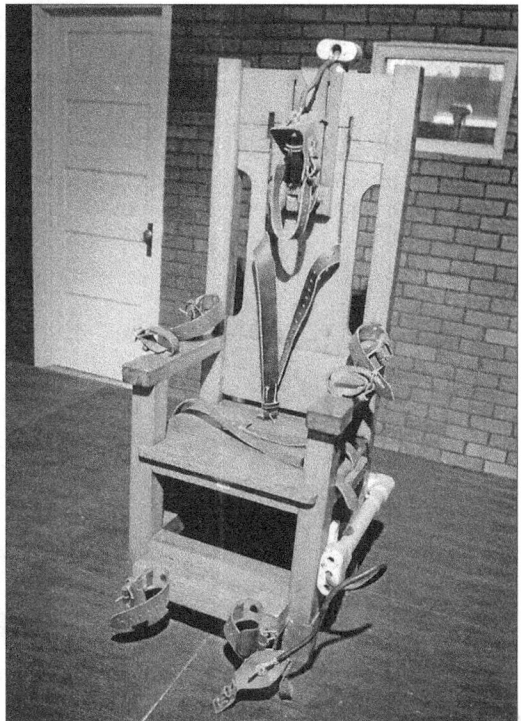

Sheriffs of Dallas County and the Years They Served

No Photos Available

John Huitt 1846 - 1848	**Rowland Huitt** 1848 - 1848	**William Jenkins** 1848 - 1850
Adam C. Haught 1854 - 1856	**Burnett M. Henderon** 1856 - 1858	**Wormley Carter** 1858 - 1860
Allen Beard 1860 - 1862	**N. O. Adams** 1862 - 1866	**Jeremiah M. Brown** 1866 - 1867 1870 - 1873
	Schuyler Marshall, Jr. 1925 - 1926	

Trezevant C. Hawpe
1850 - 1854

Norval R. Winniford
1867 - 1870

James E. Barkley
1873 - 1876

William M. Moon
1876 - 1880

Benjamin F. Jones
1880 - 1882

William H. W. Smith
1882 - 1886

William Henry Lewis
1886 - 1892

Ben Cabell
1892 - 1900

Lee H. Hughes
1900 - 1900

J. Roll Johnson
1901 - 1903

Arthur Lee Ledbetter
1904 - 1909

Ben Brandenburg
1910 - 1913

William K. Reynolds
1914 1917

Dan Harston
1918 - 1924

Allen Seale
1927 - 1928

Lula Seale
1927 - 1928

Hal Hood
1929 - 1932

Smoot Schmid
1933 - 1946

Steve Guthrie
1947 - 1948

J. E. "Bill" Decker
1949 - 1970

Clarence Jones
1970 - 1976

Carl Thomas
1977 - 1980

Don Byrd
1981 - 1984

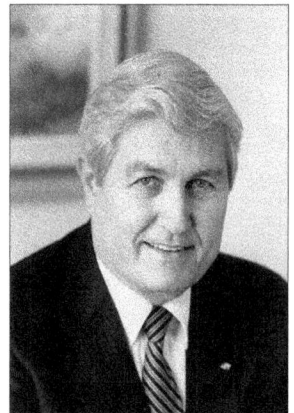

Jim Bowles
1985 - 2004

Lupe Valdez
2005 to Present

Source books:
Dallas County Sheriff's Department Commemorative Edition, 1846 – 1982.
Dallas County Sheriff's Department, 1846 – 1988.
Dallas County Sheriff's Department, 2007, A Tradition Continues.
Sheriffs Dallas County, Texas, 1846 – 1985, by O'Byrne Cox.
Texas County Sheriffs, 1989, by Sammy Tise

Bibliography

Chapter 1

Dallas County Records

Dallas County Criminal Case # 188, State of Texas vs. Jane, a slave, 1853,   Charge, murder, 14th District Court, Book A, pages 311, 316, 340 and 342. Microfilm Reel # 1993377.

Dallas County Probate Case # 179. America Elkins. Probate. Microfilm reel # 2. {She Died March 3, 1856.]

Dallas County Tax Rolls 1846-1910, Year 1852, A. C. Wisdom, 2 horses value $120, 1 wagon value $57, Reel #1.

Books

Acheson, Sam. *Dallas Yesterday. Dallas*: SMU Press, 1977. page 48.

Brown, John Henry. *History of Dallas County, Texas From 1837 to 1887*. Dallas: Milligan, Cornett & Farnham Printers. 1887. pages 12, 19, 22, 24, 62, 63, 73, 97, 105 and 112.

Cochran, John H. *Dallas County A Record of Its Pioneers and Progress*. Dallas: Service Publishing Co., 1998. pages 54, 82, 83, 84, 86, 127, 194 and 202.

Cox, O'Byrne Jr. *Sheriffs Dallas County, Texas 1846 – 1985. Dallas*: Self Published. 1985. pages 12, 13 and 14.

Dallas Genealogical Society, *Index to Probate Cases 1846 – 1900. Dallas: 1978*. page 16.

Dallas Morning News, Texas Almanac 2006 – 2007. Sesquicentennial Edition 1857 to 2007. Dallas: Texas A & M University Press Consortium. 2006. Pages 206 and 207.

Lewis Publishing Company. *Memorial and Biographical History of Dallas County, Texas*. Chicago: 1892. pages 146, 153, 157, 168, 177, 185, 193, 194, 199, 200, 202, 337 and 799.

Marquart, James W., Ekland-Olson, Shelton, and Sorensen, Jonathan R.. *The Rope, The Chair, and The Needle, Captial Punishment in Texas 1923 – 1990*. Austin: University of Texas Press. pages 1, 12, 13 and 201.

Pennybacker, Mrs. Anna J. Hardwicke. *A History of Texas For Schools*. Austin: Revised [1912] Edition. pages 263, 264, 341, 342 and 346.

Rogers, John William. *The Lusty Texans of Dallas*. Nashville: Parthenon Press. 1965. page 92.

Stout, Nancy deputy sheriff. *Dallas County Sheriff's Department Commemorative Edition 1846 – 1982*. Dallas: Dallas County Sheriffs Department. 1982. pages 18 and 19.

Tise, Sammy. *Texas County Sheriffs*. Albuquerque: Oakwood Printing. 1989. pages 146 and 147.

Wisdom, George W. *Genealogy of the Wisdom Family 1675 to 1910*. Compiled by George W. Wisdom, page 162, #544. "Andrew Wisdom, son of Pollard, lived in Dallas, Texas. He was killed and robbed by a negro in that city. He had one son." Dallas Public Library Reference #929.20973 W 811 YW.

Writers' Program of Work Projects Administration. City of Dallas. Dallas Public Library. *The WPA Dallas Guide and History*. Denton: University of North Texas Press. 1992. pages 50, 409 and 410.

Newspapers

Dallas Weekly Herald, July 10, 1875, page 4.

Galveston Daily News, August 28, 1880, page 1.

Dallas Daily Times-Herald, July 3, 1891, page1.

Dallas Daily Times-Herald, July 4, 1891, page 1.

Dallas Daily Times-Herald, July 17, 1891, page 4.

Dallas Morning News, July 15, 1892, page 8.

Dallas Morning News, August 3, 1905, pages 3 and 6.

Dallas Daily Times-Herald, June 16, 1907, page 2.

Magazines

Dingus, Anne. Deadline. *Texas Monthly, Crime, A Special Issue*. July 2002. page 96.

Enstam, Elizabeth York. *How Dallas Grew... and Why. Legacies, A History Journal For Dallas and North Central Texas*. Dallas: Dallas Historical Society, and Dallas County Heritage Society. Fall 1991. page 36.

Texas State Records

1850 Texas State Census. Dallas County. 2001. Heritage Quest.

United States Records

1850 United States Federal Census. Dallas County.

1850 United States Federal Census. Henderson County.

1850 United States Federal Slave Schedule. Dallas County.

Online

Acosta, Teresa Palomo. Handbook of Texas Online. Texas State Historical Association. Juneteeth. Accessed November 28, 2012.

Dallas Genealogical Society. 14th District Court Book A. May 1853. pages 302, 308, 311, 316, 340, 342. Accessed August 5, 2011.

Dallas Historical Society. Dallas History. Overview. Accessed September 2, 2011.

Payton, Donald. Timeline A Concise History Black Dallas Since 1842. Dallas: D Magazine. June 1998. Accessed March 26, 2012.

Underwood, Marlyn. Handbook of Texas Online. Josefa [Chipita] Rodriguez. Austin: University of Texas and Texas State Historical Association. 2002. Accessed November 5, 2002.

Wikipedia.org, John Henninger Reagan. Accessed July 11, 2012.

Chapter 2
Books

Acheson, Sam. *Dallas Yesterday*. Dallas: SMU Press, 1977. pages 35 and 36.

Betts, Vicki. *Smith County, Texas, in the Civil War*. Tyler: Smith County Historical Society. 1978. page 28.

Cox, O'byrne, Jr. *Sheriffs Dallas County. Texas 1846 – 1985*. Dallas: Self Published. 1985. page 18.

Fehrenbach, T. R. *Lone Star, A History of Texas and the Texans*. Chicago: American Legacy Press, 1983. pages 337, 338, 339, 357 and 358.

Lewis Publishing Company. *Memorial and Biographical History of Dallas County, Texas*. Chicago: 1892. page 177, 204 and 205.

Lindsey, Phillip. *A History of Greater Dallas and Vicinity*. Chicago: Lewis Publishing Company, 1909. page 63.

Reynolds, Donald E. *Texas Terror. The Slave Insurrection Panic of 1860 and the Secession of the Lower South*. Baton Rouge: Louisiana State University Press, 2007. pages 1 – 214.

Rogers, John William. *The Lusty Texans of Dallas*. Nashville: The Parthenon Press, 1965. pages 89 – 97.

World Book Encyclopedia. *Civil War*. Chicago: Field Enterprises Educational Corporation. 1974. Volume 4. page 476.

Writers' Program of Work Projects Administration. City of Dallas. *The WPA Dallas Guide and History*. Denton: University of North Texas Press, 1992. pages 53, 54 and 410.

Newspapers

Austin State Gazette, July 14, 1860, page 2.

Clarksville Standard, July 14, 1860, page 2.

Houston Weekly Telegraph, July 17, 1860, page 3.

Houston Weekly Telegraph, July 26, 1860, page 1.

Houston Weekly Telegraph, July 26, 1860, page 2.

Austin State Gazette, July 28, 1860, page 1.

Austin State Gazette, July 28, 1860, page 2.

Austin State Gazette, July 28, 1860, page 3.

Houston Weekly Telegraph, July 31, 1860, page 1.

Houston Weekly Telegraph, July 31, 1860, page 2.

Austin State Gazette, August 4, 1860, page 2.

Houston Weekly Telegraph, August 7, 1860, page 2.

Austin State Gazette, August 11, 1860, page 2.

Marshall Texas Republican, August 11, 1860, page 2.

Austin State Gazette, August 18, 1860, page 2.

Houston Weekly Telegraph, August 21, 1860, page 2.

Austin State Gazette, September 8, 1860, page 2.

Dallas Weekly Herald, October 31, 1860, page 1.

Dallas Daily Herald, July 8, 1877, pages 1 and 3.

Galveston Daily News, August 28, 1880, page 1.

Dallas Morning News, December 14, 1890, page 20.

Dallas Daily Times-Herald, July 3, 1891, page 1.

Dallas Daily Times-Herald, July 4, 1891, page 1.

Dallas Daily Times-Herald, July 7, 1891, page 8.

Dallas Morning News, July 10, 1892, page 12.

Dallas Morning News, July 15, 1892, page 8.

Dallas Times Herald, January 1, 1894, page 4.

Dallas Times Herald, January 2, 1894, page 2.

Dallas Times Herald, January 3, 1894, page 8.

Dallas Morning News, September 3, 1898, page 8.

Dallas Sunday Times Herald, July 6, 1919, page 9.

Dallas Morning News, December 26, 1920, page 10.

Dallas Morning News, September 9, 1928, page 3.

Dallas Morning News, October 14, 1928, page 14.

Dallas Morning News, July 8, 1990, pages 8-15.

Dallas Morning News, July 29, 2006, page 8 R.

Dallas Morning News, December 2, 2007, page 3 A.

Magazines

Enstam, Elizabeth York. *How Dallas Grew... and Why. Legacies, A History Journal for Dallas and North Central Texas*. Dallas: Dallas County Heritage Society. Fall 1991. page 36.

United States Records

1850 United States Federal Census. Dallas County.

1860 United States Federal Census. Dallas County.

1860 United States Federal Census. Slave Schedule. Dallas County.

1870 United States Federal Census. Dallas County.

Online

Basler, Roy P. edited by. *Collected Works of Abraham Lincoln*. Emancipation Proclamation. Accessed December 5, 2012.

Dallas Historical Society. Dallas History. Overview. Accessed September 2, 2011.

Victorian.fortunecity.com. Dallas Hanged 3 Slaves in Civil War Hysteria. Accessed March 13, 2004.

Handbook of Texas Online. Dallas County: Texas State Historical Association. Accessed December 3, 2012.

Handbook of Texas Online. Dallas, Texas: Texas State Historical Association. Accessed March 8, 2005.

Handbook of Texas Online. Pryor, Charles R.: Texas State Historical Association. Accessed December 3, 2012

Handbook of Texas Online. Slave Insurrections: Texas State Historical Association. Accessed December 3, 2012.

Handbook of Texas Online. Texas Troubles: Texas State Historical Association. Accessed September 2, 2011.

Juneteenth.com/history. History of Juneteenth. Accessed December 5, 2012.

Memory.loc.gov/ammem/cwphml/t1861.html. Time Line of The Civil War, 1861. Accessed December 5, 2012.

Chapter 3

Books
Dallas County Genealogical Society. *Dallas County, Texas Genealogical Data From Early Cemeteries, Volume 1*. 1982. page 20.

Dallas County Pioneer Association. *Proud Heritage II, Pioneer Families of Dallas County*. 1993. page 215.

Cox, O'Byrne Jr.. *Sheriffs Dallas County, Texas. 1846 – 1985*. Self-published. 1985. page 19.

Tise, Sammy. *Texas County Sheriffs*. Albuquerque: Oakwood Printing, 1989. pages 146 and 147.

Newspapers
Dallas Weekly Herald, August 14, 1861, page 1.

Marshall Texas Republican, August 17, 1861, page 3.

Dallas Weekly Herald, August 21, 1861, pages 1 and 2.

Marshall Texas Republican, August 31, 1861, page 3.

United States Records
1860 United States Federal Census, Dallas County.

1880 United States Federal Census, Dallas County.

1880 United States Federal Non-Population Schedule, Dallas County.

Online
Ancestry.com, Askey Family Tree, Josiah Record, Accessed December 11, 2012.

Ancestry.com. Find A Grave Index, 1836-2011. Josiah Record. Burial Place: Dallas County, Texas. Death Date, 13 Aug. 1861. Accessed December 11, 2012.

Ancestry.com. Josiah Record. Accessed December 11, 2012.

Ancestry.com, Worchester Family Tree, Josiah A. Record, Accessed December 11, 2012.

Blair, Wanda. Parrish Cemetery, Coppell, Dallas County. Accessed December 11, 2012.

Wheat, Jim. Jim Wheat's Dallas County, Texas. Dallas County Texas Archives. Reconstruction in Dallas County. 1867-68. List of murders and assaults with intent to kill. No. 47 and No. 355. Accessed December 22, 2005.

Chapter 4

Dallas County Records

Dallas County Probate Case. # 555. John Record, deceased Aug. 1869. Sarah S. Record, Executor of the Will. Filed September 9, 1869. Microfilm Roll # 5, Dallas County Probate Cases 500-659.

Books

Anderson, Peggy & Brittain, Lucille. *Marriage Records, Dallas County, Texas.* Books A-D, 1847-1874. Books N' Books: 1992. page 22.

Bates, Ed. F. *History and Reminiscences of Denton County.* McNitzky Printing Company: 1918 . pages 383 and 387.

Cox, O"Byrne Jr.. *Sheriffs Dallas County, Texas. 1846 – 1985.* Dallas. Self Published, 1985: pages 24, 25, 26.

Dallas Genealogical Society. *Marriages Dallas County, Texas. Books A-E. 1846-1877,* Vol. 1. 1978: page 17.

Dallas Genealogical Society. *Index to Probate Cases. 1846-1900. Dallas County, Texas.* Vol. 1. 1978: page 45.

Dallas County Pioneer Association. *Proud Heritage II. Pioneer Families of Dallas County.* 1993. page 215.

Historic Bethel Cemetery, Coppell, Texas. Dallas County. Self published. 1991. pages 1, 4, 5, Handwritten list of burials: pages 105-110. Pages 161 and 162.

Newspapers

Dallas Weekly Herald, September 4, 1869, page 3.

Galveston Daily News, September 10, 1869. page 2.

Dallas Weekly Herald, September 18, 1869. page 1.

Fort Worth Democrat-Advance, January 6, 1882. page 1.

Dallas Daily Times Herald, July 3, 1891, page 1.

Dallas Daily Times Herald, July 4, 1891, page 1.

Dallas Daily Times Herald, July 7, 1891. page 8.

Dallas Times Herald, January 1, 1894, page 4.

Dallas Times Herald, January 2, 1894, page 2.

Dallas Times-Herald, January 3, 1894, page 8.

Dallas Morning News, June 29, 1989. Section D, page 12.

Dallas Morning News, August 3, 1989, Section A. page 39.

United States Records

1860 United States Federal Census. Dallas County.

1870 United States Federal Census. Dallas County.

1870 United States Federal Census Mortality Schedules. Dallas County, Denton County and Tarrant County, Texas.

1880 United States Federal Census, Dallas, County.

Online

Ancestry.com. Headstones Provided for Deceased Union Civil War Veterans, 1879-1903. Leopold F. Bohny. Texas. 15 Jan. 1897. Accessed December 28, 2012.

Ancestry.com. Texas Muster Roll Index Cards, 1838-1900. John Record. Enlistment Feb. 1861. Civil War Index-Abstracts of Muster Rolls. Accessed December 17, 2012.

Ancestry.com. U. S. Civil War Soldiers, 1861-1865. John Record. Confederate, Texas. Capt. Good's Co. Texas Art'y [State Troops]. Accessed December 17, 2012.

Ancestry.com. U. S. Confederate Soldiers Compiled Service Records, 1861-1865. John Record, 1861. Capt. Douglas' Co., Artillery; Capt. Good's Co., State Troops, Artillery. Dallas Light Infantry; Capt. Greer's Rocket Battery. Accessed December 17, 2012.

Ancestry.com. U.S. and International Marriage Records, 1560-1900. Norval Robertson Winniford and Sarah Miranda Gilliland. Accessed December 28, 2012.

Ancestry.com. Texas Voter Registration Lists. 1867-1869. John Record. 1867 Voter Registration Lists. Dallas County. Accessed December 17, 2012.

Ancestry.com. Texas, Find A Grave Index, 1836-2011. John Record. Dallas County, Texas, USA. Accessed December 8, 2012.

Blair, Wanda. Cemeteries of Texas. Parrish Cemetery, Coppell, Texas. Slias Record, John Record. Accessed December 11, 2012.

Coppell Historical Society. A Brief History of Coppell. Accessed December 21, 2012.

Coppell Historical Society. Coppell's Historic Cemeteries. Accessed December 21, 2012.

Dallas County, Texas Cemeteries. Parrish Family Cemetery. Coppell, Dallas County, Texas. Accessed December 24, 2011.

Find A Grave Memorial. John Record. Parrish Cemetery, Coppell, Dallas County, Texas. Accessed December 8, 2012.

Find A Grave Memorial. Silas Record. Parrish Cemetery, Coppell, Dallas County, Texas. Accessed December 8, 2012.

U.S. Marshals Service, History of Northern District of Texas. A.B. Norton. Accessed December 8, 2012.

Wheat, Jim. Jim Wheat's Dallas County, Texas. Dallas County Texas Archives. Crime Related Articles. Dallas County, Texas. History of the Hangings. page 6. Accessed March 7, 2004.

Wheat, Jim. Jim Wheat's Dallas County, Texas. Reconstruction in Dallas County. List of murders and assaults with intent to kill. Accessed December 22, 2005.

Chapter 5

Dallas County Records

Dallas County 14th District Court Minutes, Case # 2734. State of Texas v. Marion Dill and Elijah T. Rice. Charge – murder. Microfilm # 1993380. Roll # 4. January 21, 1876.

Vol. I, pages 243 and 244.

Dallas County 14th District Court Minutes, Case # 2734. State of Texas v. Marion Dill, William Bell and Eligah Rice. Charge – murder. Microfilm # 1993381, Roll # 5. Sept 7, 1877, Vol. J. pages 439 and 446.

Dallas County 14th District Court Minutes. Case # 2734. State of Texas v. Marion Dill, William Bell and Eligah Rice. Charge murder. Microfilm # 1993381, Roll # 5. August 28, 1878, Vol. J. page 520. February 10, 1879. Vol. L. pages 71 and 74 and 112.

Dallas County 14th District Court Minutes, Case # 2734. State of Texas v. Marion Dill, et al. Charge – murder. Microfilm # 1993381. Roll # 5. March 4, 1879. Vol. J. page 112. Dallas County 14th District Court Minutes. Case # 3902. State of Texas v. Elijah T. Rice. Charge – murder. Microfilm # 1993381, Roll # 5. March 4, 1879. Vol. J. page 112.

Dallas County 14th District Court Minutes. Case # 2734, State of Texas v. Marion Dill, William Bell and Eilgah Rice. Micofilm # 1993382, Roll # 6. January 12, 1881. Vol. M. page 621. .

Books

Cox, O'Byrne Jr. *Sheriffs Dallas County, Texas. 1846-1985.* Dallas: Self-published, 1985. pages 24, 25, 26, 29, 30, and 31.

Gillett, James B. *Fugitives From Justice.* Austin: State House Press. Copyright 1977, City of Waco. Page 176.

Butterfield, F E. and Rundlett, C.M.. *Directory for the City of Dallas.* 1875: pages 17, 38, 39, 39, 40 and 134.

Newspapers

Dallas Daily Herald, January 24, 1875, page 4.

Dallas Daily Herald, January 26, 1875, page 4.

Dallas Weekly Herald, January 30, 1875, page 3.

Dallas Daily Herald, September 1, 1875, page 4.

Galveston Daily News, November 4, 1875, page 1.

Dallas Daily Herald, December 25, 1875, page 4.

Dallas Weekly Herald, January 16, 1876, page 3.

Galveston Daily News, January 18, 1876, page 1.

Dallas Daily Herald, January 21, 1876, page 4.

Dallas Weekly Herald, January 22, 1876, page 1.

Dallas Daily Herald, October 20, 1876, page 4.

Dallas Daily Herald, February 19, 1878, page 4.

Dallas Daily Herald, February 20, 1878, pages 1.

Dallas Daily Herald, February 21, 1878, page 4.

Galveston Daily News, February 21, 1878, page 1.

Dallas Daily Herald, February 22, 1878, page 4.

Dallas Daily Herald, February 23, 1878, page 1.

Dallas Daily Herald, February 24, 1878, page 4.

Galveston Daily News, July 10, 1878, page 1.

Dallas Weekly Herald, January 20, 1881, page 3.

United States Records

1870 United States Federal Census, Dallas County.

1880 United States Federal Census, Dallas County.

1900 United States Federal Census, Dallas County.

Online

Handbook of Texas Online. Texas State Historical Association. Silas Hare. Accessed January 3, 2013.

Wikipedia. Silas Hare, 1827 – 1908. Accessed January 3, 2013.

Wikipedia, J. M. Thurmond, 1836 – 1882. Accessed January 14, 2013.

Chapter 6

Dallas County Records

Dallas County District Court Records. 14th District Court Minutes. Case# 3196. State of Texas v. Wesley Jones. Microfilm # 1993380, Roll 4. 1875 -1876. January 21, 1876. Vol. I, pages 235 and 236.

Books

Cox, O'Byrne Jr. *Sheriffs Dallas County, Texas 1846 – 1985.*Dallas: Self Published, 1985. page 29, 30, 31 , 32 and 33.

Butterfield, F. E. and Rundlett, C. M. *Directory City of Dallas: Year 1875.* page 17 and 119.

Lewis Publishing Company. *Memorial and Biographical History of Dallas County, Texas.* Chicago: 1892. pages 336, 337 and 338.

Tise, Sammy. *Texas County Sheriffs.* Albuquerque: Oakwood Printing. 1989. Pages 146 and 147.

Writers' Program of Work Projects Administration. *City of Dallas. The WPA Dallas Guide and History.* Denton: University of North Texas Press, 1992. page 68.

Newspapers

Dallas Daily Herald, November 3, 1875, page 4.

Dallas Daily Herald, November 4, 1875, page 4.

Galveston Daily News, November 4, 1875, page 1.

Dallas Daily Herald, December 29, 1875, page 4.

Galveston Daily News, January 4, 1876, page 1.

Dallas Daily Herald, January 19, 1876, page 4.

Dallas Daily Herald, January 21, 1876, page 4.

Dallas Weekly Herald, January 22, 1876, page 3.

Galveston Daily News, January 27, 1876, page 2.

Dallas Weekly Herald, January 29, 1876, page 1.

Galveston Daily News, July 11, 1876, page 2.

Galveston Daily News, July 26, 1876, page 2.

Dallas Daily Herald, August 11, 1876, page 4.

Dallas Daily Herald, August 12, 1876, page 4.

Dallas Weekly Herald, August 12, 1876, page 3.

Dallas Weekly Herald, August 19, 1876, page 1.

Galveston Daily News, January 19, 1877, page 4.

Galveston Daily News, August 28, 1880, page 1.

Dallas Daily Times Herald, July 3, 1891, page 1.

Dallas Morning News, September 3, 1898, page 8.

Online

Handbook of Texas Online. Texas State Historical Association. Silas Hare. Accessed January 18, 2013.

Wikipedia. Silas Hare. 1827 – 1908. Accessed January 18, 2013.

Chapter 7

Dallas County Records

Dallas County District Court Records. 14th District Court Minutes Case # 4236. State of Texas vs. Allen Wright. Microfilm Roll 6. 1879 – 1881. Vol. M. March 16, 1880, page 217. May 20, 1880, page 332. June 29, 1880, pages 415 and 416.

Books

Butterfield, F. E. and Rundlett, C. M. *Directory City of Dallas: Year 1875*. page 119.

Cox, O'Byrne Jr. *Sheriffs Dallas County, Texas 1846 – 1985*. Dallas: Self Published, 1985. pages 32 and 33.

Tise, Sammy. *Texas County Sheriffs*. Albuquerque: Oakwood Printing, 1989. pages 146 and 147.

Newspapers

Dallas Daily Herald, February 8, 1880, page 4.

Dallas Daily Herald, June 30, 1880, page 5.

Galveston Daily News, June 30, 1880, page 1.

Dallas Daily Herald, July 9, 1880, page 8.

Galveston Daily News, July 9, 1880, page 1.

Galveston Daily News, July 13, 1880, page 1.

Dallas Daily Herald, August 19. 1880, page 8.

Brenham Daily Banner, August 20, 1880, page 1.

Dallas Daily Herald, August 25, 1880, page 8.

Galveston Daily News, August 25, 1880, page 1.

Dallas Daily Herald, August 28, 1880, page 5.

Galveston Daily News, August 28, 1880, page 1.

Athens [Ohio] Messenger, September 2, 1880, page 1.

Dallas Daily Times Herald, July 3, 1891, page 1.

Dallas Daily Times Herald, July 4, 1891, page 1.

Dallas Daily Times Herald, July 28, 1893, pages 1 and 2.

Dallas Morning News, September 3, 1898, page 8.

United States Records
1880 United States Federal Census.

Chapter 8

Dallas County Records
Dallas County District Court Records. 14th District Court Minutes. Case# 3380. State of Texas vs. West. Pollard and Adam Thompson. Microfilm # 1993380. Roll 4, 1875 – 1876. October 19, 20, 21, 1876. Vol. H-2, pages 635 and 636. October 23, 1876, pages 605 and 637. November 6, 1876, page 633 and 634.

Dallas County District Court Records. 14th District Court Minutes. Case # 3380. State of Texas vs. West. Pollard and Adam Thompson. Microfilm # 1993382. Roll 6, 1879 – 1881. April 28, 1880, Vol. M, pages 296 and 297. May 6, 1880, page 302. May 8, 1880, page 309. May 20, 1880, page 332.

Dallas County District Court Records. 14th District Court Minutes. Case# 3380. State of Texas vs. Adam Thompson. Microfilm # 1993382. Roll 6. 1881 – 1882. January 24 and 25, 1881. Vol. N, pages 9 and 11. April 4, 1881, pages 101 and 102.

Books
Cox, O'Byrne Jr.. *Sheriffs Dallas County, Texas. 1846 – 1985*. Dallas: Self Published, 1985. pages 35 and 36.

Texas Election Records. *Dallas County, 1880 – 1882*. Election November 2, 1880.

Tise, Sammy. *Texas County Sheriffs*. Albuquerque: Oakwood Printing, 1989. pages 146 and 147.

Newspapers
Dallas Weekly Herald, July 8, 1876, page 3.

Dallas Weekly Herald, July 22, 1876, page 3.

Galveston Daily News, October 27, 1876, page 2.

Dallas Daily Times Herald, April 27, 1880, page 5.

Dallas Daily Times Herald, April 28, 1880, page 5.

Galveston Daily News, April 28, 1880, page 1.

Dallas Daily Times Herald, April 29, 1880, page 4.

Galveston Daily News, June 10, 1880, page 1.

Galveston Daily News, June 29, 1880, page 1.

Brenham Daily Banner, June 30, 1880, page 1.

Galveston Daily News, December 21, 1880, page 1.

Dallas Weekly Herald, January 20, 1881, page 7.

Galveston Daily News, January 21, 1881, page 1.

Dallas Weekly Herald, January 27, 1881, page 2.

Galveston Daily News, April 5, 1881, page 1.

Dallas Weekly Herald, April 7, 1881, page 8.

Galveston Daily News, April 10, 1881, page 1.

Dallas Daily Times Herald, July 1, 1881, page 5.

Dallas Daily Times Herald, July 2, 1881, page 5.

Dallas Daily Times Herald, July 2, 1881, page 4.

Galveston Daily News, July 2, 1881, page 1.

Dallas Daily Times Herald, July 4, 1891, page 1.

Dallas Morning News, September 3, 1898, page 8.

United States Records
1880 United States Federal Census.

Chapter 9

Dallas County Court Records

Dallas County District Court Records. 14th District Court Minutes. Case # 5186, State of Texas vs. Frank Bell. Microfilm # 1993382. Roll 6. 1881 – 1882. November 28, 1881. Assault with Intent to Murder. Vol. N, page 428. Robbery. November 28, 1881. Vol. N, pages 428 and 429. December 8, 1881. Vol. N, page 454. December 8, 1881. Vol. N, pages 454 and 455.

Books

Cox, O'Byrne Jr. *Sheriffs Dallas County, Texas 1846 – 1985*. Dallas: Self Published, 1985. pages 35 and 36.

Texas Election Records. *Dallas County 1880 -1882*. Election November 2, 1880.

Tise, Sammy. *Texas County Sheriffs*. Albuquerque: Oakwood Printing, 1989. pages 146 and 147.

Newspapers

Dallas Daily Times Herald, April 29, 1880, page 2.

Dallas Daily Times Herald, August 6, 1881, page 5.

Galveston Daily News, August 6, 1881, page 1.

Dallas Weekly Herald, August 11, 1881.page 3.

Dallas Daily Times Herald, November 29, 1881, page 5.

Dallas Weekly Herald, December 15, 1881, page 7.

Texas State Convict Records

Convict # 9887, Frank Bell, age 18, 5' 10", 150 #, Complexion-copper, Black hair, Black eyes, Marks on person – none. Occupation – farmer. Residence Dallas, Offense- Assault to Murder and Robbery. Term of Imprisonment – 7 years, plus 7 years. When received at Huntsville prison – December 8, 1881. Expiration of Sentence – December 8, 1895. Transferred to Rusk State Prison – January 1, 1883.

United States Records

1880 United States Federal Census.

Online

Handbook of Texas Online. Rusk Penitentiary. Texas State Historical Association. Accessed on February 7, 2012.

Chapter 10

Books

Cox, O'Byrne Jr. *Sheriffs Dallas County, Texas, 1846 – 1985*. Dallas: Self-published, 1985. pages 38 and 39.

Imgmire, Frances T. *Brazos County, Texas Marriage Records, Book A & B. 1844 – 1878*. St. Louis, Missouri: 1985, page 12.

Morrison & Fourmy's *General Directory of the City of Dallas, 1884 – 85*. Self-published: 1885. Printed by Clark & Courts Printers, Galveston, Texas. pages 5, 135 and 198.

State of Texas, *Register of Elected and Appointed State and County officials, 1882 -1884*. W.H. W Smith, elected sheriff Dallas County. G. H. Miller elected constable, precinct # 1, Dallas, on Nov. 7, 1882.

Tise, Sammy. *Texas County Sheriffs*. Albuquerque: Oakwood Printing, 1989. pages 146 and 147.

Newspapers

Galveston Daily News, June 27,1884, page 1.

Dallas Weekly Herald, July 3, 1884, page 6.

Galveston Daily News, July 18, 1884, page 2.

Dallas Daily Times Herald, July 23, 1884, page 5.

Dallas Weekly Herald, July 24, 1884, page 4.

Galveston Daily News, July 24, 1884, page 1.

Galveston Daily News, August 30, 1884, page 1.

Galveston Daily News, September 5, 1884, page 1.

Dallas Daily Times Herald, September 13, 1884, page 4.

Fort Worth Daily Gazette, September 13, 1884, page 1.

Galveston Daily News, September 13, 1884, page 1.

New Haven Register, New Haven, CT. September 13, 1884, page 1.

Dallas Weekly Herald, September 18, 1884, page 2.

Galveston Daily News, January 23, 1885, page 2.

United States Records

1880 United States Federal Census

1900 United States Federal Census

Online

Ancestry.com. Family Tree. Elizabeth Lucas. Married William Henry Flippin on May 19, 1875, in Brazos County, Texas. Accessed August 10, 2013.

Ancestry.com. Family Tree. William Henry Flippin. Married Elizabeth Lucas on May 19, 1875, in Brazos County, Texas. Born – 7 March in Rome, Smith County, Tennessee, USA. Death 17 January 1891, in Dallas, Dallas County, Texas, USA. Accessed August

10, 2013.

Ancestry.com. U.S. City Directories, 1821 – 1989. William H. Flippin. Residence Year: 1902, Address: 281 Ross Av. Residence Place: Dallas, Texas. 1902 Dallas City Directory. [son of William Henry and Elizabeth Flippin]. Accessed August 8, 2013.

Chapter 11

Dallas County Records

Dallas County District Court Records. 14th District Court Minutes. Case # 17010. State of Texas vs. Henry Miller. Microfilm # 1994028. Roll 11, Vol. 3, 1892-1893, June 27 and July 4, 1892, pages 175, 179 and 180.

Dallas County Inquest Minute Book, 1889-1893. Microfilm # 2026982. Justice of the Peace S. N. Braswell, Precinct #1, Place #1. Deceased - Dallas Police Officer C. O. Brewer, May 24, 1892.

Books

Cox, O'Byrne Jr. *Sheriffs Dallas County, Texas, 1846 – 1985*. Dallas: Self-published, 1985. pages 45, 46 and 47.

Elwonger, Steve. *In the Line of Duty*. Taylor Publishing Company. Dallas, Texas. 2002. pages 8 and 9.

Lewis Publishing Company. *Memorial and Biographical History of Dallas County, Texas*. Chicago: 1892. Pages 607, 944 and 945.

Peace Officers Memorial Foundation. *CLEAT. Thirteenth Biennial Texas Peace Officers Memorial Services*. Self-published, 2011. Page 23.

Tise, Sammy. *Texas County Sheriffs*. Albuquerque. Oakwood Printing, 1989. Pages 146 and 147.

Newspapers

Dallas Morning News, May 25, 1892, page 1.

Dallas Morning News, May 26, 1892, page 10.

Saline County Review, Marshall, Missouri, May 27, 1892.

Dallas Morning News, June 11, 1892, page 7.

Dallas Morning News, June 28, 1892, page 10.

Dallas Morning News, June 29, 1892, page 8.

Dallas Morning News, June 30, 1892, page 8.

Dallas Morning News, July 1, 1892, page 8.

Dallas Morning News, July 3, 1892, page 16.

Dallas Morning News, July 4, 1892, page 8.

Dallas Morning News, July 5, 1892, page 10.

Dallas Morning News, July 7, 1892, pages 5 and 8.

Dallas Morning News, July 10, 1892, page 12.

Dallas Morning News, July 12, 1892, page 4.

Dallas Morning News, July 16, 1892, page 8.

Dallas Morning News, July 22, 1892, page 8.

Dallas Morning News, July 26, 1892, page 8.

Dallas Morning News, August 29, 1892, page 8.

Dallas Morning News, November 16, 1892, page 5.

Dallas Morning News, January 15, 1893, page 12.

Dallas Morning News, May 12, 1893, page 8.

Dallas Morning News, June 15, 1893, pages 7 and 8.

Dallas Morning News, June 25, 1893, pages 10 and 16.

Dallas Morning News, July 3, 1893, page 8.

Dallas Morning News, July 13, 1893, page 8.

Dallas Morning News, July 15, 1893, page 10.

Dallas Morning News, July 17, 1893, page 8.

Dallas Times Herald, July 19, 1893, page 8.

Dallas Morning News, July 20, 1893, page 8.

Dallas Morning News, July 27, 1893, page 8.

Dallas Times Herald, July 28, 1893, pages 1 and 2.

Dallas Times Herald, February 6, 1894, page 8.

Dallas Morning News, February 7, 1894, page 8.

Dallas Morning News, September 3, 1898, page 8.

Texas State Records

West Reporter Document. [PDF] Court of Criminal Appeals of Texas. Miller vs. State. March 25, 1893. 31 Tex. Crim. 609, 21 S. W. 925, 37 Am. St. Rep. 836. Henry Miller was convicted of murder in the first degree, and appealed. Case Affirmed.

United States Records

1850 United States Federal Census.

1870 United States Federal Census.

1880 United States Federal Census.

1900 United States Federal Census.

1930 United States Federal Census.

1940 United States Federal Census.

Online

Ancestry.com. Family Tree. Cassee Odorous "C.O." Brewer. Born 1850, in Texas. Accessed February 14, 2013.

Officer Down Memorial Page, Inc. Cassee Odorous Brewer. EOW, May 24, 1892. Accessed February 14, 2013.

Wikipedia, The free encyclopedia. Robert Emmett Burke. Wikipedia online, 2013. Accessed March 2, 2013.

Chapter 12

Books

Cox, O'Byrne Jr. *Sheriffs Dallas County, Texas. 1846 – 1985.* Dallas: Self-Published, 1985. Pages 45, 46 and 47.

Lewis Publishing Company. *Memorial and Biographical History of Dallas County, Texas.* Chicago: 1892. pages 944 and 945.

Tise, Sammy. *Texas County Sheriffs.* Albuquerque: Oakwood Printing, 1989. pages 146 and 147.

Newspapers

Dallas Morning News, July 16, 1898, page 8.

Dallas Morning News, July 17, 1898, page 2.

Dallas Morning News, July 19, 1898, page 8.

Dallas Morning News, July 26, 1898, page 8.

Dallas Morning News, July 29, 1898, page 8.

Dallas Morning News, August 7, 1898, page 24.

Dallas Morning News, August 8, 1898, page 8.

Dallas Morning News, August 9, 1898, page 4.

Dallas Morning News, August 11, 1898, page 3.

Dallas Morning News, August 21, 1898, pages 3 and 24.

Dallas Morning News, August 23, 1898, page 8.

Dallas Morning News, August 27, 1898, page 8.

Dallas Morning News, September 2, 1898, page 8.

Dallas Morning News, September 3, 1898, page 8.

Dallas Daily Times Herald, September 2, 1898, pages 1 and 8.

Dallas Morning News, September 3, 1898, page 8.

Texas State Records

Texas Bureau of Vital Statistics. Death Certificate #31281, [1926]. Mrs. Catherine Stein. Date of death September 1, 1926. Place of death – Dallas County.

United States Records

1900 United States Federal Census

1910 United States Federal Census

1920 United States Federal Census

Online

Ancestry.com, Texas Death Index, 1903-2000.Accessed February 24, 2013.

Ancestry.com. Texas Find A Grave Index, 1761-2012. Accessed February 24, 2013.

Wikipedia, The Free Encyclopedia. Earle Cabell. Wikipedia online. Accessed March 9, 2013.

Chapter 13

Dallas County Records

Dallas County Inquest Record. W. Edwards, Justice of the Peace, Pct. 1, Place 2. November 30, 1904. Deceased - Sol Aronoff. Microfilm # 2030836, Roll #2.1903-1907. page 119.

Books

Cox, O'Byrne Jr. *Sheriffs Dallas County, Texas 1846-1985.* Dallas: Self published, 1985. Pages 52, 53, 54 and 55.

Tise, Sammy. *Texas County Sheriffs.* Albuquerque: Oakwood Printing, 1989. pages 146 and 147.

Worley's *Dallas City Directory. 1903*: 253 South Houston Street, Aronoff, S. grocer, .page 62.

Writers' Program of Work Projects Administration. *City of Dallas. The WPA Dallas Guide and History.* Denton: University of North Texas Press, 1992. Pages 82 and 83.

Newspapers

Dallas Morning News, November 30, 1904, page 11.

Dallas Morning News, December 1, 1904, page 12.

Dallas Morning News, December 3, 1904, page 11.

Dallas Morning News, December 20, 1904, page 14.

Dallas Morning News, December 21, 1904, page 4.

Dallas Morning News, December 22, 1904, page 5.

Dallas Morning News, December 23, 1904, page 3.

Dallas Morning News, December 24, 1904, pages 2 and 3.

Dallas Morning News, December 25, 1904, page 3.

Dallas Morning News, December 30, 1904, pages 5 and 10.

Dallas Daily Times Herald, December 30, 1904, page 2.

Dallas Daily Times Herald, May 12, 1905, page 2.

Dallas Morning News, January 14, 1906, page 24.

Dallas Morning News, August 4, 1907, page 6.

Dallas Morning News, September 23, 1907, page 10.

Dallas Morning News, September 24, 1907, page 14.

Dallas Morning News, September 25, 1907, page 14.

Dallas Morning News, September 27, 1907, page 5.

Dallas Morning News, September 28, 1907, page 16.

Dallas Morning News, September 29, 1907, page 36.

Dallas Morning News, October 2, 1907, page 5.

Dallas Morning News, October 11, 1907, page 14.

Dallas Morning News, October 12, 1907, page 3.

Dallas Morning News, October 13, 1907, page 9.

Dallas Morning News, October 16, 1907, page 14.

Dallas Morning News, November 20, 1907, page 4.

Dallas Morning News, December 17, 1907, page 3.

Waxahachie Enterprise, March 26, 1909.

Dallas Morning News, November 17, 1909, page 3.

Dallas Morning News, November 19, 1909, page 7.

Dallas Daily Times Herald, March 1, 1910, page 1.

Dallas Daily Times Herald, March 4, 1910, page 12.

Dallas Morning News, March 18, 1910, page 16.

Dallas Morning News, March 19, 1910, page 16.

Dallas Morning News, April 10, 1910, page 10.

Dallas Morning News, September 15, 1910, page 3.

Dallas Morning News, February 14, 1911, page 16.

Dallas Morning News, July 13, 1911, page 6.

Dallas Morning News, July 31, 1911, page 7.

Dallas Morning News, March 7, 1912, page 7.

Dallas Morning News, June 27, 1912, page 11.

Dallas Morning News, November 28, 1912, page 2.

Dallas Morning News, November 29, 1912, page 16.

Dallas Morning News, November 30, 1912, page 3.

Dallas Morning News, December 4, 1913, pages 7 and 13.

Fort Worth Star-Telegram, December 17, 1913, page 3.

Dallas Morning News, April, 4, 1916, page 9,

Dallas Morning News, October 26, 1917, page 13.

Dallas Morning News, October 27, 1917, page 11.

Texas State Records

Texas Board of Health, Death Certificate # 8821 [1916] Deceased Arthur Lee Ledbetter, age 54, Date of Death, April 3, 1916. Former Sheriff Dallas County, Texas. Cause of death-accidental. Arthur Lee Ledbetter is buried in Oak Cliff Cemetery, Dallas, Texas.

United States Records

1880 United States Federal Census.

1900 United States Federal Census.

1910 United States Federal Census.

1920 United States Federal Census.

1930 United States Federal Census.

Online

Find A Grave Memorial. Solomon "Sol" Aronoff. Burial Shearith Israel Cemetery, 4626 Dolphin Road, Dallas, Texas. Accessed December 15, 2011.

Ancestry.com. Arthur Lee Ledbetter, Family Overview. Born January 11, 1863. [Died April 3, 1916]. Accessed February 26, 2013.

Texas Death Index, Arthur Lee Ledbetter,1903-2000.Death date April 3, 1916.Texas Death Certificate # 8821 [1916] Accessed February 26, 2013.

Chapter 14

Dallas County Records

Dallas County Inquest Record. Q.D. Corley, Justice of the Peace, Pct. 1, Place 1. March 3, 1910. Deceased- Allen Brooks. Microfilm # 2026983, Roll # 2, 1909-1912, Vol. 1, pages 25 and 26.

Books

Cox, O'Byrne Jr. *Sheriffs Dallas County, Texas 1846-1985*. Dallas: Self Published, 1985. Pages 52, 53, 54 and 55.

Dealey, Ted. *Diaper Days of Dallas*. Nashville: Abingdon Press, 1966. pages 61, 62, 71 and 72.

Tise, Sammy. *Texas County Sheriffs*. Albuquerque: Oakwood Printing, 1989. pages 146 and 147.

Writers' Program of Work Projects Administration. *City of Dallas. The WPA Dallas Guide and History*. Denton: University of North Texas Press, 1992. page 86.

Newspapers

Dallas Morning News, January 19, 1908, page 5.

Dallas Morning News, July 12, 1908, page 1.

Dallas Morning News, July 26, 1908, page 11.

Dallas Daily Times Herald, February 24, 1910, pages 1 and 14.

Dallas Morning News, February 24, 1910, page 2.

Dallas Daily Times Herald, February 25, 1910, pages 1 and 16.

Dallas Morning News, February 25, 1910, page 4..

Dallas Morning News, February 25, 1910, page 2.

Dallas Daily Times Herald, February 26, 1910, page 1.

Dallas Morning News, February 26, 1910, page 3.

Dallas Daily Times Herald, February 27, 1910, page 1.

Dallas Daily Times Herald, February 28, 1910, page 12.

Dallas Morning News, February 28, 1910, page 2.

Dallas Daily Times Herald, March 1, 1910, page 2.

Dallas Morning News, March 1, 1910, page 5.

Dallas Daily Times Herald, March 2, 1910, page 1.

Dallas Morning News, March 2, 1910, page 14.

Dallas Daily Times Herald, March 3, 1910, pages 1 and 2.

Dallas Morning News, March 3, 1910, page 14.

Dallas Daily Times Herald, March 4, 1910, pages 1 and 12.

Dallas Morning News, March 4, 1910, page 2.

Dallas Daily Times Herald, March 5, 1910, pages 1 and 10.

Dallas Daily Times Herald, March 6, 1910, page 2.

Dallas Daily Times Herald, March 7, 1910, pages 1 and 2.

Dallas Daily Times Herald, March 8, 1910, page 7.

Dallas Daily Times Herald, March 10, 1910, page 9.

Dallas Daily Times Herald, March 13, 1910, page 17.

Dallas Morning News, April 1, 1910, page 16.

Dallas Daily Times Herald, April 2, 1910, page 10.

Dallas Morning News, April 3, 1910, page 16.

Dallas Morning News, April 6, 1910, page 16.

Dallas Morning News, July 3, 1910, page 19.

Texas State Records

Texas Death Index, 1903-2000. Deceased – Arthur Lee Ledbetter, Date of Death, 3 April 1916. Death County: Dallas.

Texas Board of Health. Death Certificate # 8821 [1916]. Deceased - Arthur Lee Ledbetter, age 54. Date of death April 3, 1916. Former sheriff of Dallas County, Texas. Cause of death – accidental.

United States Records

1880 United States Federal Census.

1900 United States Federal Census.

1910 United States Federal Census.

Online

Anderson, Brian, Hidden History of Dallas, 1901-1925. 1910: Historical eyesore. Lynching turned downtown centerpiece into disgraceful reminder. Accessed August 29, 2005.

Ancestry.com Overview of Arthur Lee Ledbetter. Accessed February 26, 2013.

Chapter 15

Dallas County Records

Dallas County Inquest Record. Q. D. Corley, Justice of the Peace, Pct. 1, Place 1. October 8, 1909. Deceased – Walter West. Microfilm # 2026883, Roll # 2. 1909 – 1912. Vol. 1, page 43.

Books

Cox, O'Byrne Jr. *Sheriffs Dallas County, Texas. 1846 – 1985.* Dallas: Self-Published, 1985. pages 52, 53, 54 and 55.

Tise, Sammy. *Texas County Sheriffs.* Albuquerque: Oakwood Printing, 1989. Pages 146 and 147.

Newspapers

Dallas Morning News, October 21, 1908, page 14.

Dallas Dispatch, October 22, 1908, page 1.

Dallas Morning News, November 12, 1908, page 4.

Dallas Daily Times Herald, November 12, 1908, page 3.

Dallas Morning News, November 13, 1908, page 14.

Dallas Daily Times Herald, November 13, 1908, page 2.

Dallas Morning News, November 14, 1908, pages 1 and 5.

Dallas Daily Times Herald, November 14, 1908, page 5.

Dallas Morning News, November 15, 1908, page 32.

Dallas Morning News, November 17, 1908, page 4.

Dallas Morning News, November 20, 1908, page 10.

Dallas Morning News, November 22, 1908, page 4.

Dallas Morning News, November 24, 1908, page 4.

Dallas Morning News, November 26, 1908, page 14.

Dallas Morning News, November 28, 1908, page 14.

Dallas Morning News, December 1, 1908, page 4.

Dallas Morning News, December 2, 1908, page 10.

Dallas Morning News, December 3, 1908, page 4.

Dallas Morning News, March 3, 1909, page 4.

Dallas Morning News, June 22, 1909, page 4.

Dallas Morning News, June 23, 1909, pages 3 and 4.

Dallas Morning News, June 25, 1909, page 5.

Dallas Morning News, June 26, 1909, page 4.

Dallas Morning News, October 9, 1909, page 14.

Dallas Morning News, March 24, 1910, page 14.

Dallas Morning News, April 1, 1910, page 16.

Dallas Morning News, April 2, 1910, page 5.

Dallas Morning News, April 5, 1910, page 3.

Dallas Morning News, April 29, 1910, page 4.

Dallas Daily Times Herald, May 12, 1910, pages 1 and 5.

Dallas Morning News, May 13, 1910, page 16.

Dallas Daily Times Herald, May 13, 1910, pages 1 and 6.

Dallas Morning News, May 14, 1910, page 16.

Dallas Morning News, November 26, 1912, page 3.

Texas State Records
Texas Board of Health. Death Certificate # 18972 [1910]. Deceased – Julius Robinson, age 28. Date of death –Hung May 13, 1910. Place of death – Dallas County Jail. "hanged by the neck by law." Place of burial – Paris, Texas.

United States Federal Census

1860 United States Federal Census

1870 United States Federal Census

1880 United States Federal Census

1900 United States Federal Census

1910 United States Federal Census
Online
Ancestry.com. Family Tree of Franklin Wolford. Born – April 15, 1869, Dallas, Texas. Death – November 12, 1908, Dallas, Texas. Accessed March 21, 2013.

Ancestry. Com. Find A Grave Index. 1761 – 2012. Frank F. Wolford. Birth date – April 15, 1869. Death date – November 12, 1908. Burial – Sunnyvale, Dallas County, Texas. Accessed March 21, 2013.

Ancestry.com. U.S. Confederate Soldiers Complied Service Records, 1861-1865. Name Willis L. Woolford, sic. [Wolford]. Enlistment date – 1862. Military Unit – Nineteenth Cavalry [Buford's Regiment]. Accessed March 21, 2013.

Ancestry.com U.S. Federal Census Mortality Schedule, 1850 – 1885. Name – Willis Wolford. White, married, place of birth Kentucky. Estimated birth year – 1829. Cause of death – Diarrhea. Census location – Dallas, Texas. Accessed March 21, 2013.

Ancestry.com. Web. Texas Find A Grave Index, 1761-2012. Name – Willis L. Wolford. Birth date – September 15, 1827. Death date – August 7, 1869. Place of burial – Sunnyvale, Dallas County, Texas. Accessed March 21, 2013.

Chapter 16

Books
Cox, O'Byrne Jr. *Sheriffs Dallas County, Texas 1846 – 1985*. Dallas: Self-Published, 1985. Pages 56, 57, 58, and 59.

Tise, Sammy. *Texas County Sheriffs*. Albuquerque: Oakwood Printing, 1989. pages 146 and 147.

Newspapers
Dallas Morning News, December 27, 1896, page 18.

Dallas Daily Times Herald, March 1, 1897, page 8.

Dallas Daily Times Herald, June 12, 1898, page 2.

Dallas Morning News, May 5, 1911, page 6.

Dallas Morning News, May 6, 1911, page 11.

Dallas Morning News, May 8, 1911, page 16.

Dallas Morning News, June 22, 1911, page 7.

Dallas Morning News, July 18, 1911, page 16.

Dallas Morning News, October 1, 1911, page 28.

Dallas Morning News, October 3, 1911, page 16.

Dallas Morning News, December 4, 1911, page 3.

Dallas Morning News, December 6, 1911, page 5.

Dallas Morning News, December 7, 1911, page 9.

Dallas Morning News, December 9, 1911, page 5.

Dallas Morning News, December 12, 1911, page 5.

Dallas Morning News, December 14, 1911, page 10.

Dallas Morning News, November 7, 1912, page 6.

Dallas Dispatch, November 7, 1912, page 6.

Dallas Dispatch, November 25, 1912, page 1.

Dallas Morning News, November 26, 1912, page 3.

Dallas Morning News, November 30, 1912, page 4.

Dallas Dispatch, November 30, 1912, page 1.

Dallas Morning News, January 10, 1913, page 5.

Dallas Daily Times Herald, January 10, 1913, pages 1 and 6.

Dallas Dispatch, January 10, 1913, pages 1 and 2.

Dallas Daily Times Herald, January 11, 1913, page 6.

Dallas Morning News, February 23, 1934, page 1.

Dallas Morning News, September 8, 1951, pages 4 and 7.

Texas State Records

Texas State Board of Health. Standard Certificate of Death. # 10346 [1911]. Deceased – Otto Kalkhoff, white male, age 60, Married. Birthplace – Germany. Occupation – Machinist. Date of Death – May 7, 1911. Cause of Death – Fracture of skull and injury to brain. Place of Death- Dallas, Dallas County, Texas. Place of Burial – Oakwood Cemetery, Austin, Travis County, Texas.

Texas State Board of Health. Standard Certificate of Death # 831 [1913]. Deceased – John Roberson, Negro male, age 32. Married. Birthplace – Texas. Cause of Death – Hanged by Sheriff. Place of Death – Dallas, Dallas County, Texas. Place of Burial – Hempstead, Texas.

State of Texas Penitentiary Records. Convict Record Ledger 1849 – 1954. Convict # 33384, Will Flowers, age 22, 6'1", 166 pounds, Born in Texas, Charge – Murder in 1st Degree. Sentence – Life in Prison. Received at Huntsville Prison – June 9, 1912. Expiration of Sentence – at death. REMARKS – ESCAPED APRIL 4, 1923.

United States Records

1880 United States Federal Census

1900 United States Federal Census

1910 United States Federal Census

Online

Ancestry.com. Kalkhoff Family Tree. Christoph Friedrich Eduard [Otto] Kalkhoff. Born – Feb. 6, 1851 in Germany. Arrival New York, United States on January 15, 1870, at age 18. Married to Emily Walke on January 22, 1879, in Alton, Madison, Illnois, USA. Residence in 1900 - Austin, Texas. Residence in 1910 – Dallas, Texas. Murdered in Dallas, Texas. Died May 7, 1911, at age 60. Buried – Oakwood Cemetery, Austin, Travis County, Texas. Accessed March 21, 2013.

Ancestry.com New York Passenger Lists, 1820 -1957. Name - Otto Kalkhoff. Arrival Date – January 15, 1870. Birth year – 1851. Age 19. Male. Port of Departure – Hamburg, Germany. Port of Arrival – New York, New York. Ship Name – John Bertram. Accessed – March 21, 2013.

Ancestry.com. U.S. City Directories, 1821 1989 {Beta]. Name – Otto Kalkhoff. Residence in 1910, 891 Main Street, Dallas, Texas. Occupation – Pressman. Dallas City Directory, 1910. Accessed – March 21, 2013.

Ancestry.com. U.S. City Directories, 1821 – 1989 [Beta]. Name – Otto Kalkhoff. Residence in 1911, 1722 Chestnut, Dallas, Texas. Occupation – Machine Operator. Dallas City Directory, 1911. Accessed March 21, 2013.

Ancestry.com. Texas Death Index, 1903 – 2000. Name – Otto Kalkhoff, Death Date – May 7, 1911. Death County – Dallas. Death Certificate # 10346, [1911]. Accessed June 17, 2011.

Chapter 17

Dallas County Records

Dallas County Inquest Records. S.L. Stewart, Justice of the Peace and acting coroner. Deceased Naomi Stanton. Microfilm # 2026983, Roll # 2. 1912-1914. Vol. 2, page 25. Cause of death is gunshot wounds. [The date of death in the Inquest record is incorrectly recorded as December 1, 1912. THE CORRECT DATE OF DEATH FOR NAOMI STANTON IS DECEMBER 3, 1912.]

Books

Cox, O'Byrne Jr. *Sheriffs Dallas County, Texas 1846 – 1985.* Dallas: Self-Published, 1985. pages 56 and 57.

Tise, Sammy. *Texas County Sheriffs.* Albuquerque: Oakwood Printing, 1989. Pages 146 and 147.

Newspapers

Dallas Morning News, December 4, 1912, page 4.

Dallas Morning News, December 17, 1912, page 18.

Dallas Morning News, December 18, 1912, page 5.

Dallas Dispatch, January 10, 1913, pages 1 and 2.

Dallas Morning News, May 29, 1913. Page 6.

Dallas Morning News, July 16, 1913, page 18.

Dallas Daily Times Herald, July 29, 1913, page 1.

Dallas Morning News, July 30, 1913, page 18.

Dallas Daily Times Herald, July 31, 1913, pages 1 and 4.

Dallas Morning News, August 1, 1913, page 18.

Dallas Daily Times Herald, August 1, 1913, page 1.

Dallas Morning News, August 2, 1913, pages 2 and 18.

Dallas Morning News, February 23, 1924, page 1.

Dallas Morning News, September 8, 1951, pages 4 and 7.

Texas State Records

Texas Board of Health. Death Certificate # 27048 [1912]. Deceased – Naomi Stanton, age 26. Date of Death – December 3, 1912. Negro female, Cause of death – gunshot.

S.L. Stewart, J.P. Burial – Terrell, Texas. People's Undertaking Company.

Texas Board of Health. Death Certificate # 17059 [1913]. Deceased – Floyd Stanton, male, colored, age at death 38. Date of Death – August 1, 1913. Place of Death – Dallas County Jail. Cause of Death – Hanged by the neck until dead. Burial – Woodland Cemetery, Dallas, Texas. Peoples Undertaking Company.

United States Records
1910 United States Federal Census

Chapter 18

Books

Cox, O'Byrne Jr. *Sheriffs Dallas County, Texas 1846-1985*. Dallas: Self-Published, 1985. pages 56 and 57.

Mesquite Historical & Genealogical Society. *Mesquite City Cemetery*, Mesquite: Self-Published, 1995. Page 7.

Tise, Sammy. *Texas County Sheriffs*. Albuquerque: Oakwood Printing, 1989. pages 146 and 147.

Worley, John F. *Directory of Greater Dallas, Texas, 1910*. Dallas, Texas: John F. Worley Printing Company. 1910. page 235.

Newspapers

Dallas Morning News, September 11, 1910, page 40.

Dallas Daily Times Herald, September 11, 1910, page 1.

Fort Worth Record, September 11, 1910, page 7.

Dallas Morning News, September 12, page 12.

Dallas Daily Tines Herald, September 12,, 1910, pages 1 and 12.

Dallas Morning News, September 13, 1910, page 14.

Dallas Daily Times Herald, September 13, 1910, pages 3 and 14.

Fort Worth Record, September 14, 1910, page 3.

Mesquite Texas Mesquiter, September 16, 1910, pages 1 and 8.

Dallas Morning News, September 21, 1910, page 5.

Dallas Morning News, September 27, 1910, page 14.

Dallas Morning News, April 30, 1911, page 12.

Dallas Morning News, August 27, 1912, page 14.

Dallas Dispatch, January 10, 1913, pages 1 and 2.

Dallas Morning News, February 6, 1913, page 4.

Dallas Morning News, February 9, 1913, page 5.

Dallas Morning News, February 28, 1913, page 3.

Dallas Daily Times Herald, October 16, 1913, page 2.

Dallas Morning News, October 19, 1913, page 7.

Dallas Morning News, October 23, 1913, page 28.

Dallas Morning News, November 6, 1913, pages 2 and 3.

Dallas Morning News, December 10, 1913, page 13.

Dallas Morning News, December 12, 1913, page 20.

Dallas Morning News, December 19, 1913, page 18.

Dallas Daily Times Herald, December 19, 1913, pages 1 and 7.

Dallas Morning News, December 20, 1913, page 18.

Dallas Morning News, December 31, 1913, page 3.

Dallas Morning News, February 20, 1914, pages 7 and 18.

Dallas Morning News, March 14, 1914, page 20.

Dallas Morning News, March 25, 1914, pages 3 and 4.

Dallas Morning News, September 8, 1951, pages 4 and 7.

State of Texas Records

Texas Board of Health. Death Certificate #1566 [1910]. Deceased – Thomas H. Bennett, age 32, Male, White, Single, Occupation – Peace Officer, T. & P. Date of Death – September 11, 1910. Cause of Death – Gunshot wound. Burial – Mesquite City Cemetery, Mesquite, Dallas County, Texas.

Texas Board of Health. Death Certificate #24953 [1913]. Deceased – Ed Long, age 34, male, negro, single. Occupation – None listed. Date of Death – December 19, 1913. Cause of Death – "Legally Hanged." Burial by People's Undertaking Company. Location – unreadable on Death Certificate.

Court of Criminal Appeals of Texas. Cause #2608. Ed Christian vs. The State. November 5, 1913, Decided. Appeal from a conviction of murder in the first degree, penalty, death. The opinion states the case. DISPOSITION: Affirmed.

Texas State Convict Record Ledger. Convict #35808, Ed Christian, age 33,complextion black, eyes black, hair black. Occupation farmer. Case Affirmed November 5, 1913. Commuted to life February 8, 1914. Charge Murder 1st Degree. Received at Huntsville Penitentiary on March 14, 1914. Remarks - Died September 27, 1920.

United States Records

1900 United States Federal Census

1910 United States Federal Census

Online

Ancestry.com. Wheeler, Bennett, Howell, Jones and cousins. Thomas Henry Bennett, born December 18, 1878, in Dallas, Texas, USA. Died September 11, 1910, Mesquite, Dallas, Texas, USA. No Spouse. Parents - John Calhoun Bennett, 1847 – 1932. Arabelle Leach, 1850 – 1925. Accessed May 21, 2012.

Ancestry.com. United States, Officer Down Memorials, 1791 -2009. Name – Special Officer Thomas Henry Bennett. Department – Texas and Pacific Railroad Police Department. Date of Incident – September 10, 1910. Date of Death [EOW – End of Watch] September 11, 1910. Age 32, Time of duty – about 2 months. Cause of death. Gunfire. Weapon – Handgun. Suspect – Sentenced to death. Accessed – May 21, 2012.

Chapter 19

Books

Cox, O'Byrne Jr. *Sheriffs Dallas County, Texas 1846 -1985*. Dallas: Self-Published, 1985. pages 60 and 61.

Tise, Sammy. *Texas County Sheriffs*. Albuquerque: Oakwood Printing, 1989. pages 146 and 147.

Newspapers

Dallas Daily Times Herald, July 26, 1917, page 14.

Dallas Dispatch, June 26, 1917, pages 1 and 2.

Dallas Dispatch, June 27, 1917, pages 1 and 2.

Dallas Daily Times Herald, June 28, 1917, page 1.

Dallas Morning News, June 28, 1917, page 16.

Dallas Daily Times Herald, June 29, 1917, page 1.

Dallas Daily Times Herald, July 8, 1917, page 1.

Dallas Daily Times Herald, July 9, 1917, page 3.

Dallas Dispatch, July 9, 1917, pages 1 and 2.

Dallas Daily Times Herald, July 10, 1917, page 1.

Dallas Dispatch, July 10, 1917, pages 1 and 2.

Dallas Daily Times Herald, July 12, 1917, pages 1 and 2.

Dallas Daily Times Herald, July 13, 1917, pages 1 and 2.

Dallas Dispatch, July 13, 1917, pages 1 and 6.

Dallas Daily Times Herald, July 14, 1917, page 1.

Dallas Morning News, July 14, 1917, page 7 and 14.

Dallas Dispatch, July 14, 1917, pages 1 and 4.

Dallas Morning News, July 15, 1917, page 12.

Dallas Daily Times Herald, July 16, 1917, pages 1 and 2.

Dallas Daily Times Herald, July 17, 1917, page 1.

Dallas Morning News, July 17, 1917, page 16.

Dallas Daily Times Herald, July 18, 1917, page 1.

Dallas Daily Times Herald, July 19, 1917, pages 1 and 9.

Dallas Daily Times Herald, July 20, 1917, pages 1 and 2.

Dallas Morning News, July 20, 1917, page 5.

Dallas Daily Times Herald, July 21, 1917, page 1.

Dallas Dispatch, July 21, 1917, pages 1 and 2.

Dallas Morning News, July 28, 1917, page 5.

Dallas Morning News, August 4, 1917, page 13.

Dallas Morning News, August 11, 1917, page 14.

Dallas Morning News, August 18, 1917, page 13.

Dallas Morning News, August 22, 1917, page 5.

Dallas Morning News, August 23, 1917, page 16.

Dallas Morning News, August 24, 1917, pages 6 and 9.

Dallas Morning News, September 2, 1917, page 9.

Dallas Morning News, September 23, 1917, page 9.

Dallas Morning News, September 27, 1917, page 6 and 9.

Dallas Morning News, December 2, 1917, page 14.

Dallas Morning News, December 8, 1917, page 3.

Dallas Morning News, December 30, 1917, page 5.

Dallas Morning News, January 29, 1918, page 8.

Dallas Morning News, January 31, 1918, page 5.

Dallas Morning News, February 14, 1918, page 3.

Dallas Morning News, March 7, 1918, page 13.

Dallas Morning News, March 26, 1918, page 16.

Dallas Morning News, April 4, 1918, pages 3 and 5.

Dallas Morning News, April 9, 1918, page 9 and 18.

Dallas Morning News, May 2, 1918, page 16.

Dallas Morning News, May 8, 1918, page 3.

Dallas Morning News, May 10, 1918, page 3.

Dallas Morning News, May 11, 1918, page 3.

Dallas Morning News, May 21, 1918, page 7 and 9.

Dallas Morning News, May 22, 1918, page 7.

Dallas Morning News, May 23, 1918, pages 3 and 4.

Dallas Daily Times Herald, May 24, 1918, pages 1 and 5.

Dallas Morning News, May 24, 1918, pages 1, 3 and 5.

Dallas Morning News, May 25, 1918, page 7.

Dallas Morning News, June 12, 1918, page 4.

Dallas Daily Times Herald, July 18, 1918, page 7.

Dallas Morning News, September 11, 1919, page 11.

Dallas Morning News, October 19, 1919, page 4.

Dallas Morning News, August 11, 1926, page 13.

Dallas Morning News, August 12, 1926, page 3.

Dallas Morning News, August 15, 1926, page 14.

Dallas Morning News, August 17, 1926, page 9.

Dallas Morning News, December 24, 1926, page 9.

Dallas Morning News, December 29, 1926, page 1.

Dallas Morning News, March 10, 1927, page 5.

Texas State Records

Texas Board of Health. Death Certificate # 20128 [1918]. Deceased – Walter Robert Stevenson, age 34. Born November 16, 1883. Occupation - City Water Works. Date of death May 24, 1918. Cause of death "by Hanging, [Legal]." Burial, Grove Hill Cemetery, Dallas, Texas. [tombstone – yes].

Texas Board of Health. Death Certificate # 20127 [1918]. Leonard A. Dodd, age 30. Born October 3, 1887. Occupation Painter. Date of death May 24, 1918. Cause of death "Hanging by legal execution." Burial Grove Hill Cemetery, Dallas, Texas. [no tombstone].

United States Records

1910 United States Federal Census.

Chapter 20

Books

Collin County, *Texas Cemetery Inscriptions Volume I*. Complied by Mrs. Alice Pitts, Mrs. Wanda O'Roark and Mrs. Doris Posey. POP Publications, 1975: The Manney Company, Fort Worth, Texas. page 632.

Cox, O'Byrne Jr. *Sheriffs Dallas County, Texas 1846 – 1985*. Dallas: Self-published, 1985. Pages 60 and 61.

Tise, Sammy. *Texas County Sheriffs*. Albuquerque: Oakwood Printing, 1989. Pages 146 and 147.

Newspapers

Dallas Daily Times Herald, January 17, 1918, pages 1 and 3.

Dallas Morning News, July 18, 1918, page 16.

Dallas Morning News, July 19, 1918, page 14.

Dallas Morning News, July 21, 1918, page 3.

Dallas Morning News, July 22, 1918, page 7.

Dallas Daily Times Herald, July 22, 1918, pages 1 and 7.

Dallas Morning News, July 23, 1918, page 16.

Dallas Daily Times Herald, July 23, 1918, page 1.

Dallas Daily Times Herald, July 24, 1918, page 4.

Dallas Daily Times Herald, July 25, 1918, page 1.

Dallas Morning News, July 26, 1918, page 8.

Dallas Morning News, August 30, 1918, page 7.

Dallas Daily Times Herald, August 30, 1918, page 1.

Dallas Morning News, August 31, 1918, page 7.

United States Records

1910 United States Federal Census

Online

Bartek, Charlotte. Wylie Cemetery, Wylie, Collin County, Texas. January 2010. Accessed October 25, 2011.

Chapter 21

Books

Cox, O'Byrne Jr. *Sheriffs Dallas County, Texas 1846 – 1985*. Dallas: Self-published, 1985. pages 65 and 66.

Tise, Sammy. *Texas County Sheriffs*. Albuquerque: Oakwood Printing, 1989. Pages 146 and 147.

Newspapers

Galveston Daily News, April 3, 1912, page 7.

Galveston Daily News, April 11, 1912, page 9.

Dallas Daily Times Herald, May 28, 1920, page 1.

Dallas Daily Times Herald, May 29, 1920, page 1.

Dallas Morning News, May 30, 1920, page 6.

Dallas Morning News, June 1, 1920, page 6.

Dallas Morning News, June 4, 1920, page 11.

Dallas Daily Times Herald, June 5, 1920, page 1.

Dallas Morning News, June 5, 1920, page 6.

Dallas Daily Times Herald, June 8, 1920, pages 1 and 14.

Dallas Morning News, July 9, 1920, page 7.

Dallas Daily Times Herald, July 9, 1920, pages 1 and 18.

Dallas Morning News, July 10, 1920, page 16.

Dallas Morning News, July 11, 1920, page 2.

Galveston Daily News, July 11, 1920, page 15.

Dallas Morning News, July 21, 1920, page 12.

Galveston Daily News, August 12, 1920, page 5.

Galveston Daily News, January 23, 1921, page 1.

Texas State Records

Texas State Board of Health, Bureau of Vital Statistics. Death Certificate #24720 [1921]. Deceased – MRS. HATTIE A. CARPENTER. Female, white, widowed, age 57. Born July 24, 1864 in Alabama. Residence – Dallas Trinity Heights, Dallas County, Texas. Father - A. J. Busby. Mother – Adaline McPherson. Date of death – September 19, 1921. Burial – Five Mile Cemetery, Dallas County, Texas.

Texas State Board of Health, Bureau of Vital Statistics. Death Certificate # 22000 [1920]. Deceased- GREEN HUNTER, male, colored, single, age 26, born June 7, 1894 in Bryan, Texas. Residence – County Jail. Father Sam Hunter, Mother Lena Hunter. Date of death – July 9, 1920. Cause of death –" Legal execution by hanging." Place of burial – Bryan, Texas. Undertaker – E. J. Crawford Undertaking Company.

Texas State Prison Records, Convict Record Ledger 1849 – 1954. "B" Series # 32061 - # 37000, Dates covered – 1911 – 1915.Convict # 33052, BEN PERRY, 23 years old, 5'11," Bro. Bro. Black, farmer, born in Texas. Offense – Rape by force, his plea – not guilty. Trial by jury, Convicted – April 3, 1912, at Bryan, Brazos County, Texas. Sentenced to life in the State Penitentiary. Expiration of sentence – "at Death." [After Green Hunter admitted he was the guilty party, BEN PERRY WAS PARDONED ON AUGUST 23, 1920.

United States Census

1900 United States Federal Census

1910 United States Federal Census

1920 United States Federal Census

Online

Ancestry.com Hattie Carpenter, born July 1864 in Alabama. Residence J.P. Precinct # 7, West Dallas, voting Precinct Dallas, Texas, Accessed April 13, 2013.

Ancestry.com. U.S. Confederate Pensions, 1884 – 1988. Mrs. Hattie Carpenter, application date Oct. 24, 1916. Application Place: Dallas. Birth year: abt. 1865. Birth Place: St. Plain, De Kalb, Alabama. Spouse: John Robert Carpenter. Marriage place: Dallas, Texas. Spouse death date: May 10, 1902. Pension file number 04692. Application type: Widow. Accessed April 13, 2013.

Ancestry.com. Texas Death Index, 1903 – 2000. Hattie A. Carpenter. Death date: September 19, 1921. Death County: Dallas. Certificate # 24720. Accessed April 13, 2013.

Ancestry.com. Web: Texas, Find A Grave Index, 1761 – 2012. Name: Hattie Busby Carpenter. Birth date: 1864. Age at death: 57. Death date: 1921. Burial place: Dallas, Dallas County, Texas, USA. Accessed April 13, 2013.

Chapter 22

Dallas County Records

Dallas County Inquest Record. R. H. Anderson, Justice of the Peace, Precinct #1, Place #1. July 5, 1920. Deceased – Isaac T. Williams. Microfilm # 2026984, Roll #3, 1919 – 1921, Vol. 4, page 106.

Books

Cox, O'Byrne Jr. *Sheriffs Dallas County, Texas 1846 – 1985*. Dallas: Self-published, 1985. pages 65 and 66.

Tise, Sammy. *Texas County Sheriffs*. Albuquerque: Oakwood Printing, 1989. pages 146 and 147.

Newspapers

Dallas Daily Times Herald, July 5, 1920, pages 1 and 2.

Dallas Daily Times Herald, July 6, 1920, page 1.

Dallas Morning News, July 6, 1920, page 11.

Dallas Daily Times Herald, July 7, 1920.

Dallas Daily Times Herald, July 8, 1920, page 1.

Dallas Daily Times Herald, July 9, 1920, pages 1 and 5.

Dallas Daily Times Herald, July 10, 1920, pages 1 and 9.

Dallas Morning News, July 10, 1920, page 9.

Galveston Daily News, July 11, 1920, page 15.

Dallas Morning News, July 15, 1920, page 16.

Dallas Morning News, July 16, 1920, page 8.

Dallas Morning News, July 17, 1920, page 16.

Dallas Morning News, August 23, 1920, page 5.

Dallas Morning News, August 27, 1920, page 13.

Dallas Daily Times Herald, August 27, 1920, pages 1 and 18.

Dallas Morning News, August 28, 1920, page 4.

Dallas Morning News, September 1, 1920, page 10.

Texas State Records

Texas Board of Health. Death Certificate # 22026 [1920]. Deceased – Isaac T. Williams, white male, age 56, married. Occupation – Oil Station Agent. Born - March 9, 1864 in Tennessee. Date of death – July 5, 1920. Cause of death – "Skull split by sharp instrument – Homicide." Held Inquest July 5, 1920. Burial – Oakland Cemetery, Dallas, Dallas County, Texas.

Texas Board of Health. Death Certificate # 26075 [1920]. Deceased – Fred Douglas, colored male, single, age 22. Occupation – Laborer. Born January 31, 1898 in Marlin, Texas. Date of death – August 27, 1920. Cause of death – "Legally Hanged." Place of death – Dallas, Dallas County, Texas. Burial – Mt. Auburn Cemetery, Dallas, Texas.

United States Records

1900 United States Federal Census

1910 United States Federal Census

1920 United States Federal Census

Online

Ancestry.com Texas Death Index, 1903 -2000, Name 0 Isaac T. Williams, Death date – July 5, 1920. Death County – Dallas. Certificate # 22026. Accessed October 25, 2011.
Ancestry.com Texas Death Index, 1903 – 2000. Name Fred Douglas. Death date – August 27, 1920. Death County – Dallas. Certificate # 26075. Accessed October 25, 2011.

Chapter 23

Dallas County Records

Dallas County District Court Records. 14th District Court Minutes. Case #3611. State of Texas v. Jim Blake. Microfilm #1993380. Roll #4, 1875 – 1876. October 23, 1876. Vol. H-2, page 606.

Dallas County District Court Records. 14th District Court Minutes. Case # 3611. State of Texas v. Jim Blake. Microfilm # 1993381. Roll 5, 1877. September 7, 1877. Vol. J, page 439.

Books

Butterfield, F. E. and Rundlett, C. M. *Directory of the City of Dallas. For the Year 1875.* page 119.

Carlisle, Willie Flowers. *The Dallas Pioneer Park Cemetery. "The Old Cemetery."* Dallas: Williams Printery, 1948,. page 14. Reprinted 1994, James Butler Bonham Chapter, Daughters of the Republic of Texas.

Cox, O'Byrne Jr. *Sheriffs Dallas County, Texas 1846 -1985.* Dallas: Self-published, 1985.

pages 32 and 33.

Lewis Publishing Company. *Memorial and Biographical History of Dallas County, Texas. Biographical Sketch of William M. Moon*. Chicago: 1892. pages 953, 954 and 955.

Texas Election Records. Register of Elected and Appointed State and County Officials. 1878 -1880. W. M. Moon, Elected sheriff of Dallas County, November 1878.

Tise, Sammy. *Texas County Sheriffs*. Albuquerque: Oakwood Printing, 1989. pages 146 and 147.

Newspapers

Galveston Daily News, August 22, 1876, page 1.

Galveston Daily News, August 25, 1876, pages 1 and 2.

Dallas Weekly Herald, August 26, 1876, page 3.

Dallas Daily Times Herald, March 18, 1895, page 6.

United States Records

1860 United States Federal Census

1870 United States Federal Census

1880 United States Federal Census

Online

Find A Grave Memorial. Marion M. Moon, 1830 – 1895. "He Was A Famous Sheriff." Born March 18, 1830. Died March 16, 1895. Dallas, Dallas County, Texas. Burial – Pioneer Cemetery, Dallas, Texas. Accessed December 16, 2011.

Chapter 24

Books

Lewis Publishing Company. *Memorial and Biographical History of Dallas County, Texas*. Chicago: 1892.pages 607, 798. 944 and 945.

Cox, O'Byrne Jr. *Sheriffs Dallas County, Texas 1846 – 1985*. Dallas: Self-published, 1985. pages 41, 42 and 43.

Tise, Sammy. *Texas County Sheriffs*. Albuquerque: Oakwood Printing, 1989. pages 146 and 147.

Newspapers

Dallas Morning News, May 25, 1892, page 1.

Dallas Daily Times Herald, May 25, 1892, pages 1 and 5.

Dallas Morning News, May 26, 1892, page 10.

Dallas Morning News, July 5, 1892, page 10.

Dallas Daily Times Herald, July 28, 1893, pages 1 and 2.

Dallas Morning News, February 22, 1946, page 9.

Dallas Daily Times Herald, February 22, 1946, page 13.

State of Texas Records

Texas State Board of Health. Death Certificate # 7042 [1946]. Deceased – William Henry Lewis, white, male, age 94. Born – March 11, 1851, in Georgia. Occupation – Retired

Real Estate. Date of death – February 21, 1946, in Dallas, Dallas County, Texas. Cause of death – Congestive Heart Failure. Place of burial – Oakland Cemetery, Dallas, Texas.

Texas State Board of Health. Death Certificate # 38637 [1945]. Deceased – Mrs. Julia Mister Lewis, white, female, age 73. Born – October 12, 1871, in Granada, Mississippi. Occupation – Housewife. Date of death – September 22, 1945, in Dallas, Dallas County, Texas. Cause of death – Coronary Occlusion. Place of burial – Oakland Cemetery, Dallas, Texas.

Texas State Records

Texas State Election Records 1886 – 1888, page 152. Election Returns, November 2, 1886. Dallas County, Henry Lewis elected Sheriff.

Texas State Election Records 1888 – 1889, page 239. Election Returns, November 6, 1888. Dallas County, W. H. Lewis elected Sheriff.

Texas State Election Records 1889 – 1891, page 152. Election Returns, November 4, 1890. Dallas County, W. H. Lewis elected Sheriff.

United States Records

1900 United States Federal Census

1930 United States Federal Census

1940 United States Federal Census

Online

Officer Down Memorial Page. www.odmp.org Officer Cassee Odorous "C.O." Brewer. Age 42, shot and killed in the line of duty on May 24, 1892. Accessed February 18, 2013. Ancestry.com. District Judges of Dallas, 1846 – 1892. Transcribed by Dorman Holub. Accessed February 18, 2013.

Ancestry.com. Texas Death Index, 1903 – 2000. Name – William Henry Lewis. Death date – February 23, 1946. Death County – Dallas. Death Certificate # 7042. Accessed February 18, 2013.

Ancestry.com. Texas Death Index, 1903 – 2000. Name – Julia Mister Lewis. Death date – September 22, 1945. Death County – Dallas. Death Certificate # 38637. Accessed February 18, 2013.

Ancestry.com. Texas, Find A Grave Index, 1761 -2012. Name – William Henry Lewis. Birth date – March 11, 1851. Age at death – 94. Death date – February 21, 1846. Burial Place – Dallas, Dallas County, Texas USA. Accessed February 18, 2013.

Chapter 25, part 1. Sheriff Dan Harston

Books

Cox, O'Byrne Jr. *Sheriffs Dallas County, Texas 1846 – 1985.* Dallas: Self-published, 1985. page 65 and 66.

Tise, Sammy. *Texas County Sheriffs.* Albuquerque: Oakwood Printing, 1989. Pages p46 and 147.

Newspapers

Dallas Morning News, November 1, 1936, page 1.

Dallas Daily Times Herald, November 1, 1936, pages 1 and 12.

Dallas Daily Times Herald, November 2, 1936, page 14.

Dallas Morning News, November 2, 1936, page 1.

Dallas Morning News, November 3, 1936, page 2.

Dallas Morning News, November 3, 1936, page 6.

Texas State Records

Texas Board of Health. Death Certificate #49026 [1936]. Deceased – Dan S. Harston, white male, age 60, married. Date of birth – April 8, 1876. Place of birth – Kentucky. Date of death – October 31, 1936. County of death – Dallas. Cause of death – cancer. Burial – Hillcrest Memorial Park and Cemetery. Dallas, Texas.

United States Records

1880 United States Federal Census

1900 United States Federal Census

1910 United States Federal Census

1920 United States Federal Census

1930 United States Federal Census

Online

Ancestry. Com. Moore Family Tree. Daniel Simeon Harston. Birth – April 8, 1876. Allen, Kentucky. Death – October 31, 1936. Dallas, Dallas, Texas. Parents: John Loammi Harston 1842 -1918 and Anna Mumford Stovall, 1854 – 1899. Accessed April 14, 2012.

Ancestry.com. Texas Death Index, 1903 – 2000. Name: Dan B. Harston. Death date: October 31, 1936. Death County: Dallas.. Death Certificate # 49026 [1936]. Accessed April 14, 2012.

Ancestry.com. U.S. City Directories [Beta]. Name: Daniel Harston. Residence year: 1913. Street Address: Grand Prairie, Tex. I . Residence place: Dallas, Texas. Occupation: Deputy Sheriff. Publication Title: Dallas, Texas, City Directory, 1913. Accessed April 14, 2012.

Ancestry.com. U.S. City Directories [Beta]. Name: Daniel S. Harston. Residence year: 1915. Residence place: Dallas, Texas. Publication Title: Dallas, Texas, City Directory, 1915. Accessed April 14, 2012.

Ancestry.com. World War I Draft Registration Cards, 1917 -1918. Name: Daniel Simeon Harston. County: Dallas. State: Texas. Birth Date: April 9, 1876. Race: White. FHL Roll Number: 1953184. Accessed April 14, 2012.

Find A Grave Memorial. Daniel Sydney Harston. Birth: April 8, 1876, Kentucky, USA. Death: October 31, 1936, Dallas, Dallas County, Texas USA. Sheriff of Dallas County, 1918 – 1924. Burial: Sparkman Hillcrest Memorial Park, Dallas, Dallas County, Texas, USA. Accessed April 14, 2012.

Chapter 25, part 2.
Attempt to lynch Robert Grigsby on August 31, 1919

Master Thesis

Turner, William Douglas Jr. *The Dallas Express As A Forum On Lynching, 1919 – 1921*. A Thesis Presented to the Graduate Faculty of The School of Humanities and Sciences of Southern Methodist University. Partial Fulfillment of the Requirements for the degree of Master of Arts with a Major in History. 1974. Pages 90, 91 and 93.

Newspapers

Dallas Daily Times Herald, September 1, 1919, pages 1 and 6.

Dallas Morning News, September 1, 1919, page 1.

Dallas Daily Times Herald, September 4, 1919, page 1.

Dallas Morning News, September 5, 1919, page 16.

Dallas Daily Times Herald, September 9, 1919, page 1.

Dallas Morning News, September 10, 1919, page 3.

Dallas Daily Times Herald, September 16, 1919, page 1.

Dallas Morning News, September 17, 1919, page 10.

Texas State Records

Texas State Prison Ledger: Convict #44058, Robert Grigsby, black male, age 16, 5'6", 136 #, Charge: Assault with intent to rape, two counts. Sentence: 99 years and 99 years, total – 198 years. County: Dallas, Residence: Wilmer, Texas. Plead : Guilty, sentence from October 5, 1919. Sentence ends: September 16, 2117. COMMENTS: DIED JANUARY 24, 1933. [Died in prison.] NO Death Certificate was found for Robert Grigsby.

United States Records

1920 United States Federal Census

Chapter 25, part 3. Attempt to lynch David Bunn on October 7, 1921

Newspapers

Dallas Daily Times Herald, October 6, 1921, page 24.

Dallas Morning News, October 7, 1921, pages 1 and 8.

Dallas Daily Times Herald, October 7, 1921, pages 1 and 5.

Dallas Morning News, October 8, 1921, pages 1 and 2.

Dallas Morning News, October 8, 1921, page 3.

Dallas Morning News, October 10, 1921, page 2.

Dallas Daily Times Herald, October 11, 1921, page 1.

Dallas Morning News, October 12, 1921, page 9.

Texas State Records

Texas Board of Health. Death Certificate #29112. Name: Dave Bunn. Negro, male, age 21, married. Date of Birth: November 20, 1899. Place of Birth: Texas. Occupation: Laborer. Date of death: October 11, 1921. Cause of death: "Affects of Gunshot wound in hand of officers." Undertaker: People's Undertaking Company. Burial: Trinity Cemetery, Fort Worth.

United States Records

1900 United States Federal Census

1910 United States Federal Census

1920 United States Federal Census

Online

Ancestry.com. Texas Death Index, 1903 – 2000. Name: Dave Bunn. Death date: October 11, 1921. Death County: Tarrant. Death Certificate #29112.

Chapter 25, part 4. Attempt to lynch Frank Fennell on June 15, 1924

Newspapers

Garland News, May 2, 1924, page 3.

Dallas Morning News, June 15, 1924, page 2.

Dallas Morning News, June 16, 1924, page 9.

Dallas Morning News, June 18, 1924, page 13.

Garland News, June 20, 1924, page 1.

Garland News, June 27, 1924, page 8.

Garland News, July 11, 1924, page 1.

Dallas Morning News, December 4, 1924, page 22.

Texas State Records

Texas State Prison Ledger. Convict #51986, Frank Fennell. Age 43, 5'8," 162#, Black male, Bro and gray. No Church. Shoe size – 9. Born – 1881 in Texas. Occupation – farmer. Convictions – July 5, 1924, December 3, 1924 and December 20, 1924. Offense – Murder. Sentence 5 to life. County – Dallas. Residence – Garland. Plead – Not guilty. Received at Ramsey Unit January 6, 1925. Remarks: Cond. Pardon on April 13, 1939.

United States Records

1920 Untied States Federal Census

1930 United States Federal Census

Online

Find A Grave Memorial. Jack Kendall. Birth 1892. Death 1924. Burial: Garland Memorial Park, Garland, Dallas County, Texas, USA. Accessed April 13, 2012.

Chapter 26

Books

Cox. O'Byrne Jr. *Sheriffs Dallas County, Texas 1846 – 1985*. Dallas: Self-published, 1985, pages 69 and 70..

Marquart, James W. Ekland-Olson, Sheldon and Sorensen, Jonathan R. *The Rope, The Chair, and The Needle: Capital Punishment in Texas 1923 – 1990*. Austin: University of Texas Press. page 201.

Tise, Sammy. *Texas County Sheriffs*. Albuquerque: Oakwood Printing, 1989. pages 146 and 147.

Newspapers

Dallas Morning News, April 13, 1925, page 1.

Dallas Morning News, April 14, 1925, page 13.

Dallas Morning News, April 15, 1925, page 21.

Dallas Morning News, April 27, 1925, pages 1 and 8.

Dallas Morning News, April 28, 1925, pages 1 and 2.

Dallas Morning News, April 29, 1925, page 13.

Washington Post, April 29, 1925. Obituary, Milstead.

Dallas Morning News, May 5, 1925, page 4.

Dallas Morning News, May 7, 1925, page 13.

Dallas Morning News, May 8, 1925, page 13.

Dallas Morning News, May 17, 1925, pages 1 and 4.

Dallas Morning News, May 18, 1925, page 1.

Dallas Morning News, May 19, 1925, page 1.

Dallas Morning News, May 20, 1925, page 14.

Dallas Morning News, May 21, 1925, pages 1 and 8.

Dallas Morning News, May 22, 1925, pages 1, 8 and 10.

Dallas Morning News, May 23, 1925, pages 1 and 12.

Dallas Morning News, May 24, 1925, page 1.

Dallas Morning News, May 25, 1925, page 9.

Dallas Morning News, May 26, 1925, page 3.

Dallas Morning News, May 28, 1925, page 1.

Dallas Morning News, May 29, 1925, pages 1, 2, and 23.

Dallas Morning News, May 31, 1925, page 1

Dallas Morning News, June 6, 1925, page 7.

Dallas Morning News, June 7, 1925, page 1.

Dallas Morning News, June 22, 1925, page 9.

Dallas Morning News, July 2, 1925, page 13.

Dallas Morning News, July 3, 1925, pages 1 and 7.

Dallas Morning News, July 5, 1925, page 4.

Dallas Morning News, August 23, 1925, page 9.

Dallas Morning News, November 7, 1926, page 6.

Dallas Morning News, August 31, 1931, Section II, pages 1 and 10.

Dallas Times Herald, April 11, 1982, Section A, page 27.

Dallas Morning News, April 11, 1982, Section A, page 36.

Dallas Morning News, December 8, 2004, Section B, page 8.

Texas State Records

Texas Board of Health. Death Certificate #13565 [1925]. County of Death: Dallas. Deceased: Ryan Adkins. White, male, single, age 27. Born: May 26, 1897 in Texas. Occupation: Lawyer. Date of Death: April 12, 1925. Cause of Death: "Fractured skull from blow of some blunt instrument. [Homicidal]."

Texas Board of Health. Death Certificate #13510 [1925]. County of Death: Dallas. Deceased: Walter La Sour Milstead. Male, white, single, age 30. Born: March___, 1895. Occupation: Salesman. Date of Death: April 25, 1925. Cause of Death: "Gun Shot Wounds, Murder." Burial: Washington, D.C.

Texas Board of Health. Death Certificate #17263 [1925]. Name: Dwight Moody Stewart, male, white, single. Age 18. Born in Texas. Date of Death: May 22, 1925. Cause of Death: "Gun Shot wound from left to right through....." "Shot in mob riot." Place of Burial: Grove Hill Cemetery, Dallas, Texas.

United States Records

1900 United States Federal Census

1920 United States Federal Census

Online

Ancestry.com. Family Tree. H. Ryan Adkins. Born May 26, 1897. Died April 12, 1925, in Dallas County, Texas. Accessed May 13, 2012.

Ancestry.com. Texas Death Index, 1903 – 2000. Name: Ryan Adkins. Death Date: April 12, 1925. Death County: Dallas. Certificate # 13565. Accessed April 5, 2012.

Ancestry.com. Texas Death Index, 1903 – 2000. Name: Walter La Sour Milstead. Death Date: April 25, 1925. Death County: Dallas. Certificate # 13510. Accessed April 5, 2012.

Ancestry.com. Texas Death Index, 1903 – 2000. Name: Schuyler Marshall, Jr. Death Date: April 9, 1982. Death County: Dallas. Gender: Male. Accessed April 5, 2012.

Ancestry.com. Texas Death Index, 1903 – 2000. Name: Dwight Moody Stewart. Death Date: May 22, 1925. Death County: Dallas. Certificate # 17263. Accessed April 5, 2012.

Ancestry.com. Social Security Index. Schuyler Marshall. Accessed January 29, 2012.

Ancestry.com. U.S. City Directories [Beta]. Name: Walter L. Milstead. Residence year: 1924. Street Address: 4922 Junius. Residence place: Dallas, Texas. Publication Title: Dallas, Texas, City Directories, 1924. Accessed April 6, 2012.

Ancestry.com. World War I Draft Registration Cards, 1917-1918. Name: Walter La Lom Milstead. County: St. Louis. State: Minnesota. Birthplace: Maryland, United States of America. Birth Date: March 23, 1896. Race: Caucasian [white]. FHL Roll Number: 1675891. Draft Board 6. Accessed April 6, 2012.

Ancestry.com U.S. Veterans Gravesites, ca. 1775 – 2006. Name: Walter L. Milstead. Service Info: PFC FLYING CADET AIR SERV D.C. DETCHMENT. Death Date: April 25, 1925. Cemetery: Arlington National Cemetery. Cemetery Address: C/O Director Arlington, VA 22211. Buried At: Section S Site 1537. Accessed April 6, 2012.

Find A Grave Memorial. Ryan Adkins. Born: May 26, 1897. Died: April 12, 1925, in Dallas County, Texas. Burial: Live Oak Cemetery, Brady, McCulloch County, Texas. Accessed April 5, 2012.

Find A Grave Memorial. Schuyler Bailey Marshall, Jr. Born: March 3, 1895. Died: April 2, 1982 in Dallas County, Texas. Sheriff of Dallas County, 1924 – 1926. Served on the Mexican Border in 1916 and became an Army Lieutenant in 1917. He served in France in World War I, and became a captain. He was later in the oil business. Burial: Calvary Hill Cemetery, Dallas, Dallas County, Texas. Accessed December 16, 2011.

Find A Grave Memorial. Dwight Moody Stewart. Born – 1907, in Texas. Died: May 22, 1925, in Dallas, Dallas County, Texas. Burial: Grove Hill Cemetery, Dallas, Dallas County, Texas. Accessed April 5, 2012.

Index

About the Author

Tyrone W. "Terry" Baker was born and raised in west central North Dakota. His parents and family lived in a small town near the Missouri River and later bought a ranch in the area known as the Prophet Mountains.

His military service included three years in the U.S. Army Military Police stationed at Killeen Base, Texas. He was awarded the Good Conduct Medal, the Cold War Recognition Certificate and several shooting awards.

He is married to his wife, the former Joyce Ann Greear, from Lampasas, Texas. They have a son and his wife, and a daughter and her husband and four grandsons. Terry has an Associate of Arts Degree from Abilene Christian Universty at Dallas with a major in criminal justice. He is a graduate of the FBI National Academy, Quantico, Virginia, and holds the Texas Master Peace Officer Certificate.

For three years, 1981-1983, he served as captain and commander of the "Old Jail" at Main and Houston Streets in downtown Dallas. The last five Dallas County hangings from 1918-1920 were held in this jail.

Some past positions he has held were: President of the Law Enforcement Officers' Association of Texas (L.E.O.A.T.), Committee Chairman of the Criminal Justice Committee for the 1994 World Cup Soccer Games in Dallas and Supervisor on the Volunteer Security Team at the 1996 Summer Olympics in Atlanta, Georgia.

Terry retired after thirty-nine years as a sworn deputy sheriff with the Dallas County Sheriff's Department, attaining the rank of assistant chief deputy.

After he retired the author began researching cases of law enforcement officers killed in the line of duty to get their names engraved on the memorial walls in Washington, D. C. and Austin, Texas. He was able to research, verify and get approval for 246 officers' names to be

placed on the memorial walls. Many of the cases were from the 1850s through the early 1900s.

Some of his awards included: Deputy of the Year, Captain Bob Kennedy Memorial Award, Silver Spur Award, Sheriffs' Association of Texas Lost Lawman Award, FBI Director's Community Leadership Award, Sheriff's Commendation Bar and Sheriff's Certificate of Merit.

Terry is a member of the Sheriff Bill Decker Deputy Association, Retired Dallas County Employees Association, Sheriffs' Association of Texas and the FBI National Academy Associates.

He wrote an article titled "Finding the Forgotten, Texas Peace Officers Killed In the Line of Duty, it was published in the *FBI National Academy Associates Magazine.*

www.ingramcontent.com/pod-product-compliance
Lightning Source LLC
Chambersburg PA
CBHW060047100426
42742CB00014B/2725